GIFTS
of
FOOD

GIFTS of FOOD

by Susan Costner

Illustrations by Lauren Jarrett

CROWN PUBLISHERS, INC., NEW YORK

Published by Crown Publishers, Inc., One
Park Avenue, New York, New York 10016,
and simultaneously in Canada by General
Publishing Company Limited
Manufactured in the United States of America
Library of Congress Cataloging in Publication
Data
Costner, Susan.
Gifts of food.
Includes index.
1. Cookery.   2. Gifts.   I. Title.
TX652.C75   1984   641.5   84-5871
ISBN 0-517-55415-1
Book design by Dana Sloan
10 9 8 7 6 5 4 3 2 1
First Edition

The recipe for Tiger Paws contained in this
book is a variation on a recipe entitled Bear
Paws which was published in a book
entitled *The Joy of Chocolate* by Judith Olney,
copyright © 1982 by Barrons Educational
Series, Inc., and published by Barrons,
Woodbury, New York.

With love for: Grandmother Costner
With love for: Mom
With love for: Dad

Contents

Acknowledgments

I would like to thank all my generous and innovative friends who gave me their recipes and bravely tested mine, especially Gene Barnes, Sasha Clifton, Lisa and Paul D'Andrea, Ann Freegood, Devon Fredericks, Warren Padula, Miles Jaffe, Kathleen King, Barbara Remia, Sharon McNamara, Sylvia, Linda, and Dorothy Sherry, Ed Rice and Amy Rowens, Betty Wolfe, and especially Damian Wolfe, who kept the world at bay so I could finish this project.

I would like gratefully to acknowledge the help given to me by Susan Wood, Jill Levine, the Bridgehampton Library, my illustrator Lauren Jarrett, my editor Pam Thomas, Millie Becerra and the staff at the Inside Address, Dorothy Bates and her crew at Dean & Deluca, as well as all those at the Complacent Cook, Wolfman and Gold and Company, Thayer's Hardware Store, Engel Pottery, Rose Jewelers, and Balasses House. And to three very special friends, Arthur Gold, Robert Fizdale, and Camilla Turnbull, whose enthusiasm and encouragement made this book a reality.

Introduction

One of the earliest and most treasured of my childhood memories is of the special little pies my grandmother made for me with secretly borrowed crust, broken from the grownup pie, stuffed with her homemade jam, and baked in the corner of her oven. I grew up in the South—Virginia and North Carolina—in a large family where cooking and family gatherings were an important part of my life. Every visit from an aunt or cousin was proudly accompanied by homemade jellies, pickles, and of course pies. The food was unsophisticated by some standards, especially when compared to the diverse gastronomy I have learned while living in New York. However, I learned from my large family the sentiments that M.F.K. Fisher first expressed in *The Gastronomical Me*—that food is "something beautiful to be shared with people instead of as a thrice-daily necessity."

Food *is* to be shared, and for the creative cook, the spirit of giving is nowhere more alive than in the kitchen. Gifts of food show a thoughtfulness and generosity as no store-bought present can. I hope that this will soon become as treasured a tradition in your family as it is in mine.

I started cooking in Sagaponack, Long Island, at a small shoebox of a store, situated right in the middle of the celebrated Hamptons. The store was called Loaves and Fishes, a biblical expression meaning "godsend," which it was for our customers, who came from all over the world and included many famous and talented people as well as the wealthy and socially prominent. They had voracious yet discerning appetites and it was a constant challenge to satisfy them.

After six years of hard work and many unforgettable experiences, my partner, Devon Fredericks, and I sold Loaves and Fishes and moved on.

But it's hard to keep a cook out of the kitchen, and so I continued to feed and indulge my friends with gifts of food.

This book is divided into gifts for four seasons and utilizes the freshness and appeal of seasonal food. The recipes include tried and true favorites given to me by friends as well as adaptations from international, ethnic, and regional cuisines. There are gift suggestions for traditional holidays such as Christmas and Easter, along with the myriad other occasions requiring a food gift. There are presents for housewarmings, for those who are too busy to cook, along with a few cures and remedies, and even one gift for a gourmet pet. Generally, most of the ingredients and tools are easily available. However, I have included a source page at the end of the book to help you locate equipment and ingredients that may be difficult to find.

I frown on offering a gift without first wrapping it beautifully. Part of the fun of receiving a gift is that it looks special. While working at Loaves and Fishes, I noted that the presentation of the food accounted for half its appeal. After all, a wonderful homemade herb vinegar in a plain jar is rather ugly, but if placed into a beautiful bottle and sealed with colored wax and tied with ribbon, it doubles the message—"I care." I have kept my packaging ideas simple, requiring a minimum of material, time, and skill. Most of the ideas can be easily adapted to a number of recipes, and the containers can be used again when the contents are gone.

I hope these recipes and packaging ideas stimulate your imagination and encourage you to be inventive, adding your own personal touch.

GIFTS
of
SPRING

Gifts of Spring

CRYSTALLIZED VIOLETS

A violet in the youth of primy nature,
Forward, not permanent, sweet, not lasting,
The perfume and suppliance of a minute.

William Shakespeare, *Hamlet*

Unlike Shakespeare's violets, these will last almost indefinitely and are a good choice for friends who bake and decorate their own cakes. Try to use scented violets if you can find them.

METHOD

Do not wash the violets; gently shake and blow on them to remove any dust. Beat the egg white until it just begins to stiffen. Place the sugar on a saucer.

Holding each violet by its stem, dip it into the egg white. Using the paintbrush, spread the egg white evenly all over the violet, making sure to cover the back. Use the needle to hold the petals open if necessary. Next, dip the violet into the sugar, using the needle to hold the petals open while you sprinkle every surface with sugar. Place the violet on the cake rack. Cut off the stem.

Continue the process until all of the flowers are coated, placing them on the cake rack so that they do not touch one another. Sprinkle a little more sugar over any surfaces you may have missed.

Set the rack in a warm place to dry. The bottom shelf of an oven heated by a pilot light is very good for this, but don't forget the violets and turn the oven on. Drying may take several days, so if you use the oven, make sure it is completely cool before replacing the violets. They must be completely without moisture before they are packed; check the center and base of one flower—it should be milky white.

Store the violets between layers of wax paper in an airtight container. They will keep indefinitely.

Note: Rose petals may be crystallized by the same method.

INGREDIENTS

Freshly picked violets, with stems left on
Egg white of 1 large egg
Superfine granulated sugar

TOOLS

Small paintbrush
Thick needle
Cake rack
Wax paper
Airtight containers

Use a needle to hold the petals open while you sprinkle every surface with sugar.

TO PACKAGE

Celebrate spring and keep its memory permanent with a gift of Crystallized Violets packed into humble baby-food jars. Dress up the lids with silver foil muffin cups, flattened and glued in place with rubber cement. Tie on purple ribbon streamers and a small bouquet of fresh or silk violets.

Humble baby food jar decorated with a flattened silver foil muffin cup, ribbon streamers, and silk violets.

INGREDIENTS

About 30 thin-as-possible
    asparagus spears
2 quarts cold water
¼ cup coarse salt
1½ cups white vinegar
½ cup sugar
1 teaspoon coarse salt
1 teaspoon mustard seed
1 teaspoon dill seed
1 small white onion, peeled and
    sliced into very thin rings
2 small hot red chile peppers,
    fresh or dried
2 stalks of fresh dill

PICKLED ASPARAGUS

YIELD: 2 half pints

These crisp, dill-scented low-calorie pickles are a perfect cocktail snack. When the season for asparagus is long past, surprise a friend with these unusual pickles.

METHOD

Break off the tough ends of the asparagus. Cut the spears into 3½-inch lengths. Place the asparagus in a large enamel or stainless-steel bowl. Combine cold water and ¼ cup salt; cover asparagus with the solution. Let stand uncovered for 2 hours. Drain the asparagus and rinse under cool water. Pat dry.

Combine the vinegar, sugar, 1 teaspoon salt, mustard seed, dill seed, and onion rings in an enamel or stainless-steel saucepan. Bring to a boil and boil for 1 minute.

Pack the cooled asparagus, tips up, in hot, sterilized canning jars, making sure to leave ½ inch of headroom. The best way to do this is to line the asparagus around the inner edge of the jar first and then fill in the center. Tuck a hot red chile pepper and 1 dill stalk into each jar.

Pour hot pickling liquid into jars, filling to within ¼ inch of the rims, making sure all spears are thoroughly covered. Wipe rims with a clean damp cloth and seal with lids. Process in boiling water bath for 10 minutes (see instructions on page 231).

Cool to room temperature, check seal, label, and store in a cool dark place for up to 12 months.

TOOLS

Nonaluminum bowl, stainless-steel or enamel
Nonaluminum saucepan, stainless-steel or enamel
Canning jars and lids

TO PACKAGE

For a typical French spring snack: Line a shallow handwoven basket with a country check dish towel. Pack in Pickled Asparagus, a large bunch of spring radishes (tops on, please), a crock of sweet butter, coarse salt, and a loaf of black bread.

ROSE PETAL TEA

There are few hours in life more agreeable than the hour dedicated to the ceremony known as afternoon tea.

Henry James, *The Portrait of a Lady*

Rose tea is a wonderfully calming and refreshing springtime drink. Grace Firth in *A Natural Year* reports that rose tea helps to expel "womanly melancholy and cure madness." It is also beautiful to look at with its faded pink rosebuds and silvery verbena leaves. Rose tea (or any herb tea) should be drunk with a little honey or sugar to bring out the flavor.

INGREDIENTS

2 cups black or Chinese tea, about 8 ounces
1½ cups dried rose petals or buds, available from an herbalist (unsprayed!)
¾ cup lemon verbena leaves, available from an herbalist
2 tablespoons dried lemon peel

TOOLS

Airtight containers for storage

METHOD

In a large bowl, mix together the tea, rosebuds, verbena leaves, and lemon peel. Strong light will affect the delicate taste of the tea, so package in airtight containers and store away from the light.

Use 2 tablespoons per cup of tea.

TO PACKAGE

Make individual servings by placing 2 tablespoons of the tea mix in the center of a double-layer, 3-inch square of cheesecloth. Tie closed with kitchen twine. Place the tea balls in an oversized porcelain teacup, like the ones you find throughout Europe for *café au lait*. Overwrap with a large lap napkin. Tie on a ribbon and a label with the directions—"2 tablespoons per cup."

Place 2 tablespoons of the tea mix in the center of a double-layer, 3-inch square of cheesecloth and tie with kitchen twine. Present the tea balls in a café au lait *cup with ribbons and label.*

Tea Breads

Probably no other food so symbolizes the heart of domestic life as homebaked bread. If you don't have the time for yeast breads or simply don't have the "knack" for making a loaf rise, try these foolproof "sweet" breads. They are naturally versatile—good in place of toast, at breakfast, or as a simple dessert or snack any time of the day.

RHUBARB NUT BREAD

YIELD: 2 loaves

Tart spring rhubarb, crunchy walnuts, and spices add up to something special in this moist fruit bread.

METHOD

Preheat oven to 325° F. Beat the brown sugar, oil, and egg together until light. Add the buttermilk and vanilla and stir well. Sift together the flour, salt, baking soda, and cinnamon and add to the liquid ingredients, stirring just enough to moisten. Fold in the rhubarb and then the walnuts. Pour into 2 generously greased and floured loaf pans. Combine the ½ cup sugar and 1 tablespoon butter and sprinkle evenly over the 2 loaves.

Bake loaves in the preheated 325° F. oven for approximately 1 hour, or until a toothpick comes out clean. Cool in the pans. When cooled, remove from pans, and wrap and store overnight before slicing. The rhubarb nut bread will keep for up to 5 days wrapped in plastic and refrigerated, or it may be frozen.

INGREDIENTS

1 cup firmly packed brown sugar
¾ cup safflower oil
1 egg
1 cup buttermilk
1 teaspoon vanilla extract
2½ cups flour
1 teaspoon salt
1 teaspoon baking soda
1 teaspoon ground cinnamon
2½ cups chopped fresh rhubarb or unsweetened frozen (If the rhubarb is frozen, do not thaw it.)
¾ cup coarsely chopped walnuts
½ cup sugar
1 tablespoon butter, softened to room temperature

TOOLS

2 loaf pans, 8½ x 4½ inches
Electric beater

TO PACKAGE

Wrap the rhubarb breads in aluminum foil. Overwrap each in a boldly patterned 16-inch square of decorative wrapping paper. Gather together the excess paper at one end of the bread and wrap the ribbon around it. Tie a knot. Extend the ribbon over the bread, gather together the excess paper at the other end, wrap the ribbon around and tie a knot, attractively forming a handle. Trim off any extra ribbon. Label.

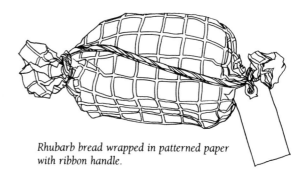

Rhubarb bread wrapped in patterned paper with ribbon handle.

MISHTI RANI'S TEA BREAD

YIELD: 1 loaf

This recipe comes from a dear friend and wonderful cook, Ed Rice. Having traveled all over the world, he has many unusual recipes and stories to tell about them. This bread is from the northern part of the Malabar Coast where the Portuguese ruled for about 450 years, in Goa. It is really a type of pound cake "Indianized" by the Portuguese with spices. Indians in this area as elsewhere have a very sweet tooth and you find throughout this region all sorts of European delicacies given a special Indian touch. The burned sugar gives the cake a slight caramel taste.

The cream of wheat is a popular ingredient in the cooking of the region. The end result is not unlike our carrot cake.

Ed says that he got this recipe by steady application of what the Indians call "the rice-pot and the rack"—persuasion and bullying.

METHOD

Preheat oven to 350° F. "Burn" or caramelize 1 cup of the sugar with 1 tablespoon water in a nonstick pan over low heat, stirring all the time, until the sugar turns a rich, deep brown color, in 2 to 3 minutes. Set aside.

Cream the butter and remaining cup of sugar until light and fluffy. Add the egg yolks, one at a time, beating after each addition.

Sift the flour, baking powder, spices, and salt together. Gradually add to the butter mixture, beating after each addition. Fold in the caramel. Add the cream of wheat, raisins, apple, and carrot. Mix well. Beat the egg whites until stiff but not dry and gently fold them into the batter.

Pour the batter into the loaf pan, which has been generously greased and dusted with flour.

Bake at 350° F. for 1 hour 20 minutes to 1½ hours, or until a cake tester comes out clean. Cool in the pan. Turn out and wrap in aluminum foil. The tea bread is best eaten the day after it is made. It can be stored wrapped in plastic in the refrigerator for about 5 days, or in the freezer for several weeks.

TO PACKAGE

See packaging for Rhubarb Nut Bread on page 8, or wrap Japanese style in a *furoshiki,* using gaily printed Indian cotton batik fabric. For directions see page 216.

INGREDIENTS

2 cups sugar

8 ounces unsalted butter

4 eggs, separated

2 cups flour

1 tablespoon baking powder

1 teaspoon ground cinnamon

¼ teaspoon ground cloves

¼ teaspoon grated nutmeg

¼ teaspoon salt

½ cup cream of wheat, cooked

1 cup raisins

1 cup golden raisins

1 small tart apple, peeled, cored, and grated

1 carrot, peeled and grated

TOOLS

Food processor or grater

Nonstick saucepan

1 loaf pan, 8½ x 4½ inches

INDIAN TEA BREAD

INGREDIENTS

1 cup raisins, dried currants, and
    golden raisins
¼ cup mixed, chopped pitted
    dates and chopped candied
    gingerroot
1½ cups strong brewed tea
1 large egg, beaten
¼ cup dark molasses
1 tablespoon butter, melted
2 cups unbleached flour
¼ teaspoon salt
3 tablespoons freshly grated
    gingerroot, or 1 tablespoon
    ground ginger
1 teaspoon baking soda
½ cup coarsely chopped walnuts
½ cup sunflower seeds (very
    popular in Indian cooking)

TOOLS

2 bread pans, 8½ x 4½ inches

YIELD: 2 loaves

Another bread from Ed Rice's travels, this recipe literally calls for strong-brewed tea. The bread is most likely an "Indianized" version of a typical nineteenth-century English fruitcake, taken to India by the English. Ed found this recipe in the Assam area of India, one of the tea-growing states. We suspect that the original recipe called for melted butter or milk as the liquid and possibly the Indian cook in the tea planter's kitchen substituted the tea. The original recipe also called for jaggery, an unrefined brown sugar, made from palm sap. Our molasses will work as well.

METHOD

Preheat oven to 350° F. Soak the dried fruits in the tea for 30 minutes. Add the egg, molasses, and butter to the tea and fruits and mix well. In a separate bowl sift together the flour, salt, ground ginger (if you are using it), and baking soda. Gradually add it to the wet ingredients, beating after each addition just enough to moisten. Stir in the nuts and seeds, and grated fresh gingerroot (if you are using it). Do not overbeat.

Pour into 2 greased and floured bread pans and bake at 350° F. for approximately 1½ hours, or until a cake tester comes out clean. Cool in the pans for 10 minutes. Remove and cool completely on a wire rack. Wrap loaves in aluminum foil.

The bread slices best the next day. If wrapped in plastic and refrigerated, it will keep for up to 5 days, or can be stored in the freezer for several weeks.

TO PACKAGE

Refer to the suggestions under Rhubarb Nut Bread (page 8) or Mishti Rani's Tea Bread (page 9), or make a Waxed Fabric Container out of Indian batik fabric according to the instructions on page 216.

WHOLE-WHEAT AND RAISIN SCONES

YIELD: about 8 scones

The mixing of lard and butter makes these very fattening and very delicious. The whole-wheat flour adds a nutty taste reminiscent of thick graham crackers. Scones do not keep well, so eat them on the same day they are baked.

METHOD

Preheat oven to 400° F. Lightly butter the baking sheet and set aside.

In a medium-size mixing bowl stir together both flours, the sugar, baking soda, cream of tartar, and salt. Using a pastry cutter or your fingertips, cut the lard and unsalted butter into the dry ingredients until the mixture resembles oatmeal. Lightly beat the egg and mix it with the buttermilk. Add the liquid ingredients to the mixture in the bowl and quickly stir the mixture together. Add the raisins and form the dough into a ball. It will be slightly sticky.

Turn the dough onto a well-floured surface. Knead 3 or 4 times to distribute the fat, and roll dough out to 1-inch thickness. Cut the dough into 3-inch rounds with a cookie cutter or glass that has been dipped into flour. Place the scones at least 2 inches apart on the baking sheet. Brush each scone with a little milk. Bake in the preheated oven for 20 minutes, or until lightly browned.

TO PACKAGE

When completely cooled, wrap each scone individually in tissue paper; see Individual Irish Soda Breads, page 14, for wrapping instructions. Pack them into a basket with a handle, a present in itself, add a crock of Lemon Cream (page 12), and off to tea you go.

INGREDIENTS

1 cup whole-wheat flour
⅔ cup white flour
2 tablespoons sugar
1 teaspoon baking soda
1 teaspoon cream of tartar
¼ teaspoon salt
3 tablespoons unsalted butter
3 tablespoons lard
1 egg
¼ cup buttermilk
½ cup raisins
Milk

TOOLS

1 baking sheet, 17 x 14 inches
Rolling pin
3-inch cookie cutter or glass
Pastry brush

LEMON CREAM

INGREDIENTS

5 eggs
2 cups sugar
5 ounces unsalted butter, melted
**Juice and finely grated rind of 3
    lemons**
1 lemon

TOOLS

Double boiler
Canning jars
Zester

YIELD: 3 cups

Found at almost every English tea, lemon cream (also known as lemon curd) has a fresh, sun-warmed flavor which adds a tangy taste to toasted scones, muffins, biscuits, or even waffles. It makes a wonderful gift for a busy hostess. But why wait for breakfast? Spread it between layers of plain cake—especially good with coconut cake—or use it as filling for lemon tarts.

METHOD

Beat the eggs at high speed until thick and lemon-colored. Gradually add the sugar, beating well after each addition. Add the melted butter in a steady stream, beating all the time. Add the lemon rind and juice and beat well.

Place the mixture in the top pan of a double boiler set over hot water on medium heat. Cook, uncovered, stirring constantly, making sure to get into the corners of the pan, until thick—approximately 10 minutes. Cool and pack into hot sterilized canning jars.

Using a zester, remove strips of rind from the lemon to create a striped effect (see illustration). Cut 3 very thin slices from the lemon, remove

Using a zester, remove strips of rind from the lemon to create a striped effect.

Decorate jar with white paper doily "hat" and lemon leaves.

the seeds, and place 1 slice on the top of each jar. Seal jars with lids and store in the refrigerator.

The lemon cream will keep for several weeks, refrigerated.

TO PACKAGE

Give the jars fabric "hats" of white paper doilies. Tie on a few lemon leaves from the florist and include a label with a few appropriate uses. See instructions for Top It Off Hats on page 219.

INDIVIDUAL IRISH SODA BREADS

YIELD: 16 large buns

A classic for St. Patrick's Day

METHOD

Preheat oven to 375° F. Combine the flour and butter, working it with your fingers until it has the consistency of coarse oatmeal. Add the sugar, baking powder, baking soda, salt, and currants, still mixing with your fingers. Beat the egg and buttermilk together. Make a well in the center of the dry ingredients and add the egg-buttermilk mixture. Stir until well blended. Form into a ball.

Lightly dust a clean surface with flour and knead the dough for 3 to 4 minutes, until smooth. Divide it into 16 equal portions. Shape each portion into a ball and place the balls at least 3 inches apart on the greased baking sheets. Gently press the top of each bun with a palm of your hand to flatten it slightly. Using a very sharp knife dipped into flour, cut a ¼-inch-deep cross on the top of each bun. Bake in the preheated oven for 20 to 25 minutes, or until golden and crusty. Cool on a wire rack.

INGREDIENTS

4 cups unbleached flour
4 tablespoons unsalted butter, softened
2 tablespoons sugar
1 tablespoon baking powder
1 teaspoon baking soda
1 teaspoon salt
2 cups dried currants
1 egg
1¾ cups buttermilk

TOOLS

2 baking sheets, 17 x 14 inches, greased

Place each Irish Soda Bread in the center of a square of paper and twist all edges upward to resemble a flower.

TO PACKAGE

Buns and muffins look special when individually wrapped. To emphasize their simple origin, place each Irish Soda Bread in the center of a 12-inch square of brown butcher paper or tan tissue paper and twist all edges upward to resemble a flower. Present the soda breads in a low basket with a shamrock-shaped label.

Present the individually wrapped Irish Soda Breads in a low basket with a shamrock-shaped label.

EASTER BREAD

YIELD: 1 ring

In many countries the baking and giving of ornamental breads at Easter is traditional. In Greece the godchild often gives this decorative bread to the godparents, and in Italy children find their Easter eggs on top of a circular Easter bread. Often the bread is then displayed on a wall as a decoration.

METHOD

Heat the milk and butter over low heat until just warm, 100° to 105° F.

In a large bowl combine 1½ cups of the flour with the sugar, salt, and dry yeast. Add the milk-butter mixture and the eggs to the dry ingredients and beat for 2 minutes by hand or with an electric mixer. Add up to 1½ cups more flour or just enough to make a soft dough.

Turn onto a lightly floured surface and knead for 6 to 8 minutes. Put the dough in a large, clear-plastic food storage bag with 1 tablespoon of flour. Close with a twist-tie. Turn the bag several times to coat all sides of the dough with the flour. Let the dough stand in a warm draft-free place, approximately 70° to 80° F., for 1 hour, or until double in bulk.

Remove the dough from the bag and punch down. Place on a lightly floured surface and knead in the raisins, almonds, and aniseeds. Divide the dough into halves and let rest for 10 minutes (this will make it easier to roll).

Roll each piece of dough into a 24-inch-long length. Twist the 2 lengths together loosely and form into a ring, pinching the ends together. Place on a greased baking sheet and brush with egg wash. Place the 5 colored eggs into spaces in the twist (see illustration). Cover and let rise until doubled, 35 to 40 minutes.

Bake the ring at 350° F. for 20 to 25 minutes. Cool on a wire rack. Spread ring with frosting and decorate with toasted almonds and sprinkles.

INGREDIENTS

⅔ cup milk
2 tablespoons unsalted butter
2¾ to 3 cups flour
⅓ cup sugar
1 teaspoon salt
1 tablespoon dry yeast
2 eggs
½ cup dark raisins
½ cup golden raisins
¼ cup chopped blanched almonds
⅔ teaspoon aniseeds
5 raw eggs that have been dyed bright colors

Egg Wash

1 egg plus 1 teaspoon water

Frosting and Topping

½ cup confectioners' sugar mixed with 1 teaspoon milk
2 tablespoons toasted sliced almonds
1 teaspoon colored sprinkles

TOOLS

1 baking sheet, 11 x 17 inches
Large clear-plastic food storage bag with twist-tie

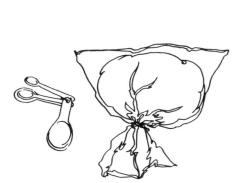

Put the dough in a large, clear-plastic food storage bag with 1 tablespoon of flour. Close with a twist-tie.

Twist the 2 lengths together.

TO PACKAGE

Place the finished bread on a round cutting board. Place a small crock of Lemon Cream (page 12) in the center of the bread. Overwrap with clear cellophane; tie in place with a ribbon. Add a humorous touch with a rabbit-shaped card.

Finished Easter Bread, showing eggs placed into spaces in the twist.

BREAD BASKET CENTERPIECE

INGREDIENTS

1 tablespoon dry yeast
2½ cups lukewarm water
2 tablespoons molasses
2 eggs, beaten
1½ tablespoons salt
8 cups white flour

This spectacular centerpiece is tailored to the skills of the average cook. It will take several hours to complete, or it may be made in stages stretched over several days.

The finished basket will make a remarkable Easter basket, filled with the traditional colored eggs and candies. Today's hostess will also enjoy it filled with spring vegetables and dips or lined with a large napkin and piled with an assortment of homemade rolls.

It is entirely edible but, if you varnish it, it will reward all your efforts by lasting for years.

STEP ONE
Basic Dark Dough for Basket Sides

In a large bowl, dissolve the yeast in the lukewarm water. Add the molasses, stirring until dissolved. Allow the mixture to rest for 3 to 4 minutes to become frothy. Add the beaten eggs and salt and blend well.

Add 3 cups of the flour and mix well. With a wooden spoon, beat the batter vigorously for 2 to 3 minutes, until it becomes elastic. Add remaining flour, cup by cup, beating well after each addition.

Turn the dough out on a lightly floured surface and knead for 6 minutes, or until it is shiny and pliable. Shape into a large ball. Place the dough in a lightly oiled bowl and cover it with plastic wrap. Refrigerate for at least 30 minutes.

Lightly oil the outside of the dish or pan you are using as a mold. Refrigerate for 10 to 15 minutes.

Remove the dough from the refrigerator. On a lightly floured surface, roll it out into a large rectangle about 12 x 18 inches and ⅓ inch thick. Using a sharp knife dipped into flour, trim away the sides of the dough so that it will have sharp clean edges. Cut the rectangle lengthwise into ten ½-inch strips. Place all but two on an oiled baking sheet, cover with plastic wrap, and chill. (The dough for the basket must be kept cold, so clear some room in the refrigerator in advance.) Pinch the remaining two strips together at one end and twist tightly. Pinch the ends together.

Remove the mold from the refrigerator and place it on a baking sheet lined with parchment paper. Wind braid around the bottom of the mold. Trim off any excess, brush the ends with cold water, and pinch together. Secure with toothpicks if necessary.

With the refrigerated strips of dough, repeat this process 4 more times, brushing each previous braid with cold water before attaching the next.

Brush the entire basket with cold water and refrigerate while the oven preheats to 425° F. Bake for 25 to 30 minutes, until dough is firm and golden brown.

STEP TWO
Basic White Dough for Basket Bottom and Handle

In a large bowl, dissolve the yeast in the lukewarm water. Add the sugar, stirring until dissolved. Allow the mixture to rest for 3 to 4 minutes to become frothy. Add the beaten eggs and salt and blend well.

Add 3 cups of the flour and mix well. With a wooden spoon, beat the

TOOLS

Rolling pin
Sharp knife
Ruler
3 baking sheets
Parchment paper
Toothpicks
Lightly flavored vegetable oil
Pastry brush
Extra heavy florist wire
8- to 10-cup metal angel-food cake pan or any similar round cake pan with sides at least 4 inches high

INGREDIENTS

2 tablespoons dry yeast
2½ cups lukewarm water
2 tablespoons sugar
2 eggs, beaten
1½ tablespoons salt
8 cups white flour

Egg Wash

1 egg plus 1 tablespoon water

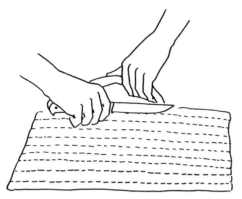

Use a sharp knife dipped into flour to trim away the sides of the dough. Cut the rectangle lengthwise into ten ½-inch strips.

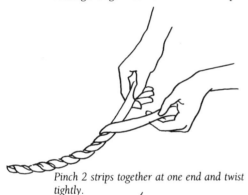

Pinch 2 strips together at one end and twist tightly.

Wind braid around the bottom of the mold.

batter vigorously for 2 to 3 minutes, until it becomes elastic. Add remaining flour, cup by cup, beating well after each addition.

Turn the dough out on a lightly floured surface and knead for 6 minutes, or until it is shiny and pliable. Shape into a large ball. Place the dough in a lightly oiled bowl and cover it with plastic wrap. Refrigerate for at least 30 minutes.

Remove the dough from the refrigerator. Roll it into a rectangle about 12 x 18 inches and ⅓ inch thick. Divide the rectangle into halves. Cut six ½-inch pieces lengthwise from one half and ten ¼-inch pieces lengthwise from the other. Place them on an oiled baking sheet and chill.

Make a tracing on a piece of parchment paper 1 inch wider than the bottom of your mold.

Remove two of the ¼-inch strips from the refrigerator. Pinch the ends together and twist tightly. Repeat the process with remaining 8 strips. Coil the braids, starting at the center of the circle, and add more braids as you go along. Seal each addition with cold water to conform to the outline of the traced circle. Brush with the egg wash.

Center the baked sides of the basket over the base and push down gently to imbed the sides into the base. Quickly remove three of the larger ½-inch strips of dough from the refrigerator. Braid together. Brush the top of the basket with egg wash. Place the braid around the circumference of the basket top (see illustration). Trim excess and seal the ends together. Secure with toothpicks. Bake the basket in a preheated 400° F. oven for 30 to 40 minutes. If the sides of the basket look too brown, cover them loosely with aluminum foil.

Bend florist wire into a handle shape, making sure to measure the diameter of the basket. Remove the remaining three ½-inch strips of dough from the refrigerator. Braid as before, this time incorporating the florist wire. Leave ½ to 2 inches of wire protruding at each end. Brush the handle with egg wash, place it on a cookie sheet lined with parchment paper, and bake at 400° F. for 15 to 20 minutes. Remove the handle from the oven and let it cool.

Insert handle into basket and remove toothpicks. Cool completely.

Coil the braids starting at the center of the circle and add more braids as you go along to conform to the outline of the traced circle.

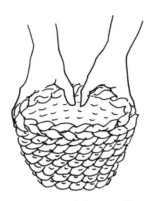

Place the braid around the circumference of the basket top. Trim excess and seal the ends together.

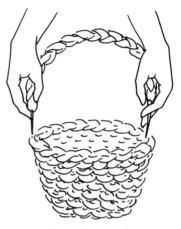

Insert handle into basket and remove the toothpicks, securing the top braid.

TO VARNISH

With a small brush, apply a satin-finish polyurethane to the handle, inside, and outside of basket, making sure to cover all areas well. Allow to dry according to directions on the can. Gently turn the basket on its side and varnish the bottom of the basket.

CHOCOLATE EASTER EGGS

YIELD: 4 large or 12 small eggs

The egg has always been a symbol of rebirth at springtime. Even in pre-Christian times, Romans held games on egg-shaped tracks and gave eggs as prizes. Gifts of eggs have become a universal custom at Easter-time.

INGREDIENTS

3½ ounces unsalted butter

1⅔ cups heavy cream

12 ounces semisweet chocolate
      bits

4 ounces bittersweet chocolate,
      broken into small pieces

2 tablespoons Grand Marnier
      liqueur

12 ounces Tobler Narcisse white
      chocolate, grated

½ cup boiling water,
      approximately

¼ pound shelled whole filberts

Unsweetened cocoa powder,
      preferably Dutch process, for
      dusting

TOOLS

Double boiler

Rounds of brightly colored
      aluminum foil (available at
      craft shops), or cut-up
      aluminum baking cups

A variation on a perennial favorite, these chocolate eggs are especially decadent yet very sophisticated, with layers of white and dark chocolate. Make them as small or as large as your conscience dictates.

METHOD

Melt the butter with the heavy cream in a saucepan over medium heat, stirring constantly. Increase the heat and bring the mixture to a slow boil. Cook until the mixture reduces by one third, about 10 minutes. Remove from the heat and add the semisweet and bittersweet chocolate, stirring until chocolate is completely melted. Stir in the Grand Marnier. Cover and place in the refrigerator to thicken for 2 to 3 hours. Stir the mixture 3 or 4 times as it cools.

Place the white chocolate in the top pan of a double boiler set over hot water. Add the boiling water to the chocolate, a little at a time, whisking until the mixture is perfectly smooth. (You may not need all the water, so only add a little at a time.) Remove the white chocolate from the heat and cool to room temperature, beating several times as it cools.

When the dark chocolate and white chocolate have the same firm consistency, begin to form into layered eggs by taking 1 filbert at a time, dipping it into the white chocolate, and placing it on a baking sheet lined with wax paper. Repeat with remaining nuts. You may make 4 large or 12 small eggs. Allow to harden slightly in the freezer, then dip the white balls into the dark chocolate mixture, smoothing and shaping into egg shapes. Chill. Continue building the layers, alternating chocolate colors, placing in the refrigerator if necessary to solidify. For smaller eggs, about 2½ inches in diameter, 2 layers of each chocolate color are best. You may make as many layers as you wish until all the dark and white chocolates are used up.

Place the "eggs" in the freezer to harden for 30 minutes.

Roll the eggs in cocoa powder and wrap them individually in variously colored thin aluminum foil, shiny side out. Refrigerate for at least 1 day before eating. The eggs will keep for several weeks in the refrigerator. To serve, remove the foil and slice the large eggs into quarters and the smaller ones into halves.

TO PACKAGE

A French wire egg basket would make a lovely centerpiece, filled with the collection of wrapped eggs. If you wish, decorate the foil-wrapped eggs with duck or chicken stickers. Attach a label or card.

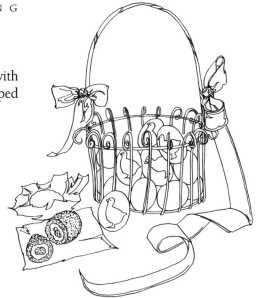

A lovely Easter centerpiece of dark- and white-chocolate layered eggs.

CHOCOLATE MADELEINES

YIELD: 24 small cakes

This simple French sweet immortalized by Marcel Proust is a cross between a small cake and a cookie, baked in a fluted scalloped mold. According to *Larousse Gastronomique,* it was the pastry makers of Commercy who popularized the madeleine about 1730 at Versailles. A welcome addition to spring picnics or, as Proust recalls, a cold remedy when dipped into hot tea. The chocolate in the recipe is untraditional but delicious.

METHOD

Preheat oven to 350° F. Lightly grease the madeleine indentations with softened unsalted butter.

Melt the butter and semisweet chocolate, uncovered, over very low heat. Set aside. Sift together the cocoa powder, sugar, flour, and salt. Set aside. Lightly beat the whole eggs and extra yolks together with the vanilla and rum. Stir the slightly warm chocolate mixture into the dry ingredients, then add the egg mixture and blend well.

Place a rounded tablespoon of the mixture in each shell form. Do not attempt to spread it, let it settle by itself. Bake for 12 minutes. Turn out on a wire rack, patterned side up, to cool. If the cakes do not slip easily

INGREDIENTS

5 ounces unsalted butter

3 ounces semisweet chocolate bits

2 tablespoons unsweetened cocoa powder, preferably Dutch process

½ cup sugar

1¼ cups unbleached flour

Pinch of salt

3 whole eggs

2 extra egg yolks

½ teaspoon vanilla extract

½ teaspoon dark rum or brandy

Confectioners' sugar, for dusting baked cakes

TOOLS

Madeleine pan with twelve 3-inch forms (See mail-order list if the pan is not available in kitchen equipment shops in your area.)

out of the molds, invert the pan and tap each mold firmly to remove cake.

Repeat the baking process with remaining batter; remember to re-grease the pans.

Sift the confectioners' sugar through a fine strainer to make a light coating on the cakes.

Stored in airtight containers between layers of wax paper, the cakes will keep for several days. They freeze well.

TO PACKAGE

What could be a better container for these small cakes then the pan they were baked in? Place 1 cake in each madeleine form. Overwrap with clear cellophane and tie with a wide, white satin bow. Include the recipe as a special surprise. If you can't part with the pan, deliver them in a decorated airtight tin, a Ribbon-Covered Box (page 228), or a Tied Paper Bag (page 220).

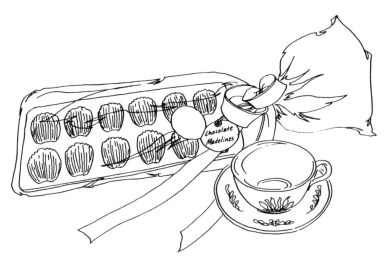

Place cookies in madeleine pan and overwrap with clear cellophane.

GINGER SHORTBREAD

YIELD: 8 wedges

Variations on the basic crisp, rich, buttery shortbread are endless (see recipes on pages 92 and 209) and some form of this pure and simple cookie traditionally belongs at every tea.

METHOD

Preheat oven to 325° F. Place butter and dark brown sugar in a medium-size bowl. Using your fingers and working quickly, cream butter and sugar until light and fluffy. Sift the flour, salt, and 1 teaspoon ginger together and add to the butter mixture. Still using your fingers, blend into a smooth dough. Gather the dough into a ball and knead on a lightly floured surface for 1 to 2 minutes. Do not let the dough become oily. Return to the refrigerator to chill before this happens, or the shortbread will have an unpleasant oily surface when baked.

With lightly floured hands, pat the dough into the pan. Crimp the edges with a fork. With a knife, mark the dough into 8 triangular wedges without cutting through to the bottom; these wedges are known as "Petticoat Tails." Prick each wedge with a fork in 3 places. Chill in the refrigerator for 30 minutes.

Bake shortbread in the preheated oven for 40 to 45 minutes, or until pale and golden. Cool for 15 minutes, then, while still warm, cut into wedges along the marks. Do not remove from the pan until fully cooled. Combine the confectioners' sugar and ¼ teaspoon ginger and dust over the baked cookies.

Tightly wrapped, the shortbread keeps for about 2 weeks. The dough freezes well and so do the baked cookies.

TO PACKAGE

Using the pie plate as your guide, cut a circle from a piece of cardboard. Cover with a large gold or silver doily. Place the shortbread on top and wrap tightly with colored cellophane or plastic wrap. Tape wrapping to back of cardboard with masking tape. Tie with a wide ribbon.

INGREDIENTS

8 ounces unsalted butter, softened to room temperature
¾ cup firmly packed dark brown sugar
1¾ cups flour
¼ teaspoon salt
1 teaspoon ground ginger
½ cup confectioners' sugar
¼ teaspoon ground ginger

TOOLS

1 round cake pan, pie plate, or shortbread mold, 8 to 9 inches across

DOUBLE CHOCOLATE COCONUT MACAROONS

INGREDIENTS

3 ounces unsweetened chocolate
3 ounces semisweet chocolate
1 egg yolk
1 teaspoon vanilla extract
1¼ cups unsweetened coconut,
    freshly grated if possible
1 cup blanched almonds, very
    finely chopped
⅓ cup egg whites
½ cup sugar
18 whole blanched almonds or
    candied cherries

TOOLS

Double boiler
Baking sheet

YIELD: 18 cookies

These chewy fudgelike macaroons are the perfect delicacies to contribute to a Seder, the Jewish service and ceremonial meal held on the first and second evenings of Passover. Forbidden during the Passover week are grains or leavening of any kind except in the form of matzo or matzo meal. These cookies substitute ground almonds for the flour and make a classic finale to this spring feast.

METHOD

Preheat oven to 325° F. Lightly butter the baking sheet.

Place all the chocolate in the top pan of a double boiler, partially covered, and set over hot water on medium heat until chocolate is melted. Transfer melted chocolate to a medium-size mixing bowl and add the egg yolk, vanilla, coconut, and chopped almonds; mix well. The chocolate mixture will be a little lumpy but it will smooth out when added to the egg whites.

Beat the egg whites until they begin to stiffen, gradually add the sugar, and continue beating until they are stiff and glossy. Gently fold the egg whites into the chocolate mixture until well mixed. Do not overbeat. Drop rounded tablespoons of dough 2 inches apart onto the prepared cookie sheet and flatten slightly with your palm. Place 1 perfect blanched almond or 1 candied cherry in the center of each cookie. Bake for 15 to 18 minutes. At the end of this time, they should still feel soft; they harden more as they cool. Remove from the oven and cool for 2 to 3 minutes before transferring to a wire rack to cool completely. Store the macaroons in an airtight container.

TO PACKAGE

Line a bamboo plate holder with a large silver doily. Stack the macaroons inside and overwrap with clear cellophane. Tie with silver and white ribbons. Using a heavy-gauge thread and needle, make a necklace of dried fruits (apples, apricots, dates, prunes), cinnamon sticks, and nuts to represent the haroset—a symbol of the hardships that Israelites suffered as slaves in Egypt. Loop necklace over the ribbons.

CHALLAH

"Challah brings nourishment to the whole world."

The Zohar

YIELD: 1 large loaf

Challah is a yeast-leavened egg bread traditionally eaten by Jews on the Sabbath. This much-prized ceremonial bread is usually a double-braided loaf—one large braid with a smaller braid set on top. The bread is brushed with egg yolk and sprinkled all over with poppy seeds to suggest manna—a sticky, candylike secretion of the desert tamarisk shrub in the spring. This honeylike food was believed to have been miraculously provided by God to deliver the wandering Israelites from hunger in their journey through the wilderness during their flight from Egypt. (Exodus 16:14–36) A blessing should be said over the challah at the beginning of the Sabbath meal.

METHOD

Combine the yeast and sugar and dissolve in 1¼ cups of warm water. Set aside to proof for 5 minutes.

In a large mixing bowl, sift together 4 cups of the flour and the salt. Make a well in the center of the flour and add the eggs, melted butter, and yeast mixture. Beat for 2 minutes by hand. Dust a clean surface with the remaining ½ cup of flour. Turn the dough out on it and knead for 6 minutes, or until smooth and elastic. (You may knead the dough with a heavy duty electric mixer fitted with the dough hook if you prefer.)

INGREDIENTS

1 tablespoon dry yeast
1 tablespoon sugar
1¼ cups warm water
4½ cups plus 1 tablespoon all-
**   purpose flour**
2 teaspoons salt
2 eggs, lightly beaten
2 tablespoons butter, melted
1 egg yolk
Poppy seeds

TOOLS

1 large clear-plastic food storage
**   bag with twist-tie**
Baking sheet
Pastry brush

Put the dough in a large clear-plastic food storage bag with 1 tablespoon of flour and close with a twist-tie. Turn the bag several times to coat all sides of the dough with flour. Let dough stand in a warm draft-free place, approximately 70° to 80° F. for about 1 hour, or until double in bulk.

Remove the dough from the bag, punch down, and divide into 2 parts, using one third of the dough for one piece and two thirds for the other piece. Divide the larger piece of dough into 3 equal pieces and roll each piece into a rope approximately 12 inches long. Braid the 3 ropes together tightly. Divide the smaller piece into 3 equal pieces and roll each piece into a rope approximately 10 inches long. Braid together tightly. Brush the larger braid all over with some of the egg yolk. Center the smaller braid on top of the larger braid and brush all over with remaining egg yolk. Sprinkle the poppy seeds generously over the entire loaf. Cover with plastic wrap or damp tea towel, and let rise again in a warm, draft-free place until doubled in bulk, approximately 40 minutes.

Bake the loaf in a preheated 375° F. oven for 40 to 45 minutes. Remove from the oven and cool on a wire rack. The challah freezes well.

TO PACKAGE

This loaf is too beautiful to hide. Show it off in a clear acrylic box tied with thick red wool.

Braid the 3 ropes together tightly.

Center the smaller braid on top of the larger braid, brush with egg yolk, and sprinkle with poppy seeds.

HAMANTASCHEN

YIELD: 3 dozen pastries

Purim is one of the great gastronomical events of the Jewish year. One of the foods most often associated with this celebration is the filled, pocketlike, triangular pastry called Hamantaschen. According to the Old Testament's Book of Esther, Haman was the villainous chief minister to King Ahasuerus of Persia who drew lots (*purim*) to determine the date on which all Jews would be killed. Queen Esther, herself a Jew, convinced the king to spare her people and Haman was later hanged.

This sweet bearing Haman's name symbolizes his pockets (*taschen*) filled with bribes or lots and, in eating this sweet, the Jews are figuratively devouring their oppressor.

Today's Hamantaschen may be filled with just about any sweet jam or filling. My favorite remains the traditional filling of poppy seeds (symbolizing manna, the food God gave the wandering Jews in Egypt to save them from starvation in the desert). Another good one is *lekvar* (prune jam).

Delicious eaten at breakfast, for tea, or as dessert.

METHOD

Sift the flour, sugar, and baking powder into a large bowl. Using your fingers or a pastry fork, cut in the butter or margarine until the mixture resembles oatmeal. This may be done in a food processor if you wish. Make a well in the middle of the dry ingredients and add the eggs and remaining ingredients for the pastry. Mix only until all the ingredients are incorporated.

With lightly floured hands, form the dough into a ball; it will be sticky. Dust lightly with flour, wrap in wax paper, then in plastic wrap, and refrigerate for at least 6 hours, or overnight.

Remove the dough from the refrigerator and let it sit at room temperature for 10 minutes. Preheat oven to 350° F. On a lightly floured board, roll the dough to ⅛-inch thickness. Cut it into circles 3 or 4 inches in diameter.

INGREDIENTS

Pastry

2 cups unbleached flour, sifted
½ cup sugar
2 teaspoons baking powder
8 ounces unsalted butter, or
    margarine for Kosher
2 eggs, lightly beaten
Grated rind of 1 orange
½ cup finely ground walnuts
2 tablespoons brandy

Filling

1 12-ounce jar prune jam, or
    prune filling (Solo brand)
Grated rind of 1 lemon
1 teaspoon brandy
½ cup finely chopped walnuts
¼ teaspoon grated nutmeg
1 teaspoon ground cinnamon or
    1 12-ounce can Solo brand
    poppy-seed filling

TOOLS

Baking sheet
Food processor or blender
    (optional)

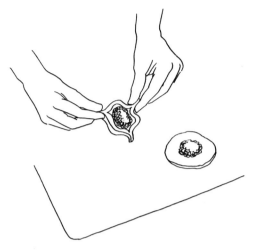

Place a rounded teaspoon of the filling in the center of each dough circle and pinch edges together to form a triangular pocket.

Combine filling ingredients in the order listed. Place a rounded teaspoon of the filling in the center of each dough circle and fold the circles to form a triangular pocket, pinching edges together (see illustration). Place these about 1 inch apart on a lightly greased baking sheet.

Bake in preheated 350° F. oven for 15 to 20 minutes, or just until the pastry is lightly browned. Cool on a wire rack.

TO PACKAGE

Send these off in a Ribbon-Covered Box (for instructions, see page 228) lined with an antique lace handkerchief.

For a thoughtful extra, include a label with a little history about the Hamantaschen.

Brioche Sandwich Basket

The quantities of butter and eggs in brioche dough produce a beautifully golden and luxurious yeast bread. The basic dough can be used to make the classic top-knotted rolls or in place of a pastry crust when wrapped around slices of Camembert cheese for individual tarts (see page 37).

Here I am giving the basic brioche dough recipe with instructions for making it into a "sandwich basket"—ideal for tea parties, cocktails, or receptions. The dough must be refrigerated overnight before baking. To facilitate the slicing of the bread into sandwich wedges, the brioche should be baked at least a day ahead, so plan accordingly.

BASIC BRIOCHE DOUGH

YIELD: 1 large brioche, about 1½ pounds

METHOD

In a large bowl dissolve the yeast and sugar in the warm milk. Let the mixture stand for 5 to 10 minutes, or until foamy. Add the eggs to the yeast mixture and stir to blend. Add 1 cup of the flour, the salt, and the melted butter and beat thoroughly to activate the yeast. Add the rest of the flour little by little, beating well after each addition.

Brioche dough is too soft and sticky to knead by hand in the conventional way. Use either a heavy-duty mixer with a dough hook or a food processor fitted with steel blade or, with your hands and a pastry scraper, slap the dough on a lightly floured surface for 3 to 4 minutes, adding as little flour as possible to prevent sticking.

Put the dough into a large, clear-plastic food storage bag with 1 tablespoon of flour; close with a twist-tie. Turn the bag several times to coat all sides of the dough with the flour. Let dough stand in a warm place, approximately 70° to 80° F., for 5 to 6 hours, until the dough has tripled in bulk and is light and spongy.

Remove the dough from the bag and punch down. Knead for 1 to 2 minutes. Return dough to the floured bag and refrigerate overnight to harden and ripen. (The dough will keep in the refrigerator for 3 to 4 days if well wrapped.) Place a 5-pound weight on the dough (such as an unopened 5-pound bag of flour) to keep it from rising. Or dough can be frozen for 1 to 2 weeks; to defrost, thaw overnight in the refrigerator.

Remove dough from the refrigerator and punch down.

Lightly butter the inside of a 1½-quart round brioche mold, charlotte mold, or soufflé dish.

Roll the dough into a cylinder on a lightly floured surface. Twist off one quarter of the dough and set aside. Roll the large piece of dough into a ball and place in the mold. Using your fingers, make a hole approximately 3 inches wide by 2 inches deep in the center of the dough. To form the distinctive "head," or "cap," of the brioche, take the small piece

INGREDIENTS

4 tablespoons milk, warmed to 100° to 105° F.

2 teaspoons dry yeast

4 tablespoons sugar

3 eggs, at room temperature

1¾ to 2 cups flour

½ teaspoon salt

5 ounces unsalted butter, melted

Fillings:

Caviar and unsalted butter, Potted Shrimp (page 31), or the Pâté (page 32)

Egg Wash

1 egg beaten with 1 tablespoon cream

TOOLS

Electric mixer, food processor, or pastry scraper

Large plastic kitchen bag

1½-quart round mold or charlotte or soufflé dish

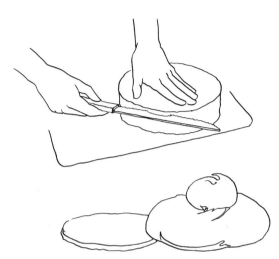

Slice off the top and bottom of the brioche and set aside. Cut the brioche into 8 slices, ¼ inch thick.

of dough and roll it into a pear shape. Place the pear-shaped cap, narrow end down, in the hole. To facilitate the shaping up of the cap during baking, make angled slits with a sharp knife just under the "head" where it joins the top of the brioche.

Cover dough with buttered plastic wrap, and let it rise in a warm place until doubled in bulk, 1 to 2 hours. Fifteen minutes before baking, pre-heat oven to 425° F. Brush the brioche with egg wash. Bake for 5 minutes, lower heat to 375° F., and bake for 30 minutes more. If the top browns too quickly, cover it loosely with foil.

Turn the brioche out on a wire rack to cool completely before storing. Refrigerate overnight before making "sandwich baskets."

TO ASSEMBLE A SANDWICH BASKET

With a long serrated flexible knife, slice off the top of the brioche; this will be the "lid of the basket." Set aside. Cut the bottom of the brioche into 9 slices, ¼ inch thick. Set the bottom slice aside. Carefully pick up slices of brioche in pairs and fill with one of the fillings. Return the slices in their original order as you fill them, to ensure that the loaf will fit together neatly. Divide the stack of slices into 8 equal wedges. Using the reserved bottom slice as a base, replace the wedges in the proper order. Replace the lid and you are ready to serve.

Spread the filling.

Invert the slices back in their original order as you fill them.

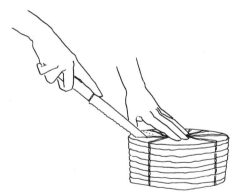

Divide the stack of slices into 8 equal wedges.

TO PACKAGE

From a heavy piece of cardboard, cut a circle in the same diameter as the base of the brioche. Cover with a paper doily. Place the finished brioche on the cardboard and overwrap in clear cellophane. Tie with ribbon streamers.

A large clay flowerpot base, a round cutting board, or a wicker paper-plate holder could also serve as a base for the finished Brioche Sandwich Basket.

Finished Brioche Sandwich Basket.

POTTED SHRIMP

YIELD: 2 cups

"Potting" is one of the oldest methods of preserving food. This classic spread, once extremely fashionable, has all but disappeared from gift-giving lists. It was most famous in England where it was developed to preserve the tiny, flavorful Morecambe Bay shrimp. There is no source for Morecambe Bay shrimp in this country—not even at Zabar's in New York City—but an acceptable substitute called "41–50 count" shrimp can be found at good fish markets, or you can use the bottled baby shrimp found in gourmet shops.

You don't need much for this—just clarified butter, shrimp, and a touch of cayenne. Both simple and quick to prepare (the only trick is to clarify the butter properly), potted shrimp makes a terrific hors d'oeuvre or first course when spread on Melba toast or on dry toast with the edges removed. You may also use it as a filling for the Brioche Sandwich Basket on page 28.

METHOD

Reserve 2 perfect shrimp and set aside.

Melt 3 tablespoons of butter in a saucepan over low heat. Remove

INGREDIENTS

4 ounces unsalted butter
**¾ pound tiny shrimp, cooked,
    peeled, and deveined**
1 tablespoon lemon juice
¼ teaspoon cayenne pepper
Salt
Freshly ground pepper

TOOL

**Two 1-cup soufflé dishes or small
    ramekins**

from the heat; skim the foam off the top of the butter and discard. Add the shrimp, lemon juice, cayenne, and salt and pepper to taste. Mix well and divide the mixture between two 1-cup soufflé dishes or small ramekins. Chill.

Melt remaining butter over low heat. When it has melted, skim the foam off the top and discard. Carefully pour off the clarified butter from the pan, leaving behind any sediment that has settled at the bottom. Pour the clean butter over the chilled shrimp and chill until the butter is partially set, about 1 hour. Press 1 perfect shrimp into each crock, cover with plastic wrap, and continue chilling for 6 hours or overnight.

The Potted Shrimp keep in the refrigerator for several months.

TO PACKAGE

Lay supple spring leaves, washed and dried, over the top of the ramekin. Laurel leaves work well. Tie in place with a thin gold satin cord. Label with 2 shrimp shapes, cut from an extra large red heart sticker.

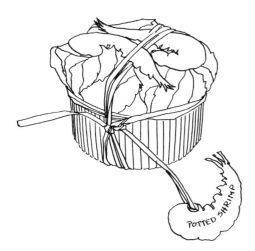

Ramekin of Potted Shrimp decorated with spring leaves and shrimp-shaped labels.

CHICKEN LIVER PÂTÉ WITH HAZELNUTS

YIELD: 2 logs, about 1 cup pâté each

This pâté is simple to prepare. It does have to be refrigerated before serving, preferably overnight, so you'll probably want to make it a day ahead.

METHOD

Melt 3 tablespoons of the butter in a frying pan. Add the onion, shallots, and garlic and cook over moderate heat, stirring occasionally, until

Carefully tear away the sides of the juice can.

onion is soft and limp but not brown, 5 to 8 minutes. Add the chopped apple and cook for about 5 minutes more, until the apple is soft enough to mash with a spoon. Transfer the mixture to the container of an electric blender, or to a food processor fitted with the steel blade, or to a large bowl.

Cut the chicken livers into halves and cut away any green spots. Pat dry.

In the same frying pan, melt 3 more tablespoons of butter. After the foam has subsided, add the chicken livers. Over high heat, cook them for 3 to 4 minutes, turning all the time. Remove pan from the heat, pour on the Cognac or Calvados, and ignite it. Let the alcohol burn out completely.

Add chicken livers and pan juices to the onion-apple mixture along with the lemon juice, salt, allspice, heavy cream, and pepper to taste. Blend in a blender at high speed until smooth, or in a food processor, or by hand. Add additional heavy cream if needed to make a smooth paste. Let cool completely.

Cream remaining softened butter until smooth. Add it little by little to the cooled chicken-liver mixture, beating well after each addition. Check the seasoning; add more salt and pepper if necessary. Remember that cold deadens flavor and the pâté will taste considerably less salted after refrigeration, so be generous with the salt and pepper.

Wrap the outside of each juice can in heavy aluminum foil. Line the inside of each can with wax paper that has been buttered on both sides. Divide the chicken liver mixture equally between the cans. Cover the ends with plastic wrap and refrigerate for at least 3 to 4 hours, or overnight.

Spread the hazelnuts on a baking sheet and toast in a 350° F. oven for 15 minutes, until lightly brown. Remove nuts from the oven and, while they are still warm, wrap them in a clean dish towel. Let them steam for 1 to 2 minutes. Rub the nuts together vigorously in the towel to remove as much of the skins as possible. Chop the nuts fine and set aside.

When the pâté is firm, cut off the closed metal end of each can, then carefully tear away the cardboard sides. Remove the wax paper from the pâté.

INGREDIENTS

8 ounces unsalted butter, softened to room temperature
⅓ cup finely minced onion
2 tablespoons finely chopped shallots
2 garlic cloves, peeled and minced
1 small green apple, peeled, cored, and coarsely chopped
1 pound chicken livers
2 tablespoons Cognac or Calvados (applejack)
1 teaspoon lemon juice
½ teaspoon salt
½ teaspoon ground allspice
¼ cup heavy cream
Freshly ground black pepper
½ cup shelled hazelnuts

TOOLS

Electric blender
Food processor or electric mixer
2 empty 6-ounce frozen-juice cans
Aluminum foil
Wax paper

Roll the pâté in the chopped hazelnuts.

Roll the pâtés in the chopped hazelnuts, and return them to the refrigerator to chill again for 1 hour. Wrap each roll first in plastic wrap, then in aluminum foil. Return to the refrigerator until ready to use.

Take the pâté from the refrigerator 15 minutes before serving to soften slightly.

TO PACKAGE

Purchase 1 bamboo sushi mat from gourmet or specialty food shops and cut into 2 equal pieces, or use old matchstick bamboo blinds, trimmed to wrap around the pâtés. Wrap a 4-inch square of lacquered origami paper catty-cornered around the roll. Label a gold seal, place it on the top of the roll, and tie with a simple piece of gold cord. Unwrapped, the bamboo mat may be used for serving the pâté.

Pâtés wrapped in sushi mat with origami paper label.

INDIVIDUAL CAMEMBERT TARTS

INGREDIENTS

½ recipe Basic Brioche Dough (page 29), or make the whole recipe using half of the dough for individual top-knotted brioche
1 egg
½ teaspoon water
1 tablespoon cornmeal
½ pound ripe Camembert cheese

Egg Wash

1 egg beaten with 1 tablespoon cream

YIELD: 1 loaf, 4 to 6 portions

The best Camembert cheese is the unpasteurized Camembert *fermier* from Normandy, available from April to October. The finest of all comes in the early spring when cows feed on the new tender young grasses. According to an article by Waverly Root in the October 1981 *Gourmet*, a document dated 1680 from the parish archives of Vimoutiers, France, praises Camembert as "a very good cheese, well suited to aid digestion . . . washed down with good wines." So take the tarts on a spring picnic along with a simple salad and a good wine to clean the digestive tract after a winter of heavy eating.

METHOD

Preheat oven to 400° F. Remove the brioche from the refrigerator and let it rest for 15 minutes. Combine the egg and water and set aside.

On a lightly floured surface, roll the brioche dough into a 14-inch square. Working quickly, cut out sixteen 3-inch rounds, using a lightly floured cookie cutter or glass. Brush each circle with egg wash and dust lightly with cornmeal. Place a 1½-inch cube of cheese in the center of half of the circles. Cover the cheese with another circle, gently pulling the dough so that it fits over the cheese and meets the edges of the bottom circle. Press the edges together to seal with the back of a fork. Place on a well-oiled baking sheet and brush each brioche with some of the remaining egg wash.

Place "sandwiches" immediately in the preheated oven. Bake for 5 minutes, reduce heat to 350° F., and continue baking for 15 minutes more, until the bread is golden brown and sounds hollow when tapped. If the top of the tart browns too quickly, cover loosely with aluminum foil, shiny side down. Remove from the oven and cool on a wire rack. The tarts may be eaten warm or at room temperature. To reheat, wrap loosely in foil and place in a preheated 350° F. oven for 5 to 10 minutes.

TO PACKAGE

Wrap each tart individually in clear plastic, then in tissue paper (see illustration on page 14). Deliver the tarts in a hand-painted mushroom basket (see page 226 for instruction), lined with a large French provincial napkin.

TOOLS

Rolling pin
1 baking sheet, 17 x 14 inches
Pastry brush
Cookie cutter or glass

Press the edges together to seal with the back of a fork.

SIMNEL CAKE

INGREDIENTS

4 ounces unsalted butter, softened to room temperature
½ cup sugar
1 egg, lightly beaten
1 cup unbleached flour
1 cup dried currants
¼ cup confectioners' sugar for dusting

TOOLS

1 springform pan, 8 inches across

YIELD: 1 cake

It is the day of all the year,
Of all the year the one day,
And here come I, my Mother dear,
To bring you cheer,
A-Mothering on Sunday.

The Oxford Nursery Rhyme Book
Iona and Peter Opie

Of all the holidays none is more filled with warm, personal expressions of gratitude than Mother's Day. This holiday, celebrated on the second Sunday in May, has its origins in the Middle Ages when Christians proclaimed "Mothering Sunday" to honor Mary, mother of Christ. "Mothering Sunday" reached its zenith in the medieval period when domestic servants and apprentices were permitted to visit their homes and their mothers, taking with them cakes baked from the scarce supply of sugar and spices. One of the most popular of these was a simnel cake, rich with butter and eggs. A cross between shortbread and cake, it is perfect today for Mother's breakfast in bed. With a little supervision, older children can prepare this one.

METHOD

Preheat oven to 325° F. Cream the butter and sugar together until light and fluffy. Add the egg, flour, and currants; mix well. Pour into a well-greased springform pan. Bake in preheated oven for 55 to 60 minutes. Allow to cool in the pan for 10 minutes. Run a knife around the edges of the cake before removing the ring of the springform pan. Dust with confectioners' sugar.

TO PACKAGE

Offer this cake as part of Mother's breakfast tray. Freshly squeezed orange juice, coffee, and this cake make a simple but special breakfast.

MAY WINE

YIELD: 1 fifth

Sweet woodruff (*Asperula odorata*) is a sweet-scented perennial ground cover redolent of vanilla and new-mown hay. In Germany it is customarily added to bottles of aromatic white wine for the popular May Day festivals. If you don't grow your own sweet woodruff, plants are available in many garden shops and markets that sell fresh herbs, and the dried leaves are stocked by herb or spice shops (see Sources on page 238).

METHOD

Using the funnel, decant the wine into the sterilized carafe or bottle. Add the woodruff, seal, and steep at room temperature for 24 hours.

Strain the wine through several layers of cheesecloth into a large bowl. Wash and resterilize the carafe. Dry thoroughly. Place the strawberries in the carafe. Using the funnel, pour the wine back into the carafe. Seal with lid or cork.

Label and date the wine and keep refrigerated until ready to use.

TO PACKAGE

May wine makes a lovely gift when accompanied by a basket of fresh strawberries and 2 long-stemmed round-bowl glasses with which to toast the flowery month of May.

For the romantic: First seal the bottle with sealing wax and ribbons; see Wax-Sealed Bottles (page 222).

INGREDIENTS

1 fifth light, flowery white wine (a
 few suggestions: German
 Rhine, California Chenin,
 Mosel, Alsatian White,
 French Colombard, or Blanc
 de Blancs)
Several sprigs of fresh woodruff,
 or 2 tablespoons dried
10 small perfect strawberries, with
 stems on

TOOLS

A widemouthed carafe or
 widemouthed bottle with lid
 or cork
Funnel

INGREDIENTS

1 fifth akvavit or vodka (for a
    flavored vodka see Lemon
    Vodka on page 157)
4 cups spring flowers (Any small
    flower will work; try pansies,
    violets, geraniums, begonias,
    or daisies; all work well; or
    use a combination. Add a few
    leaves for contrast.)

TOOLS

One ½-gallon wax milk carton

*Akvavit Frozen in Flowery Ice Block. To
present the akvavit, tear off the cardboard
carton and discard.*

AKVAVIT FROZEN IN FLOWERY ICE BLOCK

YIELD: 1 ice block

To toast the first breath of spring, assorted, colorful flowers frozen in ice make a beautiful "jacket" for a bottle of Danish akvavit or vodka.

METHOD

Bring ½ gallon of water to a rolling boil. (This makes the ice more transparent.) Remove from the heat and cool to room temperature.

Cut the top off the milk carton where it joins the sides. Place the bottle of akvavit in the center of the carton and fill with the cooled water. Pack the flowers around the sides. They will push out some of the water. Freeze until solid.

TO PACKAGE

To present the liquor, tear off the cardboard carton and discard. Wrap an ice bucket in several layers of newspaper and overwrap with a large cotton dish towel tied in place with wide ribbon. Bury the ice-encased bottle in the ice bucket filled with crushed ice. If your budget allows, tuck in a small jar of caviar, homemade Melba toast, and 2 lace-edged napkins. Move quickly.

HERBED GOAT CHEESE

YIELD: about 1 cup

Currently undergoing a vogue in this country, goat cheeses or *chèvres* are highly sought after in gourmet shops and delis. Until recently they were considered too sour and pungent for most people's taste. However, tastes change and goat cheese is all the rage. *Chèvres* are available in a large range of taste—from mild to very strong and from soft to hard, shriveled little *crottins*.

Here are a few suggestions for using them.

METHOD

Beat the goat's-milk cheese and the softened butter together until smooth. Add remaining ingredients and mix well. Transfer the mixture to a 1-cup crock and cover with plastic wrap. Refrigerate for at least 2 hours. The herbed cheese will keep for 2 weeks.

Remove the cheese from the refrigerator 15 minutes before serving to soften slightly.

TO PACKAGE

Divide the cheese into 2-tablespoon portions and shape into mounds, or *crottins* as they are called in France. Wrap each *crottin* in a vine leaf and tie with a piece of thin, rough sisal twine. If you are using bottled vine leaves, rinse them gently to remove brine. Repeat with remaining cheese.

If your budget allows, present the vine-wrapped cheese tied to a small willow cheese board or bamboo coaster. Accompany it with crusty French bread or plain crackers.

INGREDIENTS

4 ounces goat's-milk cheese
4 ounces unsalted butter, softened
    to room temperature
½ cup finely chopped parsley
¼ teaspoon dried orégano
¼ teaspoon dried thyme
¼ teaspoon marjoram
¼ teaspoon dried rosemary
¼ teaspoon freshly ground pepper
Fresh or bottled vine leaves

TOOLS

1-cup crock
1 yard of thin rough sisal twine,
    cut into 2 equal lengths
2 small willow cheese boards,
    bamboo mats, or coasters
    (optional)

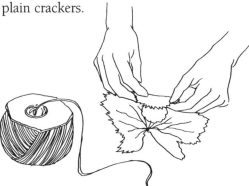

Wrap each portion of Herbed Goat Cheese in a vine leaf and tie with thin rough sisal twine.

Present the vine-wrapped cheese on a small willow cheese board.

MARINATED CHÈVRES

I. Herb Marinade with Peppers

INGREDIENTS (I)

**4 or 5 small goat's-milk cheeses
(crottins)**
**1 hot red and 1 hot green pickled
pepper, cut into strips**
**1 to 2 tablespoons *herbes de
Provence***
**1 tablespoon coarsely ground
black peppercorns**
**2 garlic cloves, peeled and left
whole**
**Best imported olive oil to cover,
approximately 1 cup**

METHOD

As you stack the *crottins* in the jar, sprinkle each one with the herbs and black pepper and drape with pepper strips before putting in the next. Add the garlic and pour on the oil to cover. Seal tightly with lid.

The *crottins* will keep in the oil at room temperature for a month.

Crottins *layered in French canning jar with simple ribbon and label.*

II. Mint and Hot Pepper Marinade

INGREDIENTS (II)

**4 small goat's-milk cheeses
(crottins)**
**Several fresh mint sprigs plus 2
tablespoons chopped fresh
mint**
1 tablespoon hot pepper flakes
3 sweet red pepper strips
**½ teaspoon coarsely ground black
peppercorns**
**Best imported olive oil to cover,
approximately 1 cup**

METHOD

As you stack the *crottins* in the jar, sprinkle each one with the mint and hot pepper flakes to taste and drape with pepper strips before putting in the next. Pour on the oil to cover. Seal tightly with lid.

The *crottins* will keep in the oil at room temperature for a month.

TO PACKAGE

Show off the Marinated Chèvres in an extravagant way by presenting them stacked in widemouthed 1-quart or 1-liter French canning jars with clamp-type lids.

Both of the Marinated Chèvres are so pretty to look at that all you need to complete the picture is to tie a bow around the jar and present it with a crusty loaf of French bread.

To serve, remove one cheese at a time along with a few pepper strips and accompany with slices of French bread or plain crackers.

For a less expensive gift, divide the recipes between two 1-pint or ½-liter widemouthed jars with clamp-type lids, keeping one for yourself.

TOOLS

1 quart or 1-liter clear widemouthed French canning jar, or decorative jar with clamp-type lid, or two 1-pint or ½-liter jars with clamp-type lids

EXOTIC OLIVES

YIELD: 4 cups

In both of the following recipes, the oil in which the olives mature becomes highly flavored and is delicious on its own for cooking or salads where a strong oil is needed. Replace the oil and the olives as they are used and this gift goes on forever.

METHOD

Drain liquid from olives and reserve.

Put 2 cups olives in each jar with 1 hot pepper, 1 bay leaf, ½ teaspoon each of coriander and fennel seeds, a sprig of fennel, and a few pieces of orange rind. Add olive oil and reserved liquid to cover. Seal each jar with a lid. Shake jar to distribute the herbs. Store in a cool place for several days to allow the flavor to develop.

Keeps in the refrigerator for 2 weeks.

TO PACKAGE

See directions, page 42.

INGREDIENTS

1 quart Calamata olives, pitted
2 fresh hot red peppers
2 bay leaves
1 teaspoon coriander seeds
1 teaspoon fennel seeds
1 branch of fresh fennel (optional)
Rind of 1 orange
Olive oil to cover, approximately 1 cup

TOOLS

Two 1-pint or ½-liter French canning jars with clamp-type lids

NIÇOISE OLIVES

INGREDIENTS

1 quart Niçoise olives with pits, drained of any liquid
2 bay leaves, broken into pieces
4 teaspoons fresh rosemary, or 1 tablespoon dried
Rind of 1 lemon
Olive oil, approximately 1 cup

TOOLS

Two 1-pint or ½-liter French canning jars with clamp-type lids

YIELD: 4 cups

METHOD

Drain any liquid from the olives and reserve. Put 2 cups olives in each jar with 1 bay leaf, 2 teaspoons rosemary, and one half of the lemon rind. Add olive oil and reserved liquid to cover olives. Shake jar to distribute the herbs. Store in a cool place for several days to allow the flavors to develop.

TO PACKAGE

Give the jars fabric "hats" according to the instructions on page 219. To complete the gift, tie on a handy wooden olive draining spoon. A welcome addition to any picnic basket or a hit at any cocktail party.

CHEESE STRAWS

INGREDIENTS

1 cup less 2 tablespoons flour
Pinch of cayenne pepper
4 ounces unsalted butter
¼ cup milk
1 cup finely grated cheese (Parmesan, Gruyère, Cheddar, or any combination of these)

YIELD: about 3 dozen 3-inch straws

These splendid hot cheese pastries replace heavy pâtés or trite corn chips as a cocktail snack.

METHOD

Preheat oven to 400° F. Rub the flour, cayenne pepper, and butter together until mixture resembles oatmeal. Make a well in the center and add the milk and grated cheese. Mix into a rough dough. Form the dough into a ball, wrap in plastic wrap, and chill in the refrigerator for at least 30 minutes. (The dough keeps for several days if wrapped tightly, or may be frozen.)

On a lightly floured surface, roll the dough into a large rectangle about ¼ inch thick. Using a pastry cutter or sharp knife, cut the dough into rectangles, roughly 3 inches x ½ inch, or "straws." They need not be the same precise length. If some are longer or shorter than others, it does not matter. Arrange the straws on an ungreased baking sheet so that they do not touch one another, and bake for 12 to 15 minutes, until barely golden brown. Cool on a wire rack.

When the cheese straws have cooled completely, carefully wrap them in aluminum foil and store in an airtight container. They will keep this way for several days. The straws can also be frozen.

Cheese straws are best served warm. To reheat them, arrange on a baking sheet loosely covered with aluminum foil and bake in a 250° F. oven for 5 to 8 minutes.

TO PACKAGE

The cheese straws are fragile, so pack them in bright red, airtight cake or cookie tins lined with several layers of tissue paper. Make your own label or stick on a large gold notary seal. Tie with thick yarn.

TOOLS

Rolling pin
Baking sheet

Food Gifts for a Child's Birthday Party

Children love birthdays and a party is their undisputed right. Kids love food that seems to have been custom-made for them and the following suggestions are guaranteed to delight children . . . of any age.

SWISS BREAD FIGURES

(Grittibanz)

INGREDIENTS

1 cup milk

4 ounces unsalted butter

½ cup sugar

1 tablespoon dry yeast

1¼ teaspoons sugar

½ cup warm water (90° to 115° F.)

2 eggs, slightly beaten

6½ cups all-purpose flour

1 teaspoon salt

Grated rind of 1 lemon

1 teaspoon ground cardamom

Egg Wash

1 egg beaten with 1 tablespoon milk

YIELD: 1 large figure or 12 small figures

Utterly charming, these gaily decorated Swiss bread figures make a lively project for a child's birthday party. Make the cardamom-scented dough ahead and let the children shape it into figures or animal shapes. Use raisins, whole almonds, filberts, walnuts, juniper berries, silver non-pareils, and candied cherries to fashion eyes, buttons, or as decoration. These make a perfect centerpiece for any celebration table.

METHOD

Place the milk and butter in a medium-size saucepan over low heat until the butter melts. Stir in the ½ cup of sugar until dissolved, and cool to lukewarm (100° to 115° F.).

In a small bowl combine the yeast, ¼ teaspoon of sugar, and ¼ cup of warm water. Stir to dissolve yeast and let stand until foamy, about 5 minutes.

When the milk mixture has cooled (check it with a thermometer if you are unsure) combine it with the foamy yeast and stir in the 2 eggs.

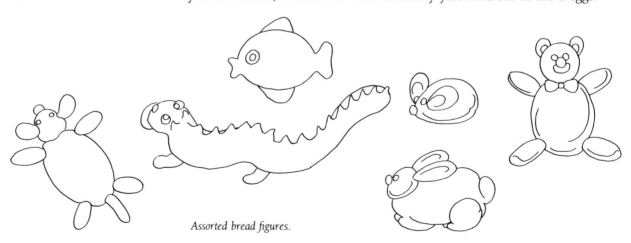

Assorted bread figures.

Set aside ½ cup of the flour for kneading. Combine 2 cups of the flour, the salt, orange rind, and cardamom. Add to the wet ingredients and beat with a wooden spoon for 2 to 3 minutes, until smooth and elastic. Add remaining 4 cups of flour, 1 cup at a time, beating well after each addition. You will have a soft, slightly sticky dough. Knead the dough on a lightly floured surface for approximately 6 minutes, adding the reserved ½ cup of flour if needed.

Put the dough in a large, clear-plastic food storage bag with 1 table-spoon of flour; close with a twist-tie. Turn the bag several times to coat all sides of the dough with flour and let stand in a warm draft-free place, approximately 70° to 80°, for 1½ to 2 hours, until double in bulk.

Remove the dough from the bag. Punch the dough down and knead for 2 to 3 minutes, or until smooth. Cover with a damp towel and let rest for 10 minutes.

TO ASSEMBLE

Preheat oven to 350° F. Line a large baking sheet with aluminum foil. Divide the dough into pieces and shape into figures or animal shapes. To attach arms, legs, and heads, moisten one end with milk. With 2 fingers make a hole into body and insert arms, etc. Pinch seam together with fingers.

Using scissors dipped into flour, make cuts to create hair or decorative patterns.

Brush the finished figure or animal with some of the egg wash. Firmly press in raisins, nuts, or candies to represent eyes, nose, mouth, belly button, etc. Cover dough and let rise for 15 minutes.

Brush again with egg wash. Bake for 40 minutes for a large figure, 25 to 30 minutes for smaller figures, or until golden brown; the figures should sound hollow when tapped. Check during baking to see if the decorations have come loose; if so, press them firmly into the dough.

Cool for 10 minutes before removing to baking rack to cool completely.

Tie a satin or grosgrain ribbon around neck or waist.

Wrapped in plastic, then foil, the bread keeps at room temperature for 3 days, or it may be frozen.

To decorate

Raisins
Whole almonds
Filberts
Walnuts
Juniper berries
Silver nonpareils
Candied cherries or citron

TOOLS

1 large clear-plastic food storage bag with twist-tie
Baking sheet
Pastry brush
Scissors

Attach arms, legs, and head by moistening one end with milk. With 2 fingers make a hole in body and insert.

TO PACKAGE

Customize 1 large figure as a personal birthday gift for a child or adult. If you wish, use the icing recipe on page 177 to paint on clothing or hair, or to write a name or message on the bread.

Place the finished figure in a large box lined with layers of tissue paper.

TIGER PAWS

INGREDIENTS

1 cup sugar
½ cup light corn syrup
1 cup heavy cream
2 tablespoons unsalted butter, chilled and cut into small pieces
½ teaspoon vanilla extract
Pinch of salt
¾ pound shelled whole, perfect pecans
12 ounces semisweet chocolate morsels

TOOLS

2 baking sheets lined with wax paper
Candy thermometer
Double boiler

YIELD: about 24

This recipe is an adaptation of a recipe of Judith Olney's from *The Joy of Chocolate*. For an amusing centerpiece, place the Tiger Paws in a walking pattern around a white paper tablecloth. Place a small stuffed tiger at the end of the trail of candies.

METHOD

Combine the sugar, corn syrup, and half of the heavy cream in a saucepan. Cook over low heat, stirring until the sugar is dissolved, about 10 minutes. Slowly add remaining ½ cup heavy cream and bring to a low boil, stirring all the time. Continue cooking for 5 minutes more.

Add the chilled butter in ½-teaspoon pieces, stirring until all is incorporated. Insert a candy thermometer and cook over low heat until the thermometer reads 244° F., about 10 minutes. Remove from the heat and stir in the vanilla and salt. Set aside to cool for about 10 minutes.

In the meantime, line 2 baking sheets with wax paper. Arrange 4 perfect pecans in a slight semicircle to represent the "toes." Place 1 nut in the center and 1 nut for the "heel" (see illustration). Use a total of 6 nuts per candy.

Spoon 1 heaping tablespoon of caramel onto each nut cluster so that it rests on the nuts, but does not cover them completely. Repeat until all nut clusters are covered. Chill the candy in the refrigerator until the caramel is set.

Place the chocolate bits in the top pan of a double boiler. Set over simmering water until melted. Stir gently.

Carefully peel the chilled candies from the wax paper. Place 1 caramel at a time, bottom side up, on a 2-prong fork or a kitchen fork, and dip the top into the melted chocolate (see illustration). Replace the candy, chocolate side up, on the paper-lined baking sheet. Repeat with remaining candies. Let the chocolate harden at room temperature. Store the candies between layers of wax papers in an airtight container, until ready to use.

Tiger Paws keep for up to 1 week.

Arrange 4 pecans in a slight semicircle to represent the "toes." Place 1 nut in the center and 1 nut for the "heel." Spoon caramel onto each nut cluster.

Place one candy, bottom side up, on a 2-prong fork, and dip into the melted chocolate.

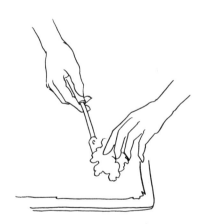

Place the candies, chocolate side up, on the paper-lined baking sheet.

Materials

Plastic wrap
Pinking shears
Six 8-inch squares of tiger-printed fabric, or any suitable fabric (burlap, printed cotton, bandannas)
6 dowels, 6 inches x ¼ inch
6 labels
Pail

TO PACKAGE

To make 6 party favors, wrap 4 candies in plastic wrap. Overwrap with an 8-inch square cut with pinking shears from a suitable fabric (cotton flannel or cotton). Tie hobo style to a birch dowel. Attach a tag shaped like a tiger paw. Repeat with remaining candies. Carry the favors to children's birthday party in a child's sand pail. Or if you like, pack 4 candies in a small, bright gift bag with a "tiger" print—just one of the many gift bags available at paper and party supply stores. Punch holes and lace with ribbon. For instructions, see Tied Paper Bags on page 220.

Tie the candies hobo style to a birch dowel. Carry to children's birthday party in a child's sand pail.

STAINED GLASS GINGER COOKIE FAVORS

YIELD: about 3 dozen 3-inch cookies

Colored sour-ball candies melt to form transparent cutout shapes, making these cookies a favorite for children of all ages. Hang them from a centerpiece at a child's birthday party, or tie them onto packages. They are also marvelous for Christmas, hung on a tree or in front of a window.

METHOD

Combine the molasses and butter in a medium-size saucepan and heat slowly over low heat until butter is melted. Cool slightly and blend in the egg. In a large bowl sift together the flour, baking soda, baking powder, salt, and ginger. Add the brown sugar and stir well.

Make a well in the center of the dry ingredients and add the molasses mixture. Mix until well blended. The dough will be slightly sticky. Gather into a large ball, wrap in plastic, then in aluminum foil, and chill for 2 hours, until stiff enough to roll without sticking.

Preheat oven to 350° F. Remove dough from the refrigerator and let it rest for 10 minutes. Line 2 baking sheets with aluminum foil. On a lightly floured surface, roll out the dough 1/4 inch thick. Using a cookie cutter or mold as your guide, cut out a shape from the center of the cookie. Be careful not to cut too close to the edges or the cookie will break. Place the cookies on the lined baking sheet. Gather up scraps, reroll, and cut, always working with chilled dough.

Note: You might use 2 different-size hearts, a heart with a star in the center, or use a sharp knife to cut initials in the center of a large circle. Use a drinking straw to cut a hole in the top of each cookie so you can later string them with ribbon for hanging.

Separate the sour balls by color and place each color group in a dou-ble-thickness of plastic bags. Place 1 bag at a time in a dish towel and crush the candies with a hammer or mallet into approximately ¼-inch

INGREDIENTS

¾ cup dark molasses
6 ounces unsalted butter
1 egg, slightly beaten
4 cups all-purpose flour
½ teaspoon baking soda
1 teaspoon baking powder
1 teaspoon salt
1 tablespoon ground ginger
1 cup firmly packed dark brown
    sugar
Two 8-ounce bags of sour-ball
    candies, assorted colors

TOOLS

Rolling pin
Baking sheet
Aluminum foil
Cookie cutters
Drinking straw
Plastic food storage bags
Ribbon

pieces. Fill the cutout shape with the crushed candies and bake for 10 to 12 minutes, until candy has melted and is bubbly.

Cool for 15 minutes, until candies harden, before peeling cookies from foil.

Thread a ribbon through the hole to hang. Stored between layers of wax paper in an airtight cookie tin, the cookies will keep for 1 week.

TO PACKAGE

For charming and edible party favors, cut each child's initials from the center of one large 6-inch round, heart-, or star-shaped cookie before filling with crushed candies and baking. Use the cookies for place cards on the birthday table.

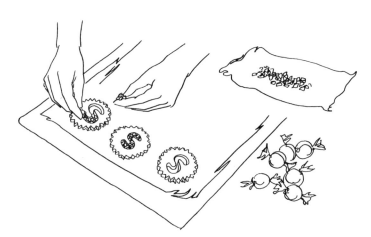

Fill the cutout shape with the crushed candies.

Gifts
of
Summer

Gifts of Summer

ROSEWATER

YIELD: 2 cups

Rosewater was first prepared as long ago as the tenth century. It is still made today by the Shakers, who use it to relieve sunburned, chapped, or dried skin. It is also a favored ingredient in Persian cuisine. It subtly enhances the flavor when added to jams, honey, even ice cream.

METHOD

Preheat oven to 450° F.

Select roses that have not been sprayed with insecticides. Rinse and dry the petals carefully and remove the white portion at the base of each petal. Place the rose petals in the casserole and cover with cold softened water (see Ingredients). Bring the mixture to a simmer on the top of the stove, place uncovered in the hot oven, and continue to simmer for 10 to 15 minutes.

Remove from the oven and allow the liquid to cool. Using the funnel, strain it into the bottles. Seal with caps or corks. The rosewater should be used within 2 weeks or it loses its healing properties and strong flavor.

TO PACKAGE

Before bestowing this elixir upon a favored one, decant into dark blue bottles using a funnel. (Such bottles are used to package antacids or are often found in antiques shops or yard sales.) Clap on the lid.

Design a rose label or cut one from old greeting cards, magazines, or garden catalogs. Use rubber cement to glue the label onto the bottle.

INGREDIENTS

2 pounds red or pink rose petals (yellow or white blossoms make a less attractive water)

Soft water to cover, either collected rain water or softened household water (Regular tap water is usually too hard and too full of minerals and chemicals.)

TOOLS

Deep enamel casserole
Funnel
Bottles with clamp-type porcelain lids or corks

SUMMER FRUITS IN LIQUEURS

INGREDIENTS

2 cups sugar
1 cup water
1 cup liqueur
2 cups fruit, clean, dry, without blemishes

TOOLS

Candy thermometer
Widemouthed canning jars with clamp-type lids

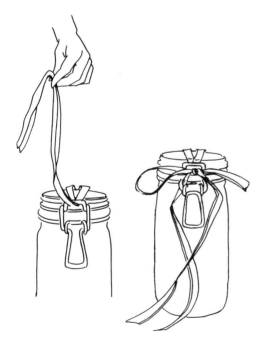

YIELD: 1 quart

In the fullness of summer, at the height of their season, steep these summer fruits in liqueur and set aside for Christmas presents.

Cherries in Brandy
Apricots in Amaretto } June

Peaches in Grand Marnier
Blueberries in Cointreau } July
Raspberries in Framboise

Plums in Mirabelle
Grapes in Grappa } August

METHOD

Make a basic sugar syrup of 2 cups sugar and 1 cup water by heating the syrup to 230° F. on a candy thermometer; stir constantly to prevent burning. Remove from the heat and cool. Add the appropriate liqueur. Pack whole fruit into a sterilized widemouthed quart jar with clamp-type lid, filling about three quarters full. Pour the hot syrup over the fruit. Wipe the rim with a clean damp cloth and seal with lid. Store in a cool dark place, or in the refrigerator, for at least 2 months.

TO PACKAGE

The sparkling glass jars showcase the contents. Merely dress up the lids by tying a ribbon in the following manner: For each jar use 1 yard of 5/16-inch-wide ribbon. Loop the ribbon through the back hinge of clamp jar. Crisscross it over the lid of jar, bringing behind, then through the pull-up clamp. Tie a knot, then a bow. If you give the fruits before the 2-month steeping time is up, attach a tag saying "Don't open until ———."

PICKLED CHERRIES

YIELD: 2 quarts

Sour or Morello cherries come in early June, and their presence in grocery stores means undoubtedly that summer is here. They don't last long and are usually available only for a couple of weeks from early to mid-June. To extend their season for many months, make them into these spicy, sweet-sour pickles, delicious as part of a mixed hors-d'oeuvre tray along with or in place of the usual olives, or as a nice accompaniment to pork, duck, or ham.

METHOD

Rinse the cherries and discard any that are damaged or bruised. Pack the rest into hot sterilized canning jars, filling to about three quarters full.

Combine the sugar, vinegar, cloves, and allspice berries in a non-aluminum saucepan and heat over high heat, stirring, until the sugar dissolves and the mixture comes to a boil. Boil for 10 minutes. Carefully pour the hot syrup over the cherries in the jars. Place 3 cloves and 1 allspice berry in each jar.

Wipe the rims of the jars with a clean damp cloth and seal with lids. Let cool on a wire rack to room temperature.

Store in the refrigerator for 1 month before using. The cherries will keep for 6 months refrigerated. Although they tend to wrinkle with age, this does not detract from their flavor.

TO PACKAGE

Show off the Pickled Cherries by packing them into widemouthed, fluted jars with corks or clamp-top lids, tying on a ribbon. If you give the cherries before the 1-month pickling time is up, attach a tag saying "Don't open until ———."

INGREDIENTS

1 pound sour Morello cherries,
    stems attached
⅓ cup sugar
¾ cup red-wine vinegar
6 whole cloves
2 whole allspice berries, crushed

TOOLS

Nonaluminum saucepan
2 widemouthed (quart) canning
    jars

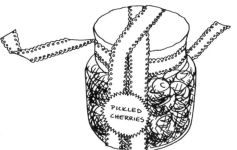

Pickled cherries packed into widemouthed jar with cork lid, tied with ribbon and gold-seal label.

DILLY BEANS

INGREDIENTS

3 pounds whole green beans
6 garlic cloves, peeled and left
whole
6 fresh dill heads, or 2
tablespoons dill seed
1½ teaspoons cayenne pepper
3¼ cups water
3¼ cups cider vinegar
6 tablespoons salt

TOOLS

Canning jars (see list of canning
equipment on page 232)

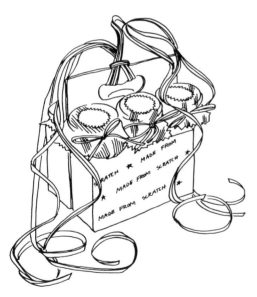

A six-pack of summer's bounty—jam, relishes, and pickles all "made from scratch."

YIELD: 6 pints

Condiments are the perfect gift for making simple summer meals into memorable gatherings. An ideal hors d'oeuvre for summer picnics or cocktail parties.

METHOD

Rinse the green beans and cut off the ends. Pack lengthwise in 6 sterilized widemouthed pint-size canning jars, leaving ¼-inch headroom. To *each* jar add 1 garlic clove, 1 head of dill, or 1 teaspoon dill seed, and ¼ teaspoon cayenne pepper.

In an enameled kettle bring to a boil the water, vinegar, and salt, and pour it, boiling hot, over the beans in the jars, filling to within ¼ inch of the rims. Wipe the rims with a clean damp cloth and seal the jars with the lids. Process in a boiling-water bath for 10 minutes (see instructions on page 231). Cool completely and store in a cool, dark, dry place.

TO PACKAGE

The following pickles, relishes, jams, and jellies packed into canning jars and topped off with fabric "hats" and/or placed in Wax Fabric Containers are sure to delight anyone on your gift list. See pages 219 and 224 for instructions.

However, if you are more ambitious and are eager to share a sampling of your efforts, give an assortment of ½-pint jars of jams, jellies, relishes, and pickles.

Spray-paint a cardboard container with a carrying handle which holds 6-packs of bottled drinks. Decorate with rubber stamps, stickers, or Prestype. (Prestype is pressure-sensitive, graphic-art tape available at art supply stores in a variety of colors.) Place one ½-pint jar topped with fabric hat and label in each hole. Tie a ribbon through the handle and carry off.

BREAD AND BUTTER PICKLES

YIELD: 5 to 6 pints

The relish tray is not complete without these crunchy pickles. This recipe comes from Betty Wolfe, who gives me a jar every Christmas but took three years to part with the recipe. Here are a few of her hints: Put up the pickles within 2 days of picking or the cucumbers become soft; when washing them, be gentle, don't scrub off the "prickles"—they add to the crunch.

METHOD

Sprinkle the cucumbers and onions with ¼ cup coarse salt and let soak in ice water for 3 hours. Rinse with cold water, drain, and pat dry.

Chop the peppers and mix with the cucumbers and onions.

Combine the sugar, vinegar, water, and spices in a large kettle and bring to a rapid boil. Gradually add the vegetables, stirring just to distribute the vegetables and prevent them from settling to the bottom of the kettle. Bring to a boil again and immediately remove from the heat.

Pack pickles and liquid into sterilized canning jars, leaving ½-inch headspace. Wipe the rims with a clean damp cloth and seal with lids. Process in a boiling-water bath for 5 minutes (see instructions on page 231). Cool completely and store in a cool, dark, dry place.

TO PACKAGE

See page 56.

INGREDIENTS

8 cups medium to small pickling cucumbers, sliced into ⅛-inch-thick rounds

4 small white onions, peeled and sliced into thin rounds

¼ cup coarse salt

1 green pepper, finely chopped

1 red pepper, finely chopped

1½ cups sugar

2 cups distilled white vinegar

½ cup water

1 teaspoon ground turmeric

1 teaspoon mustard seeds

½ teaspoon celery seeds

¼ teaspoon whole cloves

½ cinnamon stick, broken

TOOLS

Canning jars (see list of canning equipment on page 232)

ZUCCHINI PICKLES

INGREDIENTS

4 pounds *small* **zucchini,**
**   unpeeled, sliced into ¼-inch**
**   rounds, about 2 quarts**
2 onions, sliced into thin rounds
**   and separated**
¼ cup coarse salt
2 cups cider vinegar
2 cups sugar
1 teaspoon celery seeds
2 teaspoons mustard seeds
1 teaspoon ground turmeric
½ teaspoon dry mustard

TOOLS

Canning jars (see list of
**   equipment on page 232)**

YIELD: about 4 pints

Zucchini is as versatile a vegetable as it is prolific—which is really saying something. I had considered this productive summer squash a pest in the garden until I discovered this delicious recipe for bread and butter pickles, calling for zucchini in place of the traditional cucumber. If you still have a large amount of zucchini around after making the pickles, move right along to the zucchini muffins on page 88. A pest no more.

METHOD

Toss the sliced zucchini and onion rounds with the salt, place in a bowl, cover with ice water, and let stand for at least 2 hours. Drain, rinse with fresh water, drain again, and pat dry.

Combine the remaining ingredients in an enamel saucepan and bring to a boil. Cook for 2 minutes. Add the zucchini and onions and remove from the heat. Let the mixture stand for 2 hours, uncovered. Bring to a boil again and cook for 3 to 5 minutes.

Transfer the vegetables to hot, sterilized canning jars and pour the liquid over the vegetables, filling to within ¼ inch of the rims. Wipe the rims with a clean damp cloth and seal the jars with the lids. Process in a boiling-water bath for 10 minutes (see instructions on page 231). Cool completely and store in a cool, dark, dry place.

TO PACKAGE

See page 56 for suggestions.

PICKLED WATERMELON RIND

YIELD: 3 cups

Along with outdoor barbecues, corn on the cob, and minted iced tea, watermelon has the power to conjure memories of my Southern up-bringing. On hot summer days, as I sat on the side porch with my many cousins, concentrating on the watermelon seed-spitting contest, my grandmother moved quickly to gather the discarded rinds for her famous pickles.

METHOD

Remove the green peel from the watermelon with a sharp knife and cut the rind into 1-inch cubes. Boil the rinds in 2 quarts of water for 8 to 10 minutes, or until just tender. Drain and transfer to a glass, ceramic, or nonaluminum bowl.

In a nonaluminum saucepan, combine remaining ingredients and bring to a boil, stirring to dissolve the sugar, and simmer uncovered for 5 minutes. Pour the liquid and spices over the watermelon and let stand, covered with plastic wrap, at room temperature for 2 days.

Transfer the rind, spices, and liquid to a nonaluminum saucepan and bring to a boil. Remove from the heat and immediately pack the pickles and liquid into sterilized canning jars, filling to within ¼ inch of the rims. Wipe the rims with a clean damp cloth and seal the jars with the lids. Process in a boiling-water bath for 10 minutes (see instructions on page 231). Cool completely. Store in a cool, dark, dry place.

TO PACKAGE

See suggestions on page 56.

INGREDIENTS

Rind from 5-pound watermelon
2 cups cider vinegar
2 cups sugar
2 cinnamon sticks
2 teaspoons cloves
4 slices of gingerroot, each about the size of a quarter, peeled and flattened
½ teaspoon whole allspice berries
2 thin lemon slices, seeds removed

TOOLS

Nonaluminum bowl
Nonaluminum saucepan
Canning jars (see list of canning equipment on page 232)

CORN RELISH

INGREDIENTS

7 large ears of sweet corn
4 green peppers, finely chopped,
about 2 cups
4 red peppers, finely chopped,
about 2 cups
6 pounds tomatoes, finely
chopped, about 3 quarts
2 large onions, finely chopped,
about 2 cups
2 cups sugar
2 cups cider vinegar
2 tablespoons salt
2 teaspoons dry mustard
1 teaspoon ground turmeric
1 teaspoon hot pepper flakes

TOOLS

Very large saucepan, 8-quart size
Canning jars (see list of canning
equipment on page 232)

YIELD: six ½-pint jars

Always a favorite. Bring on the "dogs."

METHOD

With a sharp knife, cut the corn from the cobs, scraping the ears. There should be 4 cups of kernels. Mix the corn with the chopped vegetables. Place the vegetables in a large saucepan and add all remaining ingredients. Bring to a boil and simmer the relish over low heat, stirring occasionally, until fairly thick, about 30 minutes.

Transfer the relish to sterilized canning jars, filling to within ¼ inch of the rims. Wipe the rims with a clean damp cloth and seal the jars with the lids. Process in a boiling-water bath for 10 minutes (see instructions on page 231). Cool completely and store in a cool, dark, dry place.

TO PACKAGE

Adorned with a fabric "hat," this one pairs perfectly with homemade Tomato Ketchup and Barbecue Sauce. If your time and budget allow, include all three in a picnic hamper lined with a classic red-check tablecloth. See pages 68 and 70.

SUNSHINE STRAWBERRY PRESERVES

YIELD: 4 pints

The strawberry plant has long suggested both purity and passion. In *Othello,* Shakespeare embroidered the pure Desdemona's handkerchief with this symbolic berry.

What could be more pure than strawberries and sunshine? Once you've tasted it, you'll be overwhelmed. This recipe is not entirely fool-proof, but if you are prepared to make an adjustment or two at the last minute, you will be rewarded with the most delicious jam imaginable. Attempt this recipe only on 2 consecutive dry, sunny days.

METHOD

In a large ceramic or glass dish, arrange half of the strawberries in a single layer and sprinkle them with half of the sugar. Make a second layer with the rest of the berries and sprinkle with remaining sugar. Let stand uncovered for 3 to 4 hours.

Pour the mixture into a deep enamel or stainless-steel pot and stir very gently. Bring slowly to a boil and cook for 10 minutes, stirring occasionally until the sugar dissolves and making sure the mixture does not stick to the bottom of the pot. Add the lemon juice and cook for 10 minutes more.

Pour the mixture into a large shallow roasting pan, cover with plastic wrap, and place in direct sunshine for 2 days; bring it inside at night. Stir gently several times during the day. If the syrup has not thickened at the end of this time, transfer the berries with a slotted spoon to a bowl and boil the syrup for about 10 minutes. Add the berries and stir gently.

Pack the preserves in sterile canning jars, leaving ¼-inch headroom. Seal with paraffin (see instructions on page 235). Or, if using lids, process in a boiling-water bath for 10 minutes (see instructions on page 231). Cool completely and store in a cool, dark, dry place.

TO PACKAGE

Carefully unscrew and remove the outside rim of a canning jar. Place a label, which has been trimmed to fit, over the metal seal. Gently replace the rim. Along with a strawberry-shaped tag, attach a few strawberry blossoms for extra panache.

INGREDIENTS

2 quarts strawberries (Use small whole, firm, ripe berries; berries with hollow cores should be discarded.)
6 cups sugar
¼ cup lemon juice

TOOLS

Enamel or stainless-steel pot
Large shallow roasting pan
Canning jars (see list of canning equipment on page 232)

CHOCOLATE-DIPPED STRAWBERRIES

INGREDIENTS

4 ounces chocolate—sweet,
    semisweet, bittersweet, or
    milk, depending on your taste
1 pint strawberries, about 1 pound
    (Use ripe, not soft, small
    berries with stems attached.)
1 tablespoon lecithin (a pure
    liquid vegetable product
    available in health-food
    stores) (optional)

TOOLS

Double boiler
Baking sheet lined with wax paper

YIELD: about 20 strawberries

Chocolate-dipped fruits have become an after-dinner show of sophistication in recent years. This gift is obviously lavish and yet it can be mercifully small: Just give a few; remember that there is a certain psychological reverence for small amounts and the recipient can enjoy a luxurious binge without undoing a month's worth of dieting. It is even easier for you. The quality depends entirely on the ripeness of the berries and the choice of chocolate.

METHOD

Refrigerate the berries for about 1 hour before dipping. The chocolate will set faster if you do.

Break the chocolate into small pieces and place it in the top pan of a double boiler set over warm water on low heat. Cover the chocolate and heat until melted. Do not let the water boil. Uncover and stir until the chocolate is melted and very smooth. If the chocolate is too thick, add up to 1 tablespoon of lecithin, 1 teaspoon at a time. This will thin the chocolate and give it a satiny sheen. Remove the double boiler from the heat but leave the chocolate over the warm water.

Hold a berry by the stem or leaves and dip it to about half of its length. Let the excess chocolate drip back into the pot. Place the dipped berry on a baking sheet lined with wax paper. Repeat until all berries are coated. If the chocolate starts to thicken, reheat the water until the chocolate is melted. Again, do not let the water boil.

Place the tray of dipped berries in the refrigerator for about 15 minutes, or until the chocolate is firm. Remove from the refrigerator and lift each berry by the stem or leaves to remove it from the paper. The dipped berries should be stored between layers of wax paper in the refrigerator, to be eaten within 24 hours.

TO PACKAGE

Give each chocolate-dipped strawberry the wrapping it deserves—individual, silver-foil, petit-four cups available from kitchen supply stores.

Place the gleaming berries against white for a dazzling display. Line a shallow heart-shaped basket with several layers of doilies, slightly ruffling their edges. Nestle the strawberries and their cups in the basket. Tuck a few sprigs of glossy green leaves near the edge of the berries.

Place each dipped strawberry in a silver-foil petit-four cup and nestle in a doily-lined, heart-shaped basket.

RASPBERRY JAM

YIELD: about four ½-pint jars

For centuries the raspberry has been associated with Venus and the sorrows that follow misplaced love. Remembering this, what could better satisfy the lovelorn than a comforting homemade gift of raspberry jam to spoon over buttered muffins?

METHOD

Do not wash the raspberries but carefully pick over the fruit and use only firm, blemish-free fruit.

Place the raspberries and sugar in a nonaluminum saucepan and crush the fruit with a spoon or potato masher. Slowly bring the mixture to a boil, stirring frequently to dissolve the sugar and prevent scorching. Boil for 20 to 30 minutes, no more or jam will be tough. Remove from the heat and skim off any foam. Add the lemon juice.

Pour into sterilized canning jars, filling to within ¼ inch of the rims.

INGREDIENTS

2 pounds raspberries, about 4 cups

3 cups sugar

Juice of 1 lemon

¼ cup brandy (optional)

TOOLS

Nonaluminum saucepan

Canning jars (lids optional) (see list of canning equipment on page 232)

4 strips of clean, white paper, 3 inches x ¾ inch (optional)

Wipe the rims with a clean damp cloth. To impart a sophisticated flavor to the jam, dip strips of paper in the brandy and insert one into each jar. Seal each jar with paraffin (see instructions on page 235) or lids and process in a boiling-water bath for 10 minutes (see instructions on page 231). Cool completely and store in a cool, dark, dry place.

TO PACKAGE

Give the jars fabric "hats" of shiny red-lacquered origami paper, tied in place with a gold cord. Place a gold notary seal or gold star on the top of the jar. Everything about the package should suggest an aristocratic jam.

BLUEBERRY JAM

INGREDIENTS

4 cups blueberries
½ cup water
2 cups sugar
3 thin lemon slices, seeds removed
1 cinnamon stick

TOOLS

**Canning jars (see list of
    equipment on page 232)**

YIELD: four ½-pint jars

Precious spoonfuls of summer sapphire, traditional in Scotland served on hot scones.

METHOD

Carefully pick over the fruit. Put 2 cups of berries in the bottom of a deep saucepan and crush with a potato masher or the back of a spoon. Place remaining berries over the crushed fruit, add the water, and bring to a boil. Simmer over low heat, stirring occasionally, for 5 minutes, or until berries are tender. Add the sugar, lemon slices, and cinnamon and continue to cook, stirring constantly, to the jell point (page 234).

Remove lemon slices and cinnamon stick. Pour the jam into sterilized canning jars, filling to within ¼ inch of the rims. Wipe the rims with a clean damp cloth and seal the jars with the lids. Process in a boiling-water bath for 10 minutes (see instructions on page 231). Cool completely. Store in a cool, dark, dry place.

TO PACKAGE

For a very American spoonful, stick masses of gold stars on 6-inch circles of white tissue paper. Place the tissue paper over the lid of the jar and hold in place with a rubber band. Tie with thin double-sided red satin ribbon and add a tiny American flag.

BLUEBERRY BUTTER

YIELD: 4 cups

Very thick and spicy, blueberry butter turns plain toast, muffins, or pancakes into a real treat.

METHOD

Combine all the ingredients in a large saucepan and cook over low heat until the sugar dissolves, stirring as needed. Bring to a boil, reduce heat, and simmer uncovered for about 45 minutes, until the mixture thickens. Stir occasionally to prevent sticking.

Pour the butter into sterilized canning jars, filling to within ¼ inch of the rims. Wipe the rims with a clean damp cloth and seal the jars with the lids. Process in a boiling-water bath for 10 minutes (see instructions on page 231). Cool completely. Store in a cool, dark, dry place.

TO PACKAGE

There will be no excuses for skipping breakfast when you present that lazy someone with homemade Blueberry Butter and a wholesome bag of sourdough pancake mix from the health-food store.

Give the Blueberry Butter a pale blue tissue paper "hat." See instructions on page 219.

INGREDIENTS

4 cups blueberries
6 large Granny Smith apples, peeled and chopped, about 4 cups
2 cups white sugar
1 cup firmly packed light brown sugar
1 teaspoon ground cinnamon
¼ teaspoon ground allspice
¼ teaspoon grated mace
¼ teaspoon grated nutmeg

TOOLS

Canning jars (see list of canning equipment on page 232)

PEACH HONEY

INGREDIENTS
5 pounds ripe peaches
8 cups sugar

TOOLS
Food mill
Enamel saucepan
**Canning jars (see list of canning
   equipment on page 232)**

YIELD: 3 pints

One of my most delightful food memories is of devouring peach honey on homemade biscuits with sacramental reverence on warm Southern Sunday mornings—a pure epicurean blessing.

Fruit honeys are thick sauces made with sugar and fruit pulp, much like fruit butters only clear. Spread them on toast or muffins or spoon them over ice cream, waffles, or pancakes.

This is a basic recipe. Vary it according to your taste. Experiment with other fruits, taking the proportions in this recipe as your guidelines.

METHOD

Blanch, peel, and stone peaches, and cut into pieces. Purée through a food mill fitted with the medium plate, to make 4 cups peach pulp. Combine pulp with the sugar in an enamel saucepan and stir over moderate heat until sugar is dissolved.

Bring the sauce to a boil, stirring frequently to prevent scorching. Reduce heat and simmer for about 30 minutes, or until thick, stirring frequently.

Pour the "honey" into hot sterilized canning jars, filling to within ¼ inch of the rims. Wipe rims with a clean damp cloth and seal the jars with the lids. Process in a boiling-water bath for 10 minutes (see instructions on page 231). Cool completely. Store in a cool, dark, dry place.

TO PACKAGE

The Peach Honey and Ginger Pear Honey (page 67) fit perfectly into small gift bags decorated with whimsical bear stickers, available in stores that carry Gordon Fraser paper products. Fold over approximately 2 inches of the top of the bag, make holes with a hole puncher through folded layers, weave ribbon through holes (see Tied Paper Bags, page 220).

GINGER PEAR HONEY

YIELD: 3 pints

METHOD

Put the fruit through the food mill fitted with the medium plate. Combine pulp with remaining ingredients in an enamel saucepan and stir over moderate heat until sugar is dissolved.

Bring the sauce to a boil, stirring frequently to prevent scorching. Reduce heat and simmer for 2½ to 3 hours, or until thick.

Pour the "honey" into hot sterilized canning jars, filling them to within ¼-inch of the rims. Wipe rims with a clean damp cloth and seal the jars with the lids. Process in a boiling-water bath for 10 minutes (see instructions on page 231). Cool completely. Store in a cool, dark, dry place.

TO PACKAGE

See Peach Honey (page 66).

INGREDIENTS

5 pounds pears, peeled, cored, and cut into cubes
1 tablespoon ground ginger
2½ to 3 pounds sugar, depending on your "sweetbuds"
Grated rind and juice of 2 lemons

TOOLS

Food mill
Enamel saucepan
Canning jars (see list of canning equipment on page 232)

RASPBERRY KETCHUP

YIELD: about 1½ cups

Keep half of this for yourself. Delicious served over roasted duck or pheasant.

METHOD

Do not wash the raspberries but carefully pick over the fruit and use only firm, unblemished berries.

Combine the raspberries, vinegar, and water in a nonaluminum saucepan and boil for about 5 minutes. Put the mixture through a food

INGREDIENTS

2 cups raspberries, about 1 pound
½ cup cider vinegar
½ cup water
1 cup firmly packed dark brown sugar
½ teaspoon ground cloves
½ teaspoon ground ginger
¼ teaspoon cayenne pepper
1 teaspoon ground cinnamon
½ teaspoon salt
2 tablespoons butter

TOOLS

Nonaluminum saucepan
Food mill
**Canning jars (see list of canning
    equipment on page 232)**

INGREDIENTS

**10 pounds ripe tomatoes, peeled,
    seeded, and coarsely
    chopped, 5 to 6 cups**
3 onions, finely chopped
1 red pepper, finely chopped
1 green pepper, finely chopped
4 garlic cloves, minced
**½ cup firmly packed light brown
    sugar**
1 cup distilled white vinegar
1 teaspoon peppercorns
1 teaspoon whole cloves
**1 teaspoon whole allspice berries,
    crushed**
1 teaspoon celery seeds
1 cinnamon stick, broken
1 tablespoon salt
2 teaspoons paprika
**¼ to ½ teaspoon cayenne pepper,
    depending on how spicy you
    like ketchup**

mill fitted with the fine plate and set over a bowl. Discard the pulp.

Put the liquid and all remaining ingredients in a saucepan and boil for 8 to 10 minutes, or until slightly thick. Pour the ketchup into sterilized canning jars or bottles with clamp-type lids, filling to within ¼ inch of the rim. Wipe the rim with a clean damp cloth and seal with the lid. Process in boiling-water bath for 10 minutes (see instructions on page 231). Cool completely. Store in a cool, dry, dark place.

TO PACKAGE

Because this recipe is so extravagant, make sure it gets a beautifully designed label and real satin ribbon.

TOMATO KETCHUP

YIELD: about 8 pints

This ketchup is so often requested by friends who prefer it to the store-bought variety that I could be making ketchup forever.

METHOD

Combine the tomatoes, onions, peppers, and garlic in a large kettle and cook over medium heat, uncovered, for 20 to 30 minutes, until the vegetables are soft.

Press the mixture through a food mill fitted with the medium plate and return the purée to the pot. Add the sugar and vinegar and simmer for 30 to 45 minutes, until the mixture is reduced by half.

Tie the whole spices and broken cinnamon stick together in a square of cheesecloth and add them to the tomato mixture. Season with the salt, paprika, and cayenne and simmer, uncovered, stirring frequently to prevent sticking, until the ketchup is very thick, about 30 minutes. Remove spice bag. Adjust seasoning by adding more salt or cayenne if you wish.

Spoon immediately into sterilized canning jars or bottles with clamp-type lids, leaving ¼-inch headspace. Wipe rims with a clean damp cloth and seal with lids. Process in a boiling-water bath for 10 minutes (see instructions on page 231). Cool completely and store in a cool, dark, dry place.

TO PACKAGE

An imaginative package for humble ketchup: Wrap the bottle in a loosely woven Japanese rice straw mat (the type used to roll sushi), or cut an old bamboo matchstick blind to fit around the bottle. Secure the base and neck of the bottle with straw rope. Glue a red shiny tomato cutout on the front and label "Tomato Ketchup."

FREEZER TOMATO SAUCE

YIELD: 6 quarts

I am never prudent in the spring when it comes time to set out tomato plants in the garden. I know the rule is to plant only half the amount you think you want but, for me, there really is no such thing as too many tomatoes. By the end of August, I have become bored with the beach and lapse quite contentedly into the old-fashioned business of converting every last tomato into sauce, chutney, or conserve.

METHOD

Heat the oil in a large kettle and in it sauté the onions until translucent. Add the garlic, celery, and green peppers and continue cooking over low heat for 3 to 4 more minutes. Add the tomatoes, tomato paste, beef broth, bay leaves, and salt and pepper to taste. Bring to a boil and

TOOLS

Large kettle
Food mill
Cheesecloth
Canning jars or bottles with clamp-type lids (see list of canning equipment on page 232)

Tomato ketchup wrapped in a Japanese sushi mat and tied at both ends with straw rope.

TOOLS

Large kettle
Food mill
Freezer containers

INGREDIENTS

1½ cups olive oil

6 large yellow onions, finely chopped, about 6 cups

6 garlic cloves, finely chopped

4 celery stalks, finely chopped, about 2 cups

4 green peppers, finely chopped, about 2 cups

16 pounds fresh tomatoes, peeled, seeded, and chopped, about 6 quarts (The more liquid you squeeze from the tomatoes, the less time it will take for the sauce to thicken . . . be ruthless.)

Six 6-ounce cans tomato paste

3 cups beef broth

5 bay leaves

Salt

Pepper

½ cup chopped fresh basil

2 tablespoons fresh thyme, or 1 tablespoon dried

3 tablespoons fresh orégano, or 1½ tablespoons dried

simmer uncovered, stirring occasionally, for about 45 minutes, or until the sauce is thick and a thin layer of oil is visible around the side of the kettle. Add the herbs and simmer for 5 minutes longer.

Pass half of the sauce through a food mill fitted with the medium blade, set over a large bowl. Discard the pulp and add the purée to the remaining sauce. Check the seasonings and add more salt and pepper if you wish. Cool completely.

Pack the sauce into freezer containers, leaving 1 inch of headroom. This sauce will keep for up to 6 months with very little loss of flavor, so make lots. The recipe works well when doubled. Or make several batches as the tomato crop comes in. You will be sorry to run out in January.

TO PACKAGE

Make sure to tape the lids firmly in place before packaging. Wrap each container in tissue paper and overwrap with a large clear-plastic bag, gathering the top and tying with a bow. Stick a label on the outside bag or tie on a label with a favorite recipe for lasagne, eggplant parmigiana, or spaghetti sauce. Remind the recipient to remove wrapping before freezing.

BARBECUE SAUCE

YIELD: 5 cups

In the New World, French hunters combined words—*barbe* for whiskers and *queue* for tail—to describe the process, learned from the Indians, of slowly roasting an entire animal from whiskers to tail over a hickory wood fire. Over the years, nothing has become more American than the outdoor barbecue. Various meats can be treated this way—beef, pork, chicken, or lamb. Pork is my favorite, but everyone knows that it is not only the hickory smoke or the choice of meat that makes those succulent bits of barbecue special, it also depends on the sauce. Mild or hot, sauce makes the barbecue. This is a medium-hot one.

METHOD

Sauté the onions and garlic in the butter until limp but not brown. Add remaining ingredients in the order listed, stir to combine, and bring to a boil. Lower the heat and simmer, uncovered, for 45 minutes to 1 hour, stirring occasionally to prevent sticking.

Transfer the sauce to hot sterilized canning jars or bottles with clamp-type lids, leaving ¼-inch headspace. Wipe the rims with a clean damp cloth and seal with the lids. Process in a boiling-water bath for 10 minutes (see instructions on page 231). Cool completely and store in a cool, dark, dry place.

TO PACKAGE

A great Father's Day present, sure to please any grill fanatic on your list. See Tomato Ketchup (page 68) or Wax-Sealed Bottles (page 222) for suggestions for wrapping bottles. Make the gift complete by pairing it with assorted grill paraphernalia—tongs, basting brush, hot mitts, a bag of mesquite wood chips for authentic flavor.

INGREDIENTS

2 cups finely chopped onions
4 garlic cloves, minced
4 ounces butter
2 cups ketchup (I like Heinz or homemade)
1 cup brandy
2 tablespoons dark brown sugar
1 tablespoon dry mustard
⅛ teaspoon cayenne pepper (vary according to hotness desired)
2 tablespoons freshly squeezed lemon juice
1 cup white vinegar
1 tablespoon Worcestershire sauce
⅔ cup water

TOOLS

Canning jars (see list of canning equipment on page 232)

HELLFIRE AND DAMNATION MEXICAN SALSA

YIELD: 6 cups

A dish of *salsa* or Mexican tomato sauce is as indispensable to the Mexican table as chutneys are to the Indian cuisine. *Salsas* run the gamut from mild to nutty to fiery depending on the type of chiles used. This recipe calls for chile *ancho,* probably the most commonly used chile in

INGREDIENTS

**6 large, dried chiles *ancho,*
    available at specialty food
    shops
6 large tomatoes, 2½ to 3 pounds
6 garlic cloves, peeled
1½ teaspoons salt
3 teaspoons mild white vinegar
1 to 2 tablespoons finely chopped
    fresh coriander**

TOOLS

**Flat iron skillet
Rubber gloves
Canning jars (see list of canning
    equipment on page 232)**

Mexico. It is deep maroon in color, 4 to 5 inches long, and 2 to 3 inches wide. It may vary in strength from gentle to piquant. You might want to ask how hot they are before you buy. Diana Kennedy's book *The Cuisines of Mexico* (Harper & Row) has an excellent section on chiles if you want more information.

You may not take to *salsa* at first, but it will grow on you, and soon you may find yourself thinking of many ways to use it. A few suggestions: Start the day by adding *salsa* to scrambled eggs; use it as a side dish with cold meats at lunch; offer it as a light and snappy dip for corn chips when you have drinks; try it on fresh clams and oysters in place of the usual horseradish and ketchup mixture.

Make this at the end of August when the tomatoes are ripening faster than you can eat them.

METHOD

Heat a flat iron skillet and toast the chiles for about 1 minute, turning constantly so that they do not burn. They will soften and become a dark reddish brown. Remove from the heat. Wearing rubber gloves (a must if you don't want stinging hands for the rest of the day), slit open the chiles, remove the seeds, and set them aside. Discard the vein and stem. Toast the seeds on the same skillet for 15 to 20 seconds, turning constantly so that they do not burn.

Blend all the ingredients (except the coriander) together in the container of a blender or in a food processor for 1 minute. Do not overblend; the sauce should be lumpy in texture and slightly loose in consistency.

Add the chopped coriander and transfer the sauce into sterilized Mason jars, filling to within ¼ inch of the rims. Wipe the rims with a clean damp cloth and seal the jars with the lids. Store in the refrigerator. *Salsa* is best eaten within a few days, but it will keep for as long as 2 weeks.

TO PACKAGE

As a gift for more devilish friends, place the jar of *salsa* with a package of whole-grain corn chips, or tostados, in a Mexican basket lined with a brightly woven napkin. Attach a label and remind the recipient that the sauce needs to be refrigerated.

CAPONATINA

YIELD: 4 pints

Caponatina can best be described as a cross between a vegetable and a condiment. Intensely flavored and rich, taking its seasonings from the countries bordering the Mediterranean, it makes an excellent accompaniment to cold meats or serves as a delicious first course.

METHOD

Toss the cubed eggplant with the coarse salt and lemon juice and place in a colander set over a large bowl. Cover the eggplant with a large plate and place a 5-pound weight on the plate. (A 5-pound bag of flour is good for this.) Let the eggplant stand at room temperature for 1 hour to extract the extra water and remove the bitter taste.

Heat about ¼ cup of the oil in a large skillet. Sauté the eggplant cubes in small batches for 1 to 2 minutes on each side until barely brown. Transfer the eggplant as it is done to a large flameproof casserole. Continue to add more oil to the skillet as necessary, using as much as 1 cup. Repeat until all the eggplant is browned.

Pour the remaining ½ cup of oil into the same skillet, and over low heat sauté the onions for about 5 minutes, or until limp but not brown. Add the celery and cook for 5 minutes more. Add the tomato sauce and continue cooking until the celery is tender, adding a little water if necessary. Transfer the mixture to the casserole with the eggplant. Add the olives and pine nuts. Stir and set aside.

Combine the apples, raisins, and vinegar in an enamel saucepan over low heat and cook until the apples are soft. Add to the eggplant and vegetables in the casserole. Season to taste with salt and freshly ground pepper.

INGREDIENTS

4 medium-size eggplants, peeled and cut into 1½-inch cubes
¼ cup coarse salt
2 tablespoons freshly squeezed lemon juice
1½ cups olive oil
4 yellow onions, finely chopped
4 celery ribs, finely chopped
½ cup tomato sauce
12 green olives, pitted and quartered
½ cup pine nuts
3 apples, peeled, cored, and cut into cubes
¼ cup raisins
½ cup red-wine vinegar
Salt
Freshly ground pepper

TOOLS

Colander
5-pound weight (see Method)
Flameproof casserole
Enamel saucepan
Canning jars (see list of canning equipment on page 232)

Simmer the *caponatina* over low heat on top of the stove, uncovered, for 2 to 2½ hours, stirring occasionally to prevent sticking. Correct the seasoning and pour into hot sterilized canning jars, filling to within ¼ inch of the rims. Wipe the rims with a clean damp cloth and seal with the lids. Cool completely and store in the refrigerator for up to 2 weeks. Serve warm or at room temperature.

TO PACKAGE

Slip the jars into small fabric sacks with drawstring cords or give them fabric "hats" (see page 219 for instructions).

Fabric sacks for jars of caponatina.

INGREDIENTS

**4 cups firmly packed fresh basil
    leaves**
1 cup parsley
**8 to 10 garlic cloves, peeled and
    chopped**
2 cups shelled walnuts
1½ cups best-quality olive oil
½ cup walnut oil
**2 cups freshly grated best-quality
    Parmesan cheese**
**½ cup freshly grated best-quality
    Romano cheese**
Coarse salt
Freshly ground pepper

PESTO

*If I had to choose just one plant for the whole herb garden,
I should be content with basil.*

Elizabeth David, *Italian Food*

Nothing evokes the pleasures of summer like the heady, aromatic scent of basil. Too good to limit to summer alone, its pungent flavor can be enjoyed year round if you make it into *pesto Genovese*. This recipe can be doubled or even tripled, depending on your access to large amounts of basil.

In Genoa there has always been only one way to prepare *pesto*. Using only fresh basil, the best Italian Parmesan and Romano cheeses, garlic, and pure virgin olive oil, they pound these classic ingredients into a fine paste with a marble pestle in a marble mortar. Today, with our more hurried life-styles, most cooks own a blender or food processor, either of which is a reasonable substitute for the mortar and pestle, especially in the preparation of large quantities for freezing or gifts.

I have added walnuts, walnut oil, and a little parsley in this slightly different version of the classic recipe. Don't limit *pesto* to pasta. Add it to soups or stews, use it to bind a cold chicken salad, toss it with small red potatoes, or stuff it into cherry tomatoes or mushrooms for an unusual hors d'oeuvre. The possibilities are endless.

METHOD

Combine the basil, parsley, garlic, and walnuts in the bowl of a food processor, or quarter the recipe and use a blender, or pound by hand in a mortar. Process to a coarse paste. Gradually add the olive oil, then the walnut oil, in a slow steady stream until all the oil is used. Add the cheese, a large pinch of coarse salt, and a liberal amount of fresh pepper; process briefly to combine. Scrape out into four 1-cup plastic containers for freezing (1 cup of *pesto* is enough for 1 pound of pasta), leaving about 1 inch of headroom in the containers, or scrape into four 1-cup sterilized glass canning jars. Pour a thin layer of olive oil over the *pesto,* to prevent discoloration, before sealing with the lids. The *pesto* freezes indefinitely or will keep refrigerated for several weeks.

TO PACKAGE

Viva Italia! A complete dinner presented in a reusable stainless-steel colander.

Directions

Line the colander with several layers of pages from an Italian magazine or red, green, and white tissue paper.

Pile in the pasta, *pesto,* cheese, and pasta server.

Overwrap in clear cellophane and tie with a big red or green bow.

Tie on a label with directions for making *pesto.* (See label suggestions on page 216.) Remind your recipient that the *pesto* should be either frozen or refrigerated if not used immediately.

TOOLS

Blender, food processor, or mortar and pestle
Plastic freezer containers

Materials

For each gift
1 stainless-steel colander
Pages from an Italian fashion magazine or red, green, and white tissue papers (the colors of the Italian flag)
1 pasta server—an ingenious device made for lifting and serving pasta
½ pound wedge of imported Parmesan or Romano cheese
Several 8-ounce boxes or bags of assorted pasta—shells, corkscrews (*fusilli*), wheels (*rotelle*), linguine, spaghettini—in an assortment of flavors—green (spinach), red (tomatoes), semolina, or Jerusalem artichoke
Pesto
Clear plastic
Wide red or green ribbon

TAPENADE

INGREDIENTS

½ cup imported Alfonso olives
    (black), pitted
¼ cup imported Sicilian olives
    (green), pitted
3 anchovy fillets
1 garlic clove
2 tablespoons capers, drained
¼ cup oil-packed tuna, drained
1 tablespoon lemon juice
1 cup fresh parsley
¼ cup best-quality olive oil
Freshly ground black pepper

TOOLS

Blender or food processor

YIELD: 1½ cups

Straight from Provence where summer cooking is a bundle of lusty tastes and smells, this poor man's caviar is traditionally spread on crackers or French bread as a first course or an hors d'oeuvre. Try using it as a garnish for a fresh tomato salad or deviled eggs. Ideal for dipping raw vegetables or to toss with fresh pasta. A welcome house gift full of summer warmth.

METHOD

In a blender or food processor combine the pitted olives, anchovy fillets, garlic, capers, tuna, lemon juice, and parsley. Process until smooth.

With the motor running, add the olive oil, dribble by dribble, as if making mayonnaise, to make a thick sauce.

Add a few grinds of pepper to taste. Store in an airtight container. The *tapenade* will keep refrigerated for up to 1 week.

TO PACKAGE

In keeping with the region, give this one a hat cut from a French Provincial print fabric, adding a tag with serving suggestions. Remind the recipient to keep the *tapenade* refrigerated.

COLD SPICY SESAME SAUCE

YIELD: about 4 cups

With this sauce on hand, all you need to enjoy the cold sesame noodles that have become so popular in Chinese restaurants is a package of whole or buckwheat noodles, fresh scallions, and sesame oil. You can use the sesame sauce in place of the habitual mayonnaise for cold salads of leftover chicken, turkey, or duck. Try it as a good nutty-flavored dip for raw vegetables or experiment with it as a marinade for chicken, lamb, or beef.

METHOD

Heat the oil in a medium-size saucepan. Add the onion and garlic and sauté over low heat for 1 minute. Stirring constantly, whisk in the coconut cream, ground red pepper, and Szechuan peppercorns, ginger, cuminseed, lemon juice, and soy sauce. Bring to a boil and remove from the heat. Stir the sesame paste thoroughly to incorporate all the oil at the top and gradually add it to the coconut cream mixture, stirring until very smooth.

Cool the sauce and pour it into clean sterilized jars. Seal with lids and store in the refrigerator until ready to use. The sauce will keep for up to 1 week.

TO PACKAGE

For the perfect take-along meal, line a woven basket or decorated mushroom basket with burlap (see instructions on page 226). Pack in the sesame sauce, add buckwheat noodles, a bottle of hot sesame oil, a bunch of fresh scallions, and a set of chopsticks tied with a ribbon. Include a card with directions for serving.

To serve over buckwheat noodles, cook the noodles according to the directions on the package, adding ¼ cup of oil to the water. Drain the noodles and rinse with cold water to prevent their sticking together. Add a few drops of sesame oil to the noodles and toss. While the noodles are still warm, toss with the sesame sauce. Cool completely, sprinkle with finely chopped scallions, and serve.

INGREDIENTS

1 tablespoon peanut oil
¼ cup finely chopped onion
4 garlic cloves, minced
1½ cups canned coconut cream
1 teaspoon red pepper, pounded
    to a fine powder
1 teaspoon Szechuan peppercorns,
    pounded to a fine powder
1 teaspoon ground ginger
½ teaspoon ground cuminseed
Juice of 2 lemons
5 tablespoons soy sauce
1½ cups sesame seed paste or
    butter (available in health-
    food stores or gourmet shops)

TOOLS

Canning jars, two 1-pound jars or
    four 8-ounce jars

Fruit and Herb Vinegars and Oils

As more and more Americans follow the trend to lighter eating habits, fruit and herb vinegars play an increasingly important part as low-calorie flavorings to sauces and dressings. They have an inimitable edge to their taste which is a pleasant surprise when encountered in salads or in glazes for meats or poultry. The variations on the basic concept are countless.

These are a few of my favorites. They take a couple of days to make, but they are a great treat for summer salad days.

HERB VINEGAR

YIELD: 1 quart

Herb vinegars are simple to prepare and improve with age. This is a good basic recipe, which you can flavor with your own choice of herbs or the special favorite of a friend. Use only fresh herbs, picked just before the plants are in full bloom.

METHOD

Stud the onions with the cloves. Place the onions, mint, parsley, fennel, peppercorns, coarse salt, sugar, and brandy in a ceramic or stainless-steel bowl.

Bring the vinegar to a boil and then pour it over the mixture in the bowl. Cover loosely and let stand for 2 weeks.

Strain the flavored vinegar through a colander lined with cheesecloth. Using a funnel, pour the vinegar into a sterilized bottle. Add a few sprigs of the herb or herbs of your choice. Seal with cork or lid.

INGREDIENTS

2 small white onions, peeled
4 cloves
1 small bunch of mint
1 small bunch of parsley
1 small head of fennel (optional)
    } combined to make 2 cups
1 teaspoon peppercorns
⅛ teaspoon coarse salt
1 teaspoon sugar
1 teaspoon best brandy
1 quart white vinegar
A few sprigs of any combination of the following: fennel with flowers, tarragon, dill with flowers, chervil, lemon thyme, summer savory, marjoram, chive blossoms, rosemary, green or purple basil

TO PACKAGE

For a simple yet professional way to seal and show off herb or fruit vinegars, see Wax-Sealed Bottles (page 222).

A perfect partner for Herb-Flavored Oils (page 81).

TOOLS

Ceramic or stainless-steel bowl
Cheesecloth
Funnel
Bottles with tight-fitting lids or
      corks
Colander

CRANBERRY MINT VINEGAR

YIELD: about 6 cups

Excellent for deglazing fish or poultry or as a refreshing addition to a fruit salad dressing.

METHOD

Reserve 12 whole cranberries. Coarsely chop remaining cranberries and place them in an enamel or stainless-steel bowl. Bring the rice vinegar to a boil and pour over the chopped berries. Cover with several layers of cheesecloth and let the mixture stand in a cool place (but not in the refrigerator) for 24 hours.

Strain the vinegar through a colander lined with a double layer of cheesecloth set over a large bowl. Press all the juice from the cranberries. Bring the juice to a boil, then cool slightly. Using a funnel, pour the vinegar into a sterilized bottle. Place the whole cranberries on a bamboo skewer, with a fresh mint leaf between each 3 or 4 berries. Repeat until the skewer is full, allowing 1 inch on each end. Gently place the skewer in the bottle and seal with the lid or cork.

The vinegar keeps in a cool place for about 4 months.

TO PACKAGE

For a simple yet professional way to seal and show off herb or fruit vinegars, see Wax-Sealed Bottles (page 222).

INGREDIENTS

1½ pounds fresh cranberries
6 cups rice vinegar
About 12 fresh mint leaves

TOOLS

Enamel or stainless-steel bowl
Bamboo skewer
Cheesecloth
Colander
Funnel
Bottle with tight-fitting cork or lid

BLUEBERRY VINEGAR

INGREDIENTS

1 quart blueberries
1 quart rice vinegar
½ cup sugar

TOOLS

Glass or enamel bowl
Cheesecloth
Funnel
Bottles with tight-fitting corks
    or lids

YIELD: 5 cups

METHOD

Pick over the blueberries and discard any blemished fruit. Put the clean berries in a large glass or enamel bowl. With the back of a wooden spoon or a potato masher, coarsely mash the berries, leaving some whole. Bring the rice vinegar to a boil and pour over the mashed berries. Let stand, covered with several layers of cheesecloth, for 2 to 3 days; stir occasionally.

On the third day, remove the fruit with a slotted spoon and discard all but some of the whole berries. Strain the liquid through the cheesecloth into an enamel saucepan. Add the sugar and bring the mixture to a boil, stirring to dissolve the sugar. Simmer for 10 minutes. Using a funnel, pour the vinegar into hot sterile bottles; add a few whole berries to the bottles for identification and seal with corks or lids. Store the vinegars in a cool, dark place.

TO PACKAGE

For a simple yet professional way to seal and show off herb or fruit vinegars, see Wax-Sealed Bottles (page 222).

RED RASPBERRY VINEGAR

INGREDIENTS

3 quarts red raspberries
1 quart rice vinegar
1 cup sugar

YIELD: 5 cups

Raspberries are always expensive. They don't keep very long and you never have enough of them. However, if you have your own private patch or access to a generous neighbor's, or if you are given to lavish expenditure, consider making 3 quarts of berries into Red Raspberry

Vinegar. (Sometimes called Shrub by our ancestors, it was used to relieve symptoms of flu or sore throat.)

METHOD

Do not wash the raspberries, but carefully pick over the fruit and use only firm, blemish-free berries. Put 1 quart of the berries into a large glass or enamel bowl. Pour the rice vinegar over them and let stand, covered with plastic wrap, for 24 hours. Remove the berries with a slotted spoon and reserve the fruit for other uses (pies, jams, sauces). Add another quart of fresh raspberries to the vinegar. Let steep, covered, for another 24 hours. Again, remove berries and replace with the final quart of fresh fruit. Let steep, covered, for a final 24 hours.

On the fourth day, remove berries and strain liquid through cheesecloth into an enamel saucepan. Add the sugar, bring to a boil, and simmer for 10 minutes. Using a funnel, pour into hot sterile bottles and seal with corks or lids. Store in a cool, dark place.

TO PACKAGE

For a simple yet professional way to seal and show off herb or fruit vinegars, see Wax-Sealed Bottles (page 222).

HERB-FLAVORED OILS

These look and smell as delicious as they taste, either in salad dressings or in recipes for roast meats or vegetables. Try basting a roast chicken with tarragon oil, or add a few tablespoons of rosemary oil to steamed green beans.

METHOD

Place the herbs, peppercorns, and bay leaf (if you are using it) in the bottle. Using a funnel, pour the oil over the herbs and seal with the cork

TOOLS

Glass or enamel bowl
Enamel saucepan
Cheesecloth
Funnel
**Bottles with tight-fitting corks
   or lids**

INGREDIENTS

**Olive oil to fill any bottle with a
   tight-fitting cork or lid (Try
   using a white-wine bottle
   with the label removed.)
   Experiment with different
   types, from extra, extra
   virgin, to fine. They vary
   greatly in taste—from an
   intense, green olive flavor to a
   light fruity one. I prefer
   French to Italian or Greek.**
**8 to 10 sprigs of fresh herbs or
   herbs dried on their stalks
   (Suggestions: basil, fennel,
   rosemary, marjoram, thyme,
   tarragon, or, for an unusual
   taste, lavender)**
1 teaspoon peppercorns
1 bay leaf (optional)

TOOLS

**Bottle with tight-fitting corks
   or lids**
Funnel

or lid. Place the oil in strong summer sunlight to release the aromatic oils of the herbs into the olive oil; shake the bottle periodically. Allow to sit for at least 1 week before using. The longer it sits, the more pronounced the flavor.

TO PACKAGE

The complementary look of gold foil glued in place over the cork, paired with a hand-lettered gold seal label, will immediately suggest the quality of the product inside. If you wish, tie on a sprig of dried herbs.

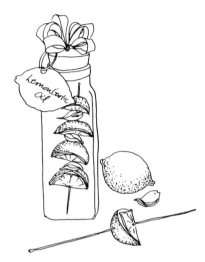

Use a bamboo skewer to pierce the lemon wedges.

LEMON-GARLIC OIL

INGREDIENTS

Virgin olive oil to fill a bottle. See Herb-Flavored Oils for hints on oil.
3 garlic cloves, peeled
½ lemon, cut into 3 pieces, seeds removed

TOOLS

Bamboo skewer
Funnel
Widemouthed bottle with tight-fitting cork or lid

METHOD

Pierce a garlic clove with the bamboo skewer and add a lemon slice, alternating the lemon and garlic until it is all used. Place the skewer inside the bottle and then, using a funnel, fill the bottle with the oil and cork it. Place the oil in strong summer sunlight to release the garlic and lemon flavors into the olive oil; shake the bottle periodically.

Allow to sit for at least 1 week before using. The longer it sits, the more pronounced the flavor.

TO PACKAGE

See suggestions under Wax-Sealed Bottles (page 222), or refer to Herb-Flavored Oils (page 81).

CAPERS AND OIL

YIELD: 1 quart

The capers give a nice bite to the oil. Choose only the best virgin oil, strongly flavored. See Herb-Flavored Oils for hints on oil. Use the caper oil to dress fresh tomato-basil-red-onion salad.

METHOD

Drain the capers. Using a funnel, put capers into a clean, sterilized bottle. Add the rosemary sprigs and fill to the top with olive oil. Seal with a lid and place in strong summer sunlight. Shake the bottle periodically for at least 1 week to allow the flavors to develop.

TO PACKAGE

See suggestions under Wax-Sealed Bottles (page 222) or refer to Herb-Flavored Oils (page 81).

INGREDIENTS

One 7-ounce jar of capers,
    vinegar-packed
24 ounces virgin olive oil,
    approximately 3⅓ cups
Several sprigs of fresh rosemary
    (optional)

TOOLS

Bottle with tight-fitting cork or lid
Funnel

FRESH GINGER IN SHERRY

As interest grows in Oriental and Indian cooking, fresh gingerroot is in great demand. However, it is a perishable food item which greengrocers and supermarkets stock mostly during the summer months. It will keep for several weeks in the refrigerator if stored in a plastic storage bag tightly closed with a wire twist, but for longer storage or as a gift for the experimental cooks on your list, try preserving the peeled "hands"— as they are called in the produce trade—in a good dry sherry or vodka. As a by-product, the ginger-flavored sherry or vodka makes an unusual flavoring for sauces or soups as well as a special drink.

INGREDIENTS

Fresh gingerroot
Dry sherry or vodka

TOOLS

Funnel
Ceramic or earthenware
    widemouthed bottle or crock
    with tight-fitting cork or lid,
    or glass bottle or jar with lid

METHOD

Peel the skin from the gingerroot and pat root dry. Slice the gingerroot into pieces the size of a quarter and about ⅛ inch thick. Put the gingerroot in a jar. Using a funnel, add enough sherry or vodka to cover the pieces, and cap tightly.

Gingerroot will keep indefinitely this way when stored in the refrigerator.

TO PACKAGE

Dramatize the ordinary bottle or crock by covering the cork or lid with a circle of loosely woven reed or bamboo wallpaper fabric* held in place with a rubber band. Tie with hemp twine. Design a charming tag shaped like a gingerroot, and put a favorite recipe on the back.

*Most decorators or stores carrying wallpaper will give you free samples from out-of-print books.

Summer Breads

Summer is the time for picnics and picnics demand sandwiches. The following three breads—dill, tomato, and cheese—will lend a delightful difference to anything spread between them.

DILLY BREAD

YIELD: 2 loaves

This soft herb bread is perfect for summer's egg salad sandwiches. It freezes well.

METHOD

In a large bowl dissolve the yeast in the warm water; add the sugar and let stand for 10 minutes.

Over low heat, sauté the onion in the butter for 5 minutes, or until limp but not brown. Toss in the dill and set aside to cool.

Add the flour, egg, salt, baking soda, and cottage cheese to the yeast mixture and beat for 2 to 3 minutes. Add the cooled dill and onion and beat for 1 minute more. The dough will be quite sticky. Place it on a floured surface and knead for 6 to 10 minutes, adding more flour to prevent sticking. Don't overdo the flour or the bread will be tough. Try using a pastry scraper to lift the dough while kneading.

Put the dough in a large, clear-plastic food storage bag with 1 tablespoon of flour. Close with a twist-tie. Turn the bag several times to coat all sides of the dough with the flour and let stand in a warm draft-free place (approximately 70° to 80° F.) for about 1 hour, or until double in bulk.

Remove the dough from the bag. Punch down the dough, divide, shape into 2 loaves, and place in well-greased loaf pans. Place the loaves in a warm place to rise for 30 to 40 minutes, or until doubled in size. Brush the tops with the egg wash and sprinkle with coarse salt.

Bake in a preheated 375° F. oven for 45 minutes, or until the loaves sound hollow when tapped. Cool on a cake rack for 20 minutes before slicing.

TO PACKAGE

Place the loaves on a wooden cutting board and overwrap with clear cellophane, cutting a hole for the handle. Tie with a red checkered ribbon and add a few dill sprigs for color.

INGREDIENTS

1 tablespoon dry yeast
¾ cup warm water
1 tablespoon sugar
4 tablespoons chopped onion
1 tablespoon butter
4 tablespoons chopped fresh dill
2 cups white flour
1 egg, beaten
1 teaspoon salt
1 teaspoon baking soda
1 cup cottage cheese

Egg Wash

1 egg white, lightly beaten with 1
     teaspoon water

Coarse salt

TOOLS

2 loaf pans, 9 x 5 x 2½ inches
1 large clear-plastic food storage
     bag with twist-tie
Pastry scraper (optional)

TOMATO BREAD

INGREDIENTS

8 ounces canned whole tomatoes
1 package dry yeast
1 tablespoon sugar
½ teaspoon coriander seeds
    (optional)
3½ to 4 cups unbleached flour
½ cup finely chopped onion (1
    small onion)
1 teaspoon salt
2 tablespoons unsalted butter,
    softened to room temperature

TOOLS

2 loaf pans, 9 x 5 x 2½ inches
1 large clear-plastic food storage
    bag with twist-tie
Food processor or blender

YIELD: two 1-pound loaves

The color is a little strange, being light pink, but delicious nonetheless, especially for grilled cheese sandwiches.

METHOD

In a blender or food processor, purée the tomatoes with their juice. Heat the purée over low heat until just warm (100° to 110° F.). Remove from the heat, cool for 2 minutes, and pour into a large bowl. Add the yeast and sugar and let stand until foamy, about 10 minutes.

Roast the coriander seeds in a heavy skillet (iron is the best) over medium-high heat, stirring constantly, for 2 to 3 minutes, or until the seeds begin to darken. Be careful not to burn them. Coarsely grind the seeds in a mortar with a pestle, or in a spice grinder.

In a separate bowl, combine 3½ cups of flour, the onion, salt, and coriander seeds. Cut in the butter until the mixture resembles coarse meal. Add the tomato-yeast mixture and beat until you have a resilient dough, adding as much as ½ cup more flour if needed.

Knead the dough on a lightly floured surface for 4 to 6 minutes, until smooth and elastic. Put the dough in the large clear-plastic food storage bag with 1 tablespoon of flour; close with a twist-tie. Turn the bag several times to coat all sides of the dough with the flour. Let dough stand in a warm draft-free place, approximately 70° to 80° F., for about 1 hour, until double in bulk.

Remove the dough from the bag and punch down. Divide it into 2 equal balls. Shape into loaves and place in greased loaf pans. Cover with a damp tea towel or oiled plastic wrap and leave in a warm place to rise just to the top of the pans, about 40 minutes.

Bake in a preheated 375° F. oven for 35 to 40 minutes, until loaves sound hollow when tapped. Remove from the pans and cool on a wire rack.

TO PACKAGE

Choose a basket and line it with deep-red tissue paper or a checkered tea towel. Wrap the bread in plastic wrap and tie a black-handled serrated bread knife on top of the bread with a ribbon. Place it in the basket along with a small wheel of Cheddar cheese, or try Crottin Poivre (with coarse black peppercorns), or for a very dramatic look, white Cheddar from Lancaster, Pennsylvania, coated with black wax. Add several ripe tomatoes, leaving a little of the stem and some leaves on for color. Lunch is ready.

CHEESE BREAD

YIELD: two 1-pound loaves

METHOD

Dissolve the yeast in the warm water and let stand until foamy, about 10 minutes.

Combine the cheeses, flour, cornmeal, sugar, and salt. Mix well. Cut the butter into the flour mixture until it resembles coarse meal. Add the egg, then the yeast mixture. Beat very hard to mix. Gradually add the water and beat until you have a resilient dough.

Knead the dough on a lightly floured surface for 4 to 6 minutes, until smooth and elastic. Put the dough in a large clear-plastic food storage bag with 1 tablespoon of flour. Close with a twist-tie. Turn the bag several times to coat all sides of the dough with flour. Let dough stand in a warm draft-free place, approximately 70° to 80° F., for 1 to 1½ hours, until double in bulk.

Remove the dough from the bag and punch down. Divide into 2 equal balls. Shape into loaves and place in greased loaf pans. With a pastry brush, brush some egg wash over the top of each loaf. Cover with a

INGREDIENTS

1 tablespoon dry yeast
¼ cup warm water (100° to 115° F.)
½ cup grated sharp Cheddar cheese, about 1½ ounces
½ cup freshly grated Parmesan cheese, about 1½ ounces
3⅔ cups unbleached flour
⅓ cup yellow cornmeal
2 tablespoons sugar
1 teaspoon salt
3 tablespoons butter, softened to room temperature
1 egg, lightly beaten
¾ to 1 cup water

Egg Wash

1 egg beaten with 1 teaspoon water

TOOLS

2 loaf pans, 9 x 5 x 2½ inches
1 large clear-plastic food storage bag with twist-tie
Pastry brush

Stitch the middle of the straw hat together with heavy thread; add a bow and fresh flower. Place a bread in both openings.

damp tea towel or oiled plastic wrap and leave in a warm place to rise just to the top of the pans, about 40 minutes.

Preheat oven to 375° F. Brush the breads again with remaining egg wash and bake for 35 to 40 minutes, or until loaves sound hollow when tapped. Remove from the pans and cool on a wire rack.

TO PACKAGE

For the summer sun lover, a handy hat basket holds the cheese breads. Choose a soft natural-straw hat approximately 12 inches in diameter. Gather the middle together and secure with a few stitches, using heavy-gauge thread. Tack on a large bow and a few fresh flowers. Line the hat with tissue paper. Place a bread in both openings.

INGREDIENTS

1½ cups unbleached flour
½ teaspoon baking powder
½ teaspoon baking soda
½ teaspoon salt
¾ teaspoon ground cinnamon
1 cup firmly packed light brown
    sugar
1 egg, lightly beaten
½ cup pure vegetable oil
1 cup firmly packed grated
    zucchini (1 large or 2 small
    zucchini)
¼ teaspoon vanilla extract
½ cup chopped walnuts
½ cup golden raisins

ZUCCHINI MUFFINS

YIELD: about 1 dozen
Delicious with whipped cream cheese and honey

METHOD

Preheat oven to 350° F. Generously grease muffin tins or line tins with muffin papers.

Sift together flour, baking powder, baking soda, salt, and cinnamon; set aside. Combine brown sugar and egg and beat until light. Add oil and beat for 1 to 2 minutes. Add zucchini and vanilla and blend well. Stir in walnuts and raisins. Quickly fold in dry ingredients, just until evenly blended. Do not overmix.

Spoon batter into prepared muffin tins, filling to the rims. Bake for 25 to 30 minutes, until lightly browned on top. Cool on a wire rack.

TO PACKAGE

For a pleasingly homey presentation for the muffins, wrap the base of each muffin in a 5-inch white doily and tie in place with cord or ribbon. Place muffins on a bamboo paper-plate holder, around a crock of whipped cream cheese. Overwrap with clear cellophane and tie with more cord or ribbon.

TOOLS

Muffin tins and papers
Grater

Bamboo paper-plate holder filled with individually doily-wrapped muffins and Lemon Cream.

CRÈME FRAÎCHE

YIELD: about 1 cup

This heavy French cream with a slightly nutty-acid flavor is the perfect gift during berry and fruit seasons. It will keep in the refrigerator for about 2 weeks. You will want the security of having this thick cream on hand to spoon on pies and berries at all times. Over strawberries *crème fraîche* is sublime. Unlike heavy cream or sour cream, it will boil without curdling. Easy to make and exceedingly useful in sauces, too.

A gift of *crème fraîche* can be a continuous gift if you present the recipe right along with the cream, and remind the recipient to reserve 2 tablespoons from the original recipe to start the next batch.

METHOD

Combine the heavy cream and sour cream in a heavy saucepan. Over very low heat, warm the mixture to about 80° to 90° F., no warmer or the heat will kill the ferment. Pour the mixture into a sterilized jar, cover loosely with cheesecloth or a dish towel, and let stand at room temperature for about 8 hours, or overnight, until thickened. Stir up, cover with plastic wrap or lid, and refrigerate. Will keep for up to 2 weeks, if refrigerated.

INGREDIENTS

1 cup heavy cream, either ultrapasteurized or pasteurized
2 tablespoons dairy sour cream

TOOLS

Food thermometer
Jars or container
Cheesecloth

TO PACKAGE

Decorate a pint-size, plastic berry basket by weaving a red checkered ribbon through the side holes. Fill the basket with ripe strawberries and present it along with the *crème fraîche*. Don't forget to include a label with the recipe.

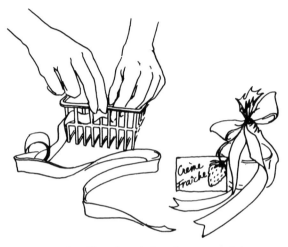

Starting at one end, weave the ribbon through the side openings of the top row of the basket. Repeat with bottom row.

Summer Cookies

Cookies! Traditionally baked in quantity only at holiday times, they are just as important to have on hand in the summer. Serve them to impromptu guests with iced tea, take them on picnics, or include them as the perfect accompaniment for ice cream.

FILLED GINGER COOKIES

YIELD: about 4 dozen 2-inch cookies

Ginger cookies are traditionally served at holiday time in November and December, but I have discovered that in warm weather they taste delectable with homemade ice cream. Perfect for picnics, too.

METHOD

Sift the flour, baking soda, and salt together. Mix in the gingerroot and set aside.

Cream the butter and brown sugar together until light. Add the molasses and egg and beat until smooth.

Gradually add the dry ingredients to the wet, stirring after each addition until the dry ingredients are thoroughly incorporated and the mixture is smooth. Form the dough into a ball, wrap it in plastic, and refrigerate it for at least 2 hours, or overnight. (For longer storage, wrap it in foil. It will keep in the refrigerator for about 1 week.)

Preheat oven to 350° F. Lightly grease baking sheets. Remove half of the dough from the refrigerator; keep the other half chilled until ready to use. On a lightly floured surface, roll out the dough to ¼-inch thickness. Using a 2-inch fluted round cookie cutter, cut out the cookies and place them on the baking sheets. Cut a ½-inch hole (I used the metal tip of my cake decorator for this) in the center of half of the cookies. Bake for 10 to 12 minutes, until lightly brown. Repeat until all the dough is used.

Melt the ginger preserve over low heat until sugar dissolves. Spread about ½ teaspoon of the preserve on the bottoms of all the cookies without holes. Cover with the cookies with holes and press gently together. Dust lightly with confectioners' sugar.

Store the cookies in a tightly covered jar or an airtight box to keep them crisp.

TO PACKAGE

Line a hand-painted, Shaker design box (see page 226) with several white doilies. Gently stack the cookies inside. Place a piece of wax paper between each layer of cookies. Tie on a ribbon in a crisscross manner.

INGREDIENTS

2½ cups all-purpose flour
1½ teaspoons baking soda
½ teaspoon salt
1 tablespoon grated peeled fresh gingerroot
6 ounces unsalted butter, softened to room temperature
1 cup firmly packed dark brown sugar
¼ cup dark molasses
1 egg, lightly beaten
1 16-ounce jar Dundee Ginger Preserve, or homemade
Confectioners' sugar

TOOLS

Baking sheets
Rolling pin
Cookie cutters, 2-inch-round fluted and half-round
Airtight container

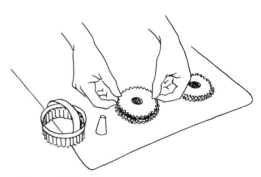

Cover with the cookies with holes and press gently together.

CHOCOLATE SHORTBREAD COOKIES

INGREDIENTS

12 ounces unsalted butter, chilled
1 cup confectioners' sugar
1 teaspoon coffee extract
2 cups all-purpose flour
½ cup unsweetened cocoa powder, Dutch process preferred
¼ teaspoon salt

TOOLS

Rolling pin
Cookie sheet
2-inch cookie cutter
Airtight container

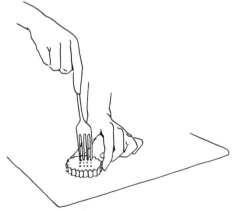

Make 3 vertical rows of holes in each cookie.

YIELD: 4 dozen 2-inch cookies

This old-fashioned cookie gets a new twist when you add chocolate and coffee extract. A simple, sweet treat. Incredibly easy when you use a food processor or electric mixer, the recipe takes a little longer when done by hand. A splendid foil for homemade ice cream.

METHOD

Preheat oven to 325° F. Put butter and confectioners' sugar in a medium-size bowl. Using your fingers and working quickly, cream butter and sugar until light. Add the coffee extract and blend well. Sift the flour, cocoa powder, and salt together and gradually add the sifted ingredients to the butter and sugar. Blend together with the tips of your fingers until the mixture holds together.

Form the dough into a ball; with the heel of your hand, knead it on a smooth surface for 1 to 2 minutes, until dough is perfectly smooth and the butter well blended. Form into a ball. Lightly dust a smooth surface with flour. Gently flatten the dough; with a lightly floured rolling pin, roll the dough until it is ½ inch thick. Using a 2-inch plain or fluted cookie cutter dipped into flour (shake off any excess flour), cut the cookies as close to each other as possible. Place them on an ungreased cookie sheet. Dip a fork into flour, shake off any excess, and make 3 vertical rows of holes in each cookie. Press together all dough scraps, roll again, and cut remaining cookies until all the dough is used. Refrigerate for 30 minutes. Bake for 20 to 25 minutes, watching carefully. Transfer cookies to a wire rack to cool.

The dough will keep in the refrigerator for several days and may be frozen. Store cookies in an airtight container. They freeze well.

TO PACKAGE

Pack into Personally Stamped Containers (page 221), or Ribbon-Covered Boxes (page 228), lined with pale blue tissue paper.

DOUBLE CHOCOLATE FUDGE COOKIES

YIELD: about 5 dozen 3-inch cookies

Chocolate desserts are the most popular in any season. These double chocolate cookies are incredibly rich, keep well, and are simple to make. You could become a legend with this recipe alone.

METHOD

Preheat oven to 375° F. Sift together flour, baking soda, and salt and set aside.

Melt both chocolates with the butter in the top pan of a double boiler, covered, set over hot water over moderate heat. Uncover, remove from the heat, and stir in the sugars, eggs, and vanilla until smooth and shiny.

Transfer the chocolate mixture to a large bowl and gradually add the sifted ingredients, stirring just until the flour is absorbed. Do not over-beat. Fold in the nuts if you are using them. Chill the dough in the refrigerator for about 15 minutes, to make the shaping of the cookies easier.

Remove from the refrigerator and form the dough by hand into 1-inch balls. Place them 2 inches apart on an ungreased cookie sheet. Bake for 10 minutes. Let them cool on the cookie sheet for 2 minutes before transferring them to a wire rack to cool.

Store in an airtight container or freeze.

TO PACKAGE

Package the cookies in hand-decorated brown paper bags or place them in brightly colored gift bags. Furnish the bags with woven ribbon streamers of deep-chocolate-colored ribbon. See Tied Paper Bags (page 220).

INGREDIENTS

2 cups unbleached flour

1 teaspoon baking soda

½ teaspoon salt

4 ounces German chocolate, broken into 1-inch pieces

6 ounces unsweetened chocolate, broken into 1-inch pieces

8 ounces unsalted butter, softened to room temperature

1 cup granulated sugar

1 cup firmly packed light brown sugar

2 eggs, lightly beaten

1 tablespoon vanilla extract

1 cup coarsely chopped walnuts (optional; for those who must have nuts with their chocolate)

TOOLS

Double boiler
Cookie sheet
Airtight container

GIFTS
of
AUTUMN

Gifts of Autumn

WINDFALL APPLE BUTTER

YIELD: about 6 cups

Here's the purest example of autumn in a jar. Make this velvety orange-spiced spread from the first apples that fall with the wind. It spreads smoothly on buttered toast or muffins or serves as a topping for plain cake. Pass the whipped cream.

METHOD

In a large nonaluminum saucepan cook the apples with the apple cider, covered, over medium heat, stirring frequently, for 20 minutes, until very tender. Purée the mixture in a food mill fitted with a medium disc set over a large nonaluminum saucepan. Add the brown sugar, orange rind, salt, and spices and cook over very low heat, uncovered, stirring occasionally, for 3 to 3½ hours, until very thick. The last half of cooking is the most crucial, so stir the apple butter frequently to prevent burning. Add the Calvados and stir.

Spoon the apple butter into sterilized jars to within ¼ inch of the rims. Wipe the rims clean and seal the jars with the lids. Let the apple butter stand in the refrigerator for at least 1 week to allow the flavors to mellow.

Windfall Apple Butter in snug basket with metallic and white paper hat.

INGREDIENTS

6 pounds Granny Smith apples, unpeeled, cored, and sliced
2 cups apple cider
1½ cups light brown sugar
Grated rind of 1 orange
¼ teaspoon salt
1 tablespoon ground cinnamon
1 teaspoon ground allspice
½ teaspoon ground cloves
½ cup Calvados (apple brandy)

TOOLS

Nonaluminum saucepan
Food mill
Mason jars with lids

Materials

6 small bamboo baskets
Six 6-inch squares of plain white paper
Six 4-inch squares of metallic paper
6 yards of hemp cord, cut into 1-yard pieces

TO PACKAGE

Dramatize this wholesome apple butter in a fitting container.
Choose baskets that hold the jars snugly. Set each 1-cup Mason jar

inside a basket, allowing the top of the jar to protrude above the basket by several inches.

Cover the top of each jar with 1 square of plain white paper. Place 1 smaller square of metallic paper over each of the white papers.

Wrap a piece of hemp cord twice around the top of the paper-covered jars. Make a tight knot. Knot the 2 ends of the hemp cord together to form a loop for carrying and attach a plain white handmade label.

APPLE-HERB JELLY

INGREDIENTS

2½ cups fresh apple juice (not the frozen or bottled type found in the supermarket; buy it from a local fruit stand where they press their own)

¼ cup coarsely chopped fresh herbs (choose savory, tarragon, sage, thyme, or rosemary)

¼ cup cider vinegar

4 cups sugar

½ bottle (3 ounces) liquid fruit pectin

Sprigs of fresh herbs

TOOLS

Cheesecloth

Canning jars, lids optional (see list of canning equipment on page 232)

YIELD: 3 cups

This fragrant, clear jelly is delicately flavored with apples and herbs. Very easy to make, almost foolproof. Use your culinary imagination to come up with other unusual combinations. Delicious with meat and game dishes, or with bread and butter.

METHOD

Bring the apple juice to a boil in an enamel or nonaluminum saucepan. Pour it over the herbs and let stand for about 30 minutes. Strain the liquid through a double thickness of cheesecloth. Discard cheesecloth and herbs.

Return the liquid to the saucepan, add the vinegar and sugar, and bring to a full, rolling boil which cannot be stirred down. Stir frequently to dissolve the sugar and keep the mixture from burning. Remove from the heat, add the pectin, and return to a full, rolling boil; boil hard for 1 minute, stirring constantly.

Remove from the heat and skim off any foam. Pour into sterilized Mason jars, filling to within ¼ inch of the rims. Add several sprigs of fresh herbs to each jar. Wipe the rims with a clean damp cloth and seal the jars with paraffin (see instructions on page 235) or canning lids. With canning lids, process in a boiling-water bath for 10 minutes (see instructions on page 231). Cool completely. Store in a cool, dark, dry place.

TO PACKAGE

Give this one a simple wrapping to show off the delicate herbs suspended in jelly—a fabric "hat" (page 219) or ribbon streamers.

FOURTEEN-CARAT MARMALADE

(Carrot-Lemon-Ginger Marmalade)

YIELD: 8 cups

This recipe comes from my friend Gene Barnes, a great cook from Indiana.

METHOD

Cook the grated carrots in boiling water for 5 minutes and drain in a sieve. Return carrots to the pot and add the sugar, lemon rind, lemon juice, and candied gingerroot.

Bring the mixture to a slow boil, stirring until the sugar dissolves. Continue cooking over low heat, stirring frequently, for 1½ hours. Remove from heat when a candy thermometer reads 220° F., or when the liquid runs off a spoon as a thick syrup.

Carefully spoon the marmalade into hot sterilized jars, filling to within ¼ inch of the top. Wipe the rims clean and seal the jars with the lids. Process the jars for 10 minutes according to canning directions on page 231.

TO PACKAGE

The beautiful orange color of this marmalade is enhanced by the addition of "hats" made of silver paper doilies (see page 219). Tie them in place with green-and-white-striped ribbon. Accent the bows with a few lemon leaves obtained from your local florist. To each jar attach a label shaped like a carrot so you will know the contents at a glance.

INGREDIENTS

3 pounds carrots, grated fine
4 cups sugar
Grated rind of 8 large lemons
1 cup lemon juice
1½ cups finely cut candied
  gingerroot

TOOLS

Food processor or grater
Candy thermometer
Mason jars with lids

GREEN TOMATO CONSERVE

INGREDIENTS

**12 to 15 medium-size green
    tomatoes, cored, and cut into
    small cubes (about 12 cups)**
**4 lemons, sliced very thin, with
    seeds removed**
4 cups sugar
Grated rind of 1 orange
1 cup golden raisins
2 tablespoons orange brandy

TOOLS

Large enameled casserole with lid
Mason jars with lids

YIELD: 2 pints

Here is the perfect way to take advantage of the supply of unripe tomatoes so often found in late autumn gardens. (For ripe tomato recipes, see the summer section.) I have used this conserve to enhance everything from ground beef to ice cream.

METHOD

In a large enameled casserole make layers of (1) 3 cups of the chopped tomatoes, (2) one third of the lemon slices, and (3) one third of the sugar. Repeat the layering twice, ending with the remaining 3 cups of tomatoes. Cover and marinate for 24 hours.

Add the orange rind to the casserole and cook the fruit over very low heat, stirring occasionally, for 2 hours.

Add the raisins and cook for 1 more hour, until the liquid becomes a glowing amber color. Stir frequently during this cooking to keep the caramel from burning. Remove casserole from the heat and stir in the orange brandy.

Spoon the conserve into hot sterilized jars, filling them to within ¼ inch of the rims. Wipe the rims clean and seal the jars with the lids.

Process the jars for 10 minutes according to canning directions on page 231.

Note: A great addition to any kitchen where a lot of low heat cooking as for jams, condiments, and stews goes on is an item called a Flame-Tamer, available at most hardware or kitchen stores for under $10. It makes any pot act like a double boiler by diffusing the heat evenly under the pot. You no longer have to worry about burned foods.

TO PACKAGE

Another candidate for easy wrapping with a fabric "hat" (page 219). Include serving suggestions on the tag.

Autumn Pickles and Condiments

The relish tray is the most overlooked ingredient in the full-fledged Thanksgiving feast. All these recipes are simple and fun to make. Their only prerequisite is a farseeing cook whose thoughts turn to the holiday season early in the fall when gardens and markets are bursting with fresh fruits and vegetables. Try one of these, or surprise your family and friends with the entire assortment. There is no limit to the combinations of pickles, relishes, and chutney you may include. (For other suggestions see the summer section.)

MAPLE PUMPKIN PICKLES

YIELD: 8 cups

Fine for the relish tray and perfect served over ice cream for the expectant mother.

METHOD

Sprinkle the pumpkin pieces with salt and let stand for 3 hours. Rinse the pieces under cold water and pat dry.

Combine all other ingredients in a saucepan and make a syrup by boiling for 5 minutes; stir constantly and wash down sugar crystals on the side of the pan with a pastry brush dipped into cold water. Add the pumpkin and simmer for 5 minutes.

Using a slotted spoon, pack the pumpkin into hot sterilized jars, filling each to within ¼ inch of the top. Pour the hot syrup over the

INGREDIENTS

1 pumpkin, 2½ to 3 pounds, peeled, seeded, and cut into 1-inch cubes (For a fancier look, try scooping out the pumpkin flesh with a 1-inch melon-ball cutter.)

Kosher salt

8 cups apple cider vinegar

4 cups pure maple syrup

4 tablespoons pickling spices

2 cinnamon sticks, broken into pieces

¼ cup thin slices of peeled gingerroot

4 garlic cloves, peeled

TOOLS

Pastry brush
Slotted spoon
Mason jars with lids

pumpkin, making sure each jar contains some of the pickling spices, gingerroot, garlic, and cinnamon stick. Seal with the lids. Process the jars for 10 minutes according to directions on page 231. Cool.

Chill the pumpkin pickles for at least 3 days before eating.

TO PACKAGE

To keep with the pumpkin theme, wrap the base of the jar in orange tissue paper. Overwrap with a 10-inch white doily. Tie in place with deep rust-colored shiny ribbon and add a pumpkin-shaped tag.

JERUSALEM ARTICHOKE PICKLES

INGREDIENTS

3 pounds Jerusalem artichokes, peeled and cut into 1-inch pieces
1½ tablespoons mixed pickling spices
1 quart white-wine vinegar
1½ cups sugar
1½ tablespoons salt
2 garlic cloves
2 teaspoons ground turmeric
1 tablespoon dry mustard

TOOLS

Mason jars with lids

YIELD: 8 cups

Most people think only of cucumbers when they consider pickling, but the imaginative pickler can pickle just about every kind of vegetable or fruit available. Everyone loves these unusual mustard pickles, which make an excellent accompaniment to cold meats and poultry. The Jerusalem artichoke has a misleading name. It tastes nothing like an artichoke and does not come from Jerusalem. This tuber of a small sunflower, often labeled "sunchoke," is very low in calories, resembles fresh gingerroot in appearance, and has a texture much like a water chestnut.

METHOD

Scrub, rinse, and dry artichokes.

Arrange the sunchokes in hot sterilized glass jars, filling them to within ½ inch of the tops.

Combine the pickling spices, vinegar, sugar, salt, garlic, turmeric, and mustard in a large saucepan and simmer for 15 minutes. Increase the heat and boil for 5 minutes.

Pour the hot mixture over the sunchokes in the jars, filling each to within ¼ inch of the top, making sure each jar contains some of the pickling spices. Seal with the lids. Process the jars for 10 minutes according to directions on page 231. Cool.

Chill the pickles for at least 3 days before eating.

TO PACKAGE

Add an extra touch—a fabric "hat" (page 219) or a Wax Fabric Container (page 224). Make the label sun-shaped and tie it on with gold cord.

CHOW CHOW

YIELD: 8 cups

In the South this is called chou chou; in France, picalillis. However, this mixed vegetable and mustard pickle is perhaps best known as chow chow. Straight from the fall harvest, this condiment is one you will truly "relish."

METHOD

In a large bowl combine the vegetables with the coarse salt and let stand at room temperature for 24 hours. Drain the vegetables in a colander and rinse with cold water. Drain well.

In a large nonmetallic saucepan combine the vinegar, sugar, mustard seeds, celery seeds, allspice, cloves, peppercorns, and cayenne pepper. Slowly bring to a boil, stirring to dissolve the sugar. Simmer for 5 minutes, add the drained vegetables, and cook for 3 minutes.

Drain the vegetables in a colander set over a large bowl to reserve the cooking liquid.

Combine the flour, dry mustard, and turmeric. Add a little of the

INGREDIENTS

2 pounds cauliflower, cut into very small pieces

2 pounds cucumber, peeled, seeded, and chopped

2 pounds zucchini, chopped

½ pound celery, chopped

3 onions, chopped

2 red peppers, chopped

½ cup coarse salt

2 cups white vinegar

1 cup sugar

1 tablespoon mustard seeds

1 teaspoon celery seeds

1 teaspoon whole allspice

1 teaspoon whole cloves

¼ teaspoon whole peppercorns

⅛ teaspoon cayenne pepper

2 tablespoons flour

2 tablespoons dry mustard

1 teaspoon ground turmeric

TOOLS

Colander
Nonmetallic saucepan
Mason jars with lids

reserved cooking liquid to the mixture to form a smooth paste. Whisk the paste into the reserved cooking liquid until smooth.

Transfer the liquid to a kettle and bring to a boil. Add vegetables and cook, stirring, for 5 minutes.

Pack the chow chow in hot sterilized jars, filling to within ¼ inch of the rim. Wipe the rims clean and seal the jars tightly with the lids. Process the jars for 10 minutes according to canning directions on page 231.

TO PACKAGE

Label this old-fashioned relish "MADE FROM SCRATCH."

Flavored Dijon Mustards

Mustard has become, next to salt and pepper, our favorite seasoning. Once merely the stripe squirted down the middle of a hot dog, mustard has moved from the prosaic to the gourmet. Food magazines and cookbooks feature recipes with mustard as a base for salad dressings, for slimming sauces, or to add a surprise bite to stews or meat dishes. Anyone who visits the gourmet food shops springing up all over the country has noticed that entire sections are devoted to the display of "status" mustards in great variety. Exotic mustards are the rage; some of the best known come from Germany, England, and France and range in taste from mellow or musky to hot and fiery. They may be smooth or grainy in texture, sweet or sharp. The French city of Dijon has long produced delicate wine-based mustards especially popular throughout the world. According to a pamphlet distributed by Grey Poupon Dijon Mustard, France's King Louis XI frequently dropped in on friends for dinner uninvited. With him he always brought a pot of mustard.

Unlike Louis, you might wait for an invitation but you can carry on the tradition by arriving with a pot of mustard of your own devising. With so many mustards readily available, it is easy to forget that they are also very quick and very easy to make.

TO PACKAGE

For a fall tailgate picnic or sports event, line a large picnic hamper with a plaid tablecloth. Include flavored mustards, a hard sausage or pâté, hard-cooked eggs, and a jar of homemade pickles.

For a gift of one jar, add an excellent finishing touch by wrapping it in a simple drawstring sack cut from mustard-colored printed fabric, topping with a fabric "hat" (page 219), or tying with ribbon streamers.

TARRAGON MUSTARD

YIELD: 4 cups

This looks and tastes extravagant but is very easy to make. This tarragon-flavored mustard is especially good with fish, shellfish, and poultry dishes.

METHOD

Finely chop tarragon leaves. Add shallots, mustard, and vermouth. Whisk together. Pour into a clean, dry jar. Seal with a tight-fitting lid and store in the refrigerator.

Keeps in the refrigerator for 1 month.

INGREDIENTS

1 cup fresh tarragon leaves, or 1 small jar of Dessaux Fils tarragon leaves in vinegar, well drained, with stems removed

½ cup finely minced shallots

4 cups Grey Poupon Dijon Mustard

1 tablespoon dry vermouth or dry white wine

TOOLS

Whisk

French canning jar with clamp-type lid

DILL MUSTARD

INGREDIENTS

1 cup fresh dill leaves
4 cups Grey Poupon Dijon
    Mustard
4 tablespoons dairy sour cream
Rind of 1 lemon, removed in long
    strips with a zester
Juice of 1 lemon

TOOLS

Citrus zester
Whisk
French canning jars with clamp-
    type lids

YIELD: 4 cups

Dill-flavored mustard complements fish, shellfish—especially shrimp—poultry, and cold beef dishes.

METHOD

Finely chop dill. Add mustard, sour cream, lemon rind, and juice. Whisk together. Pour into clean, dry jars. Seal with tight-fitting lids and store in the refrigerator.

Keeps in the refrigerator for 1 month.

TO PACKAGE

See page 105.

INGREDIENTS

4 cups Grey Poupon Dijon
    Mustard
Rind of 4 limes, removed in long
    strips with a zester
Juice of 4 limes
4 tablespoons honey
¾ cup dairy sour cream

TOOLS

Citrus zester
Whisk
French canning jars with clamp-
    type lids

LIME MUSTARD

YIELD: 4 cups

A surprise flavor when used with roast pork or grilled fish.

METHOD

Combine all ingredients in a bowl and whisk together. Pour into clean, dry jars. Seal with tight-fitting lids and store in the refrigerator.

Keeps in the refrigerator for 1 month.

TO PACKAGE

See page 105.

HOT MUSTARD SAUCE

YIELD: 2 cups

Especially pungent—use as a condiment with cold cuts, grilled sausage, tongue, or brisket of beef.

METHOD

Combine all ingredients in a saucepan and mix until smooth. Cook over low heat, stirring constantly until thickened, 5 to 8 minutes. Pour into clean, dry jars. Seal with tight-fitting lids or corks and store in the refrigerator.

Keeps in the refrigerator for 2 months.

INGREDIENTS

1 cup cider vinegar
1 cup dry mustard
1¼ cups brown sugar
2 eggs
Pinch of salt
1 teaspoon ground cloves
½ teaspoon ground turmeric

TOOLS

French canning jars with clamp-type lids

CRÈME DE DIJON SAUCE

YIELD: 3 cups

This delicate mustard sauce is delicious on cold shellfish, steamed vegetables, poultry, and pork.

METHOD

Combine the mustard, eggs, heavy cream, and vinegar in a saucepan. Cook over low heat, stirring constantly to keep the eggs from curdling, for 8 to 10 minutes. Remove from heat when mixture becomes thick. Cool the sauce and add chopped dill. Pour into clean, dry jars. Seal with tight-fitting lids and store in the refrigerator.

Keeps in the refrigerator for 1 month.

TO PACKAGE

See page 105.

INGREDIENTS

⅔ cup Grey Poupon Dijon Mustard
4 eggs, beaten
2 cups heavy cream
1 tablespoon white vinegar
½ cup tightly packed chopped fresh dill

TOOLS

French canning jars with clamp-type lids

RED PEPPER SAUCE

INGREDIENTS

5 large sweet red peppers
1 large tomato, peeled, seeded,
    and coarsely chopped
2 or 3 garlic cloves, minced
4 ounces blanched almonds
¼ teaspoon cayenne pepper
⅓ to ½ cup olive oil
Salt
Freshly ground pepper
A few pitted black olives for
    decoration

TOOLS

Blender or food processor
French canning jars with clamp-
    type lids

YIELD: about 4 cups, enough for 2 pounds of pasta

A fall pasta sauce made from roasted red peppers and the creamy richness of ground almonds. A delicious gift easily made into a quick, elegant meal.

METHOD

Char and blister the peppers on all sides under the broiler. Place them in a closed brown paper bag to rest for approximately 10 minutes (this will facilitate peeling). Remove peppers from the bag and carefully peel off the skins. Discard seeds. Reserve ½ pepper for decoration.

Squeeze all the juice from the tomato and place the peppers, tomato, garlic, almonds, and cayenne pepper to taste in a food processor or blender, and purée.

Slowly add the oil until the mixture is of fairly thick consistency. Season to taste with salt and lots of freshly ground pepper. Pour into jars with clamp-type lids. Cut the reserved ½ pepper into thin strips. Slice the olives. Use some of each to decorate the top of each jar of sauce.

If refrigerated, the sauce will keep for up to 1 week and may be frozen.

TO PACKAGE

Make this part of a theme basket. For a simple Sunday dinner, include a pound of pasta, a few extra red peppers for color, a bunch of parsley, a ramekin of niçoise olives, and of course a crusty loaf of Italian bread.

WALNUT PESTO

YIELD: about 3 cups

Delicious on grilled shellfish, pasta, and steamed vegetables. A welcome alternative to Pesto Genovese made with basil.

METHOD

Soak the bread in the milk until all the milk is absorbed. Squeeze the liquid from the bread and place it in a food processor fitted with the steel blade, or in a blender, or in a mortar. Add the toasted walnuts, parsley, garlic, salt, red pepper flakes, and vinegar, and process into a smooth paste. Slowly add the walnut oil in a thin stream, beating all the time. Correct the seasoning by adding salt and pepper to taste.

Walnut Pesto keeps well in the refrigerator for about 1 week, or it may be frozen for several months. Store in tightly capped containers. Cover the surface of *pesto* with a thin film of olive oil to prevent discoloration.

TO PACKAGE

For the nuts on your gift list, fill a small wooden crate or basket with packing straw. Add a jar of Walnut Pesto and sprinkle a handful of whole walnuts in their shells around the jar. Overwrap with clear cellophane and tie with a big bow. Add a label with serving suggestions.

INGREDIENTS

2 slices of white bread, crust removed
¼ cup milk
2 cups shelled walnuts, lightly toasted in a 300° F. oven for 5 minutes
⅔ cup chopped Italian parsley
2 garlic cloves
1 tablespoon coarse salt
½ teaspoon crushed red pepper flakes
2 tablespoons white vinegar
1¼ cups walnut oil
Salt and pepper

TOOLS

Food processor or blender, or mortar and pestle

Layered Mascarpone Torte

Beautiful to look at and equally delicious to eat, these tortes transport easily to all outdoor eating events. Italian mascarpone cheese has only recently become popular in this country. It is an acquired taste—slightly sour and buttery, reminiscent of buttermilk. Plain, it is delicious served with the cloved lemons in oil on page 82, or make it into one of the following tortes.

PESTO MASCARPONE TORTE

INGREDIENTS

8 ounces mascarpone cheese
¼ cup *Pesto* (page 74)
½ cup coarsely chopped walnuts,
**   reserving 1 whole for**
**   decoration**
2 basil leaves for decoration

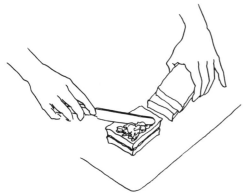

Slice the cheese horizontally into 4 equal slices and spread a thin layer of pesto *over each slice. Sprinkle with chopped walnuts.*

METHOD

Warm the knife under hot water and slice the cheese horizontally into 4 equal slices (see illustration).

Spread a thin layer of *pesto* over 1 slice of cheese and lightly sprinkle with chopped walnuts. Repeat with remaining slices. Do not spread *pesto* on the top slice.

Place the torte on a plate, cover with plastic, and refrigerate for at least 1 hour, or until cheese is firm. Remove from the refrigerator. Using your hands, press firmly on the top and sides of the cheese, molding it into a neat rectangle. To give the torte a professional look, warm a knife under hot water and use it to smooth the top and sides. Decorate the top of the torte with the basil leaves and a perfect walnut. Wrapped in clear plastic and refrigerated, the torte will keep for several weeks.

TO PACKAGE

The oil from the *pesto* tends to leak through the plastic, so overwrap the torte in clear cellophane and tie with a bow.

FIG AND MASCARPONE TORTE

INGREDIENTS

8 ounces Turkish fresh figs,
**   stemmed and chopped**
1 tablespoon Cognac
8 ounces mascarpone cheese
4 tablespoons coarsely chopped
**   pine nuts**
1 handful of whole pine nuts for
**   decorations**

METHOD

Purée the figs and Cognac into a smooth paste in a blender or food processor.

Warm the knife under hot water and slice the cheeses horizontally into 4 equal slices (see illustration). Spread a thin layer of the fig purée over 1 slice of the cheese and lightly sprinkle with chopped pine nuts.

Repeat with remaining slices. Do not spread fig purée on the top slice.

Place the torte on a plate, cover with plastic, and refrigerate for at least 1 hour, or until cheese is firm. Remove from the refrigerator. Using your hands, press firmly on the top and sides of the torte, molding it into a neat rectangle. To give the torte a professional look, warm a knife under hot water and use it to smooth the top and sides. Decorate the top of the torte with the reserved pine nuts (see illustration).

Wrapped in clear plastic and refrigerated, the torte will keep for several weeks.

TO PACKAGE

This makes an unusual dessert when served with slightly sweet crackers—Carr's Whole-Wheat Crackers or Bath Olivers and a dessert wine. Overwrap the cheese in clear cellophane and tie in place with ribbon.

Tuck the cheese into a shallow basket, including appropriate crackers, a wooden knife for spreading, and, if you like, a dessert wine.

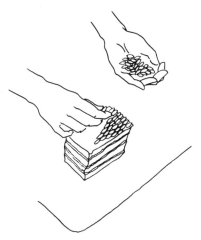

Decorate the top of the torte with the reserved pine nuts.

MACADAMIA NUT BUTTER

YIELD: about 1 cup

This rich nut butter is the perfect dip for crisp apple and pear wedges. Use it as the base for a fruit salad dressing. Try it on anything coconut. Spread it between layers of chocolate cake. The nuts are expensive but macadamias are very rich and a little of this goes a long way.

METHOD

Roast the nuts on a baking sheet in a 300° F. oven for 5 minutes, then purée in a food processor fitted with the steel blade, or in a blender for 3

INGREDIENTS

7 ounces Macadamia nuts

TOOLS

Baking sheet
Food processor or blender
½-pint jar with lid

to 4 minutes, until the nuts have a smooth consistency like peanut butter. Spoon into the jar and seal with lid.

TO PACKAGE

Tie strips of tartan ribbon onto the stems of red and green apples. Heap them in a small garden basket and nestle the jar of Macadamia Nut Butter in the center.

CASHEW BUTTER

INGREDIENTS

2 cups unsalted cashews
2 tablespoons peanut oil
Pinch of salt

TOOLS

Baking sheet
Food processor or blender
1-pint jar with clamp-type lid

YIELD: about 2 cups

Because these nut butters have no preservatives and are unhomogenized, they tend to separate. Store them in the refrigerator and stir before using.

METHOD

Roast the cashews on a baking sheet in a 300° F. oven for 5 minutes, then purée in a food processor fitted with the steel blade, or in a blender for 3 to 4 minutes, adding the peanut oil a little at a time, until the nuts have a smooth consistency like peanut butter. Spoon into the jar and seal with the lid.

Note: For homemade peanut butter, substitute peanuts for the cashews.

TO PACKAGE

Make slender, finger-shaped sandwiches of thin slices of cooked chicken, Cashew Butter, chutney, and crisp bacon. Stand the sandwiches up in a small basket lined with a cocktail napkin. Overwrap with clear cellophane. Wrap a ribbon around the basket and present it with the remaining Cashew Butter in a jar. This makes a welcome addition to a fall tailgate picnic or goes nicely with drinks at a cocktail party.

RUM CASHEWS

YIELD: 2 cups

Nuts have been used in both sweet and savory recipes for centuries. They are never more plentiful than in the fall. The ease with which these recipes are made is all out of proportion to the pleasure of the final results. These nuts are delicious as snacks but they also provide delicate accompaniments to a variety of foods. Try the rum cashews with an Indian curry, the fried walnuts with a Chinese dinner, the spiced nuts sprinkled on ice cream.

METHOD

Generously oil a baking sheet and set aside.

Bring the sugar and rum to a boil in a medium-size saucepan. Cook for 3 minutes, or until candy thermometer registers 234° F. Remove from the heat and add the cashews, stirring constantly to coat with syrup. The sugar will become white and grainy after about 30 seconds.

Return saucepan to the heat; over medium heat, remelt the sugar, adding a few drops of water if needed. Watch carefully; do not let the sugar burn. When the syrup has turned a rich caramel color, about 2 minutes, and the nuts sound hollow at the tap of a spoon, remove from the heat and stir in the butter.

Transfer the mixture to an oiled baking sheet, spreading the nuts in one layer. With a fork or toothpicks separate any pieces that have stuck together. Cool completely.

Store nuts in an airtight container until ready to use.

Keeps in an airtight container for 2 weeks.

TO PACKAGE

For a novel fall gift—all nuts, no bolts—make several of the flavored nuts and show them off in this handsome way. Improvise 6 miniature knapsacks from brightly printed squares of batik cotton. Separately pack about 1 cup of each recipe into plastic sandwich bags; tie with twists.

INGREDIENTS

1 cup sugar
¾ cup rum
2 cups whole unsalted cashews
2 ounces butter

TOOLS

Baking sheet
Candy thermometer
Airtight container

Place 1 bag in the center of each square of fabric and tie each sack with contrasting ribbon. Label them. Stuff them into a tissue-lined basket. Strew a handful of mixed nuts in their shells between the sacks.

CURRIED ALMONDS

INGREDIENTS

2 cups whole blanched almonds
3 tablespoons unsalted butter
1 teaspoon coarse salt
2 teaspoons curry powder
1 teaspoon ground cuminseed
¼ teaspoon sugar

TOOLS

Large skillet
Airtight container

YIELD: 2 cups

METHOD

In a large skillet sauté the almonds in the butter over moderate heat, tossing them until they are lightly browned. Stir in salt, curry powder, cuminseed, and sugar. Continue sautéing for 1 to 2 minutes more. Transfer the nuts to a paper towel to drain and cool.

Store in an airtight container; they will keep for 1 week.

TO PACKAGE

A snacker's delight, perfect for any occasion. Seal the almonds in a clear plastic sandwich bag to maintain freshness. Tuck into a small clay flowerpot and overwrap with clear cellophane, tying it in place with a shiny cord.

CANDIED WALNUTS

YIELD: about 2½ cups

These lightly caramelized nuts make a good snack or can accompany a spicy Indian or Chinese dinner.

METHOD

Bring 2 quarts of water to a boil, add the walnuts, and simmer for 3 minutes; drain well. Toss the nuts with the sugar. Transfer to a baking sheet and allow them to dry thoroughly.

Heat the oil in a wok or deep frying pan until hot but not smoking. Fry the nuts in several batches, turning all the time, for 3 to 5 minutes, or until golden.

Transfer nuts to a baking sheet, spreading them in one layer. Cool completely. Toss with the coarse salt.

Stored in airtight containers, they will keep for several weeks.

Note: Equally delicious made with blanched, unsalted peanuts or un-salted cashews.

TO PACKAGE

For the Chinese cook, make this into a double present. To preserve freshness, first wrap the nuts in a clear plastic sandwich bag and seal. Pack the bag of nuts into a decorative Chinese ceramic bowl.

Place a bowl of the same size over the top as a lid. Hold in place with cloth tape. Tie with shiny cord, attaching chopsticks and fortune cookies for extra fun. Once opened, the bowls can be used for serving the nuts or as part of a Chinese table setting.

INGREDIENTS

1 pound shelled walnuts
1½ cups sugar
6 cups peanut oil
1 tablespoon coarse salt

TOOLS

Baking sheet
Wok or deep frying pan
Airtight container

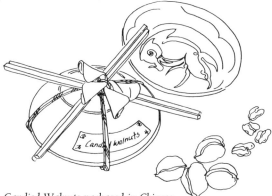

Candied Walnuts packaged in Chinese bowls, tied with shiny cord, decorated with chopsticks and fortune cookies.

GINGER NUT MIX

INGREDIENTS

2 cups shelled Spanish peanuts

1 cup candied gingerroot, cut into bite-size pieces

1 cup *pepitas* (roasted pumpkin seeds)

TOOLS

2 plastic food bags

Materials

Whole cinnamon sticks, about 4 inches long, available in bulk from most gourmet stores

Plastic container. Choose a container no higher than the cinnamon sticks, for example, 2-cup plastic Tupperware-type food containers, strawberry or mushroom baskets, clean tin cans, custard cups, small baskets

Household glue

Small paintbrush

Rubber bands

Packing straw, shredded tissue paper, or plastic grass

Assorted ribbon

Newspaper

YIELD: about 4 cups

A mix so tantalizing, you will be tempted to eat it all before you package it.

METHOD

Combine nuts, gingerroot, and *pepitas*. Toss gently to distribute evenly. Pack about 2 cups of the mix into each bag. (Freezer bags are a good size.) Secure with a twist-tie or rubber band.

TO PACKAGE

Add some spice to a friend's life by packing the Ginger Nut Mix into a container covered with cinnamon sticks. Transform ordinary household food containers into unique gift baskets. Use cinnamon sticks to give a rustic country look that can be used year round for holidays or festive occasions, especially during the Christmas season.

Curried almonds in a container covered with cinnamon sticks.

Directions

Cover a clean surface with newspaper. Using the paintbrush, cover the inside of the container with a thin layer of glue. Glue the cinnamon sticks in a vertical row, as close together as possible. Let dry.

Cover the outside of the container with a thin layer of glue. Glue the cinnamon sticks in a vertical row, as close together as possible. Hold the outer row in place with two rubber bands, one around the top half of the row and one around the bottom half. When the glue is dry, remove the rubber bands. Fill the containers with the packing straw and add the Ginger Nut Mix. (See illustration.)

Tie a ribbon around center of container. Attach an appropriate label (see Labels, page 216).

ALMOND-PECAN CORN

YIELD: 3 pounds

History has it that popped corn was the surprise gift from the Indians at the first Thanksgiving feast. It seemed like magic the way the "parched" corn turned itself inside out. The Indians believed that a demon lived inside each kernel of corn and that when his home was heated, he became so mad the kernel burst. Almonds, pecans, and freshly popped corn in a caramel glaze make this a delicious snack, suited for Halloween or munching at football games, and like all snacks utterly addictive.

METHOD

Toast the pecans and almonds on a baking sheet in a 350° F. oven for 10 to 15 minutes, until lightly browned. Combine the popcorn and nuts in a lightly oiled bowl. Toss to distribute evenly. Combine the sugar,

INGREDIENTS

2 cups shelled pecans
2 cups shelled almonds
8 cups popped corn
2 cups sugar
1 cup Golden Syrup
⅔ cup water
1 pound unsalted butter

TOOLS

Baking sheets
Pastry brush
Candy thermometer

Almond-Pecan Corn packaged in a large decorative pail.

syrup, and water in a saucepan and bring the mixture to a boil over high heat, washing down any sugar crystals clinging to the sides of the pan with a pastry brush dipped into cold water. Add the butter and continue cooking until a candy thermometer registers 300° F., about 5 minutes.

Pour the hot syrup over the popcorn and nut mixture. Quickly toss to coat the mixture with the caramel, and spread it in a thin layer on 2 lightly oiled baking sheets. Cool completely before breaking into bite-size pieces. Store in airtight containers until ready to use.

TO PACKAGE

Popcorn packed in large shiny tin pails is a hot holiday gift item from mail-order catalogs. It is simple to create your own at home. Purchase the pails from hardware stores and attach a handmade label, or use wide tape or Prestype to spell out popcorn in bold letters around the outside of the can. First, pack the Almond-Pecan Corn in a large plastic bag to maintain freshness, then attach the lid and tie a bow to the handle.

INGREDIENTS

3 cups dry-roasted peanuts
2 cups sugar
1 cup light corn syrup
½ cup water
8 ounces unsalted butter
1½ teaspoons baking soda
½ tablespoon vanilla extract

TOOLS

1 baking sheet
Candy thermometer
2 jelly-roll pans

OLD-FASHIONED PEANUT BRITTLE

YIELD: about 2½ pounds

METHOD

Lightly oil 2 jelly-roll pans. Place the peanuts on a baking sheet and warm them in a 300° F. oven. Combine the sugar, corn syrup, and water and cook over low heat until the sugar dissolves. Bring the mixture to a boil and stir in the butter. Continue cooking, stirring frequently with a wooden spoon, until a candy thermometer registers 280° F. (soft-crack stage).

Add the peanuts and continue to cook the syrup, stirring constantly, until the candy thermometer registers 305° F. (hard-crack stage). The syrup will be a rich golden color.

Remove from the heat and stir in the baking soda and vanilla. Pour the syrup onto the jelly-roll pans; with a spatula dipped into cold water, spread the candy as thin as possible.

Cool completely. Bang the pans on the sharp edge of a counter to break the candy into pieces. Place the peanut brittle in plastic sandwich bags and secure each bag with a tie.

TO PACKAGE

Perfect for Halloween trick or treaters or as favors at a Halloween party.

Directions

For each bag, lay a brown paper bag on a flat surface and draw a cute pumpkin face in the center of one side. Slide the piece of cardboard inside the bag so you don't cut through to the other side. Cut out your design, starting from the middle of the design and working outward.

Remove the piece of cardboard. Using the brush, place a thin layer of rubber cement close to the edges of 1 piece of cellophane. Open the bag and insert the cellophane piece. Glue into place over the pumpkin-shaped hole. Let dry. Divide the Old-Fashioned Peanut Brittle among the 4 plastic food storage bags and tie with twist-ties. Place 1 bag inside each brown sandwich bag.

Fold over approximately 2 inches at the top of the bag, punch holes in the folded area, and lace with black ribbon. Tie ends. For other bag ideas see Tied Paper Bags (page 220). Write a name on each bag or attach a label (see Labels, page 216).

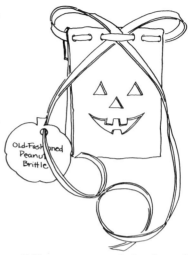

Fold over approximately 2 inches at the top of the bag, punch holes in the folded area, and lace with ribbon.

Materials

4 brown paper lunch bags
4 pieces of orange cellophane,
    3 x 4 inches
1 piece of cardboard, 9 x 4½
    inches
Scissors
Rubber cement with brush
    applicator
¼-inch-wide ribbon, orange and
    black
Label of your choice
4 small plastic food storage bags
    with twist-ties

CRANBERRY CHUTNEY

INGREDIENTS

½ cup apricot preserves
½ cup cider vinegar
½ cup firmly packed dark brown
    sugar
1 teaspoon curry powder
1 teaspoon ground ginger
1 cinnamon stick
¼ teaspoon ground cloves
1½ cups water
1 lemon, blanched in boiling water
    for 2 minutes, seeded, and
    chopped
2 medium-size green apples,
    peeled, cored, and diced
3 cups cranberries
½ cup raisins
½ cup chopped walnuts

TOOLS

Nonaluminum saucepan
Mason jars with lids
Cheesecloth

YIELD: 4 cups

A complex blend of fruits and spices in a pungent sauce, this chutney enlivens a classic Indian curry. Modify tradition and serve it with a roast Thanksgiving turkey.

METHOD

In a large nonaluminum saucepan, combine the preserves, vinegar, sugar, and the spices tied in a cheesecloth bag. Add the water and bring the mixture to a slow boil, stirring until the sugar is dissolved. Add the chopped lemon and apples and simmer for 10 minutes. Add the cranberries and raisins and simmer, uncovered, for 25 to 30 minutes, or until thick, stirring occasionally to prevent sticking.

Remove the chutney from the heat, discard the cheesecloth bag, and stir in the chopped walnuts. Transfer to hot sterilized Mason jars, filling to within ¼ inch of the rims. Wipe the rims with a clean damp cloth and seal the jars with the lids. Process the jars for 10 minutes according to canning directions on page 231. Cool.

TO PACKAGE

Cover these appropriately with festive red-tartan fabric "hats" (page 219).

CANDIED CRANBERRIES WITH CRANBERRY SYRUP

YIELD: about 2 cups syrup and 4 cups candied fruit

This is several days in the making. However, when you finish, you will have a cranberry syrup which doubles as an unusual glaze for ham or pork and a base for a fruit salad dressing, as well as a jar of dried berries to use over ice cream or as an accompaniment for roast meats that is much prettier than maraschino cherries. Make this in the fall when fresh cranberries are plentiful.

METHOD

With a zester remove the lemon peel in long strips. Heat the sugar, water, and cranberry juice to boiling. Cook for 1 minute, stirring constantly. Add the lemon peel strips.

Combine the cranberries, cinnamon, allspice, and hot syrup in an ovenproof bowl. Place the bowl on the steamer rack in a large pot or steamer over simmering water. Steam, covered, for 30 minutes, adding more water to the steamer as needed.

Remove the bowl from the pot. Cool but do not stir. Cover fruit with cheesecloth and let stand at room temperature for 2 to 3 days, stirring occasionally, until very thick. Lift the fruit from the syrup with a slotted spoon to a baking sheet lined with wax paper.

Store the syrup in a tightly covered container in the refrigerator.

Let the fruit dry, uncovered, on the paper-lined baking sheet for several days, turning occasionally. Fruit will be slightly sticky.

Pack in tightly covered containers. If stored in the refrigerator, fruit will keep for as long as 3 months.

TO PACKAGE

Accent the jars with fabric "hats" (page 219) cut with pinking shears from green taffeta moiré. Tie with ribbon.

Using a needle and heavy-gauge thread, knotted at one end, string raw cranberries into a chain approximately 17 inches long for a wide-mouthed canning jar. Secure end with double knot. Wrap the cranberry string twice around the rim of the jar. Attach a label and tuck in a sprig of holly, or an evergreen sprig with tiny cones.

INGREDIENTS

1 lemon
2½ cups sugar
1 cup water
¾ cup cranberry juice cocktail
3 cups fresh cranberries
¼ teaspoon ground cinnamon
⅛ teaspoon ground allspice

TOOLS

Ovenproof bowl
Zester
Steamer rack
Baking sheet
Slotted spoon
Jars with lids
**Steamer with tight-fitting lid or
    large pot**

Place the bowl on the steamer rack in a large pot or steamer over simmering water.

INGREDIENTS

Pastry

1¾ cups all-purpose flour
⅔ cup yellow cornmeal
3 tablespoons sugar
½ teaspoon salt
2 teaspoons minced seeded
    jalapeño peppers
4 ounces unsalted butter, chilled
2 tablespoons lard or vegetable
    shortening
¼ cup cold water, approximately

Filling

1 pound small white onions
2 tablespoons butter
4 ounces country slab bacon, cut
    into small cubes
3 large carrots, peeled and
    coarsely diced
2 tablespoons all-purpose flour
1½ cups rich chicken stock
3 whole cloves
2 whole cardamom pods, papery
    membranes removed
1 teaspoon crumbled rosemary
3 pounds cooked turkey
¼ cup heavy cream or half-and-
    half
Salt and pepper
5 ounces frozen corn
5 ounces frozen peas

Egg Wash

1 egg, beaten

DEEP-DISH TURKEY POT PIE

YIELD: 6 servings

High on everyone's gift-receiving list is a hearty turkey pot pie. It is the perfect dish to rush over to a friend in a crisis. It is also, of course, the time-honored solution for the leftover Thanksgiving turkey. Filled with vegetables and topped with a tightly woven jalapeño-spiced cornmeal crust, this variation of the classic recipe makes a complete meal with the addition of a simple salad and a good jug wine. The ambitious cook will rise to the challenge of weaving the tight basketlike crust.

METHOD

Pastry

Combine the flour, cornmeal, sugar, salt, and jalapeño peppers. Add the butter and lard in small pieces; in a food processor or with a pastry cutter, blend until the mixture resembles coarse oatmeal. Work quickly so the butter stays cold. Add the water, a little at a time, until the dough is just moist and can be gathered into a loose ball. Overmixing will produce a tough crust. Wrap the dough and chill for at least 30 minutes.

Filling

Bring a quart of water to boil in a saucepan. Add the onions and blanch for 2 to 3 minutes; drain. Trim off the tops and bottoms and peel off the skins.

Melt the butter in a large casserole over medium heat. Add the bacon and cook until very crisp. Remove the bacon and set aside. Pour off all but 3 tablespoons of fat and lightly brown the onions and carrots in the casserole. Add the flour, stirring to mix it into the fat, and cook for 2 minutes more. Add the stock, spices, rosemary, and turkey. Simmer for about 15 minutes, until the sauce is thick. Thin the sauce with the cream and simmer for 5 minutes. Season generously with salt and pepper to taste. Stir in the corn and peas and pour the mixture into a generously greased 6-cup soufflé dish or casserole.

Preheat oven to 400° F.

Remove the pastry dough from the refrigerator and let it rest for 10 minutes. Roll out the pastry on a floured surface to ⅛-inch thickness. Slice the pastry into ½-inch strips and weave a tight lattice crust (see illustration). Crimp the edges to the rim of the baking dish and brush the entire crust with half of the beaten egg.

Bake for 1 hour, brushing the crust with beaten egg again after 30 minutes. The sauce should be bubbling and the crust brown. (If the crust browns too quickly, cover the pie loosely with aluminum foil.)

The turkey pot pie can be made several days in advance and kept covered in the refrigerator. If you freeze it, thaw for 45 minutes before baking.

TO PACKAGE

Make sure you show off the crust you have taken so much time to produce. Wrap the base of the casserole in several layers of tissue paper; tie in place with a ribbon. Set the casserole in a wicker paper-plate holder; these are easily found in variety stores and groceries. Punch a hole in the corner of a pretty postcard and list instructions for reheating and a reminder to remove the wicker plate holder and tissue paper before baking. Tie it on with ribbon.

Or with a little more effort you could make a Wax Fabric Container (instructions on page 224) to hold and display the Turkey Pot Pie.

TOOLS

Food processor or pastry cutter
Rolling pin
6-cup soufflé dish or equivalent casserole

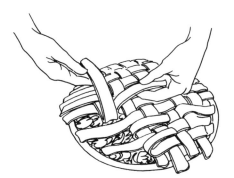

Weave a tight lattice crust over the Deep-Dish Turkey Pot Pie filling.

RILLETTES

INGREDIENTS

1½ pounds lean pork, cut into cubes

¾ pound pork fat, diced

½ pound country-style bacon, diced

⎫ or any combination of the two totaling 1¼ pounds fat

¾ teaspoon salt

Coarse-ground pepper

Pinch of grated nutmeg

1 teaspoon *herbes de Provence*

½ teaspoon whole thyme

1 teaspoon juniper berries

1 teaspoon coriander seeds

3 or 4 shallots, cut into halves

1 bay leaf

1 garlic clove

6 to 8 parsley sprigs

½ cup water

¼ cup Cognac

Bay leaves for decoration

TOOLS

Enameled casserole with lid

Cheesecloth

Strainer

Earthenware container or several ramekins

YIELD: 4 cups

Rillettes (re-et′, the "*ll*'s" are not pronounced) originated in the French region of Touraine and it is in the city of Tours that *rillettes* are still a local favorite. Similar to pâtés and terrines, *rillettes* are served slightly chilled or at room temperature, thickly spread on slices of French bread, or can be an hors d'oeuvre or snack, accompanied by tiny cornichon pickles. Practical, hearty, and easy to prepare, *rillettes* packed into handsome crocks make ideal picnic fare to lavish on crusty rolls or baguettes. This potted pork has not become as popular in this country as French pâté because traditionally *rillettes* are too bland and fatty for American taste. However, enough pâté is enough, and you may wish to join me in the headlong stampede away from that overused spread and try this spiced-up version of *rillettes*. Vouvray, a reliable, flowery white wine from the Touraine region, is the perfect companion for the potted pork.

METHOD

Put the pork, pork fat, and bacon in a large mixing bowl. Add the salt, pepper to taste, nutmeg, *herbes de Provence,* and thyme. Toss together and place the mixture in a deep enameled casserole.

Tie the juniper berries, coriander seeds, shallots, bay leaf, garlic, and parsley in a square of cheesecloth with a string attached for easy removal. Add this *bouquet garni*, the water, and the Cognac to the casserole and bring the mixture to a boil on the top of the stove.

Cover the casserole and put it in a preheated 325° F. oven to braise for about 3½ to 4 hours. Remove the *bouquet garni* after 3 hours. The liquid will evaporate and the meat should brown slightly. If the meat browns too quickly, reduce the heat to 300° F.

Transfer the meat to a strainer lined with cheesecloth set over a large bowl to catch the fat. Reserve the fat.

After the meat has cooled, shred it either with your hands or with 2 forks. Put the meat into one 4- to 5-cup earthenware container, or divide it between several small ramekins. Press down to compress the meat slightly but do not pack it too tightly. Use three quarters of the reserved fat to cover the *rillettes* so that no meat is exposed to the air. Cover and refrigerate until the fat is set.

Remove *rillettes* from the refrigerator and make an additional thin layer with the remaining fat. If there is not enough fat left from the cooking, render additional pork or bacon fat or use melted lard. Gently press bay leaves into a pattern on top of the fat and refrigerate until hard. Sealed with the fat, the *rillettes* will keep several months, refrigerated.

TO PACKAGE

Present the *rillettes* in a handsome crock accompanied by a crusty loaf of French bread, a jar of cornichon pickles, and a good bottle of Vouvray.

CARDAMOM WHEAT SHEAVES

YIELD: 12 sheaves

The inspiration for a bread in the form of wheat sheaves comes from the master baker of France, Lionel Poilane. His bread graces the best cafés, restaurants, and food shops of Paris; it was in his Paris bakery that I first saw bread shaped to resemble bundles of wheat.

This recipe is my own. I have included cardamom to impart an unusual subtle flavor. Slightly sweet, these breads make a perfect "take-along" for a fall brunch or a surprise addition to a soup and salad supper. Presented together, they also make an attractive edible centerpiece.

METHOD

Scald the milk, remove from the heat, and add the butter in small pieces to melt. When the butter has melted, add the sugar, salt, and eggs to the milk and stir well. Cool to lukewarm, 90° to 105° F., and add the yeast.

INGREDIENTS

1¼ cups milk
4 ounces butter
¾ cup sugar
1 teaspoon salt
2 eggs, beaten
1 tablespoon dry yeast
6 cups white flour
½ teaspoon ground cardamom
1 tablespoon grated lemon rind
1 cup whole-wheat flour

Egg Wash

1 egg, beaten with 1 tablespoon
      cream

TOOLS

Baking sheet
Pastry brush
Scissors
Large clear-plastic food bag with twist-tie

Add 3 cups of the white flour, the cardamom, and lemon rind. Beat for 3 minutes, until smooth and elastic. Add remaining white flour and whole-wheat flour to form a soft dough. Knead for 5 minutes or until smooth and elastic.

Put the dough in a large clear-plastic food storage bag with 1 tablespoon of flour; close with a twist-tie. Turn the bag several times to coat all sides of the dough with the flour. Let dough stand in a warm draft-free place, approximately 70° to 80° F., for about 1 hour, until double in bulk.

Remove the dough from the bag, punch down, and divide into 12 equal pieces. Cover and put all but 1 piece in the refrigerator. Divide the piece into 8 equal portions and roll 6 of them into strands ¼ inch wide and 6 inches long. With the palm of your hand flatten one end of a strand. With a sharp knife or kitchen scissors make four ⅛-inch-deep, diagonal cuts on each side of the flat end. Place the strand on a well-greased baking sheet. Repeat with five of the remaining strands or "stalks."

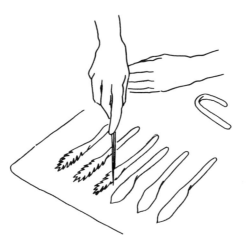

With a sharp knife or kitchen scissors make several ⅛-inch-deep, diagonal cuts on each side of the flat end.

Gently wrap the braid around the center of the "stalks."

Roll the 2 remaining pieces of dough into 8-inch strands and twist together. Gently wrap the braid around the center of the stalks, tucking the ends under the "sheaf." Spread the tops of the sheaves into a fan shape. Brush with some of the egg wash, lightly cover with wax paper, and refrigerate. Repeat the process with remaining 11 pieces of dough.

Allow the sheaves to rise in a warm place for 10 to 15 minutes. Brush with egg wash again and bake in a preheated 350° F. oven for 20 to 25 minutes.

TO PACKAGE

These make beautiful favors for a wedding shower or fall brunch. For each wheat sheaf, cut a 5-inch circle from a piece of cardboard; use boxes from the grocery or liquor store for the cardboard. Lay a 6-inch white paper doily over the circle and place 1 wheat sheaf on top. Overwrap with clear cellophane and tie with yellow satin ribbon.

FARMER'S BREAD

YIELD: 2 loaves

The following two recipes come from Lisa and Paul D'Andrea, proprietors of a perfect small bakery called Simple Pleasures in Bridgehampton, New York. Certainly by making and giving one of their breads you will be providing one of life's most "simple pleasures"—a home-baked loaf. This bread adds a lot of extra nutrition to your diet with its whole-wheat flour and bran. It could even qualify as a "health food."

METHOD

To make the starter: Combine the yeast with the warm water. Allow to proof for 10 minutes, until foamy. Stir in the rye flour and sugar. Beat for

INGREDIENTS

Starter

1 tablespoon dry yeast
¾ cup warm water, 90° to 105° F.
1 cup rye flour
1 teaspoon sugar

Dough

1 cup warm coffee, 90° to 105° F.
1½ tablespoons dry yeast
¼ cup firmly packed dark brown sugar
1 tablespoon vegetable oil
1½ cups whole-wheat flour
1 tablespoon salt
½ cup unprocessed bran
2 to 4 cups white flour

TOOLS

2 loaf pans 8½ x 4½ inches
1 large clear-plastic food storage
bag with twist-tie

2 minutes. Cover the starter and set in a warm, draft-free place for 1 to 3 days. The longer the starter sits, the more pronounced the flavor will be. If starter sits longer than 3 days, the bread tends to be too sour for most people's tastes.

To make the dough: In a large bowl, combine the warm coffee, yeast, brown sugar, and oil and let proof until foamy, about 10 minutes. Add the whole-wheat flour, the starter, the salt, and bran; beat for 2 to 3 minutes, until smooth and elastic. Add the white flour, starting with 2 cups, adding a little at a time, until the dough pulls away from the sides of the bowl and forms a sticky ball. Knead for 8 to 10 minutes, adding up to 2 more cups of white flour to make a smooth elastic dough. The kneading may be done by hand or with an electric mixer fitted with a dough hook.

Place the dough in a large clear-plastic food storage bag with 1 tablespoon of flour. Close with a twist-tie. Turn the bag several times to coat the dough with the flour. Place in a warm draft-free place, approximately 70° to 80° F., to double in bulk 1 to 1½ hours.

Remove from the bag, punch down, and divide into 2 equal pieces. Shape the pieces into loaves, place them in greased loaf pans, cover loosely with clean, damp dish towels, and allow dough to rise to the top of the loaf pans. Bake at 350° F. for 30 to 40 minutes, until the bread sounds hollow when tapped.

Remove the breads from the pans and cool completely on a wire rack before slicing or wrapping. Tightly wrapped, the bread will stay fresh for 3 to 4 days. It freezes well.

TO PACKAGE

See Rhubarb Nut Bread on page 7 or Dilly Bread on page 85 for 2 suggestions on how to wrap the breads; or tie them Japanese style in a *furoshiki* (page 216).

STRASBOURG RYE

YIELD: 2 loaves

This bread is a moist, medium-dark rye bread with plenty of flavor.

METHOD

To make the starter: Combine the yeast with the warm water and allow to proof for 10 minutes, until foamy. Stir in the rye flour and beat for 2 minutes. Cover the starter and set it in a warm, draft-free place for 1 to 3 days. The longer the starter sits the more pronounced the flavor will be. Starter that sits any longer than 3 days tends to make a bread too sour for most people's taste.

To make the dough: In a large bowl, combine the warm water, yeast, molasses, oil, and caraway seeds. Let proof for 10 minutes, until foamy. Add the rye flour, the starter, and the salt and beat for 2 to 3 minutes by hand, or with an electric mixer, until smooth and elastic. Stir in the white flour, starting with 2 cups, adding a little at a time until the dough pulls away from the sides of the bowl, forming a sticky ball. Knead for 8 to 10 minutes, adding up to 2 more cups of white flour to make a smooth elastic dough. Kneading may be done by hand or with an electric mixer fitted with a dough hook.

Place the dough in the large clear-plastic food storage bag with 1 tablespoon of flour. Close with a twist-tie. Turn the bag several times to coat the dough with the flour. Place in a warm, draft-free place, approximately 70° to 80° F., to double in size, 1 to 1½ hours.

Remove dough from the bag, punch down, and divide into 2 equal pieces. Shape the pieces into 2 round loaves and place on a well-greased baking sheet to rise for about 30 minutes.

With a sharp knife, make 4 diagonal slashes on the top of each loaf. Bake at 350° F. for 30 to 40 minutes, until the bread sounds hollow when tapped.

Cool loaves completely on a wire rack before slicing or wrapping. Tightly wrapped, the bread will stay fresh for 3 to 4 days. It freezes well.

INGREDIENTS

Starter
1 tablespoon dry yeast
1½ cups warm water, 90° to 105° F.
2 cups rye flour

Dough
1 cup warm water
1 tablespoon dry yeast
1 tablespoon molasses
1 tablespoon vegetable oil
2 tablespoons caraway seeds
2 cups rye flour
1 tablespoon salt
2 to 4 cups white flour

TOOLS
1 baking sheet, 11 x 17 inches
1 large clear-plastic food storage bag with twist-tie

TO PACKAGE

The deep brown crust is the wrapping for this round loaf; add a final touch by tying with wide brown velvet ribbon.

INGREDIENTS

2 cups grated peeled carrots
1½ cups grated homemade bread crumbs
1 cup dark brown sugar
4 large eggs, beaten
2 tablespoons Grand Marnier liqueur
6 ounces unsalted butter, melted, with foam removed
4 tablespoons ground cinnamon
1 teaspoon ground cloves
1 teaspoon grated nutmeg
1¼ cups flour
1½ teaspoons baking soda
¼ teaspoon salt
1 cup seeded raisins
¾ cup chopped pitted dates

TOOLS

Food processor or grater
1-quart steamed pudding mold
Rack or steamer rack
Large pot to hold steamed pudding mold

STEAMED CARROT PUDDING

YIELD: 8 to 10 portions

The steamed pudding has all but disappeared from the American dessert table. Not long ago every grandmother owned a pudding mold and could produce far more with it than the obligatory Christmas plum pudding. The name of these desserts is misleading since we think of a pudding as a soft, custardlike dessert eaten with a spoon. Steamed pudding is actually moist, fragrant cake produced by steaming a batter in a closed mold. It is what pudding cakes—those horrible combinations of cake mix and instant pudding—dream of becoming.

Dried or fresh fruit is the standard base for this dessert, but I particularly like this recipe for carrot steamed pudding. It is a delectable switch from the carrot cake we are so often served.

A food processor for grating the large quantity of carrots will make this recipe a little easier.

METHOD

In a large bowl, combine the carrots, bread crumbs, and sugar. Add the eggs, Grand Marnier, and butter and mix well. Sift together the spices, 1 cup of flour, the baking soda, and salt. Add this to the carrot mixture and blend well. Toss the raisins and dates in the remaining ¼ cup of flour and add to the batter, stirring well.

Fill a well-buttered 1-quart steamed pudding mold with the batter and cover with a layer of heavy-duty foil tied in place with kitchen twine. Cover with the lid.

Set the mold on a rack or steamer in a large pot with a tight-fitting lid. Add enough boiling water to the pot to reach two thirds of the way up the sides of the mold. Cover the pot and steam the pudding over medium heat for 2 hours.

Remove the mold from the water and let the pudding stand uncovered for 10 minutes before unmolding. To unmold, run a knife around the edges of the mold and then place a plate over the mold and invert the pudding onto the plate. Serve warm with Orange Hard Sauce (following recipe).

Wrapped and refrigerated, the pudding will keep for 3 to 4 weeks.

TO PACKAGE

If more of us had pudding molds, the revival of the steamed pudding would be ensured. Pass on the tradition by presenting the carrot pudding in the same mold in which it was steamed.

Wrap the mold in layers of tissue paper, leaving the top and handle of the mold free. Tie a large bow around the top and attach a label with directions for reheating the pudding. (To reheat, steam the dessert in the fashion described above for 30 minutes, until hot.) Complete your gift with a jar of fluffy Orange Hard Sauce.

Pass on the tradition by presenting the Steamed Carrot Pudding in the steamed pudding mold.

ORANGE HARD SAUCE

YIELD: 1 cup

METHOD

In a bowl, cream the butter until light and fluffy. Add the confectioners' sugar a little at a time, beating constantly. Add the grated orange rind and liqueur and beat the mixture until it is very fluffy.

INGREDIENTS

6 ounces unsalted butter
1 cup sifted confectioners' sugar
2 tablespoons grated orange rind
3 teaspoons Grand Marnier liqueur
Strips of orange rind for decoration

Transfer the sauce to ramekins or small serving bowls. Decorate the top of the hard sauce with a few strips of orange rind.

Covered with plastic wrap and stored in the refrigerator, this keeps for 3 to 4 weeks.

TO PACKAGE

Tie a shiny orange ribbon around the rim of the dish and present with Steamed Carrot Pudding.

CHOCOLATE PUMPKIN LOAF

INGREDIENTS

1 cup fine unseasoned bread crumbs, approximately, for dusting pans

2½ cups sifted all-purpose flour

2 teaspoons baking soda

½ teaspoon salt

1½ teaspoons ground cinnamon

½ teaspoon ground ginger

¼ teaspoon ground cloves

¼ teaspoon grated nutmeg

½ cup unsweetened cocoa powder, preferably Dutch process

2 eggs

2 cups firmly packed light brown sugar

YIELD: 4 small loaves or 2 large loaves

Seasonally spiced, not too sweet, but very chocolaty and moist (because of the pumpkin, which you don't taste), this is a perfect cake for the holiday season. Easy to make, with good keeping power, it seems to belong especially to Thanksgiving.

METHOD

Preheat oven to 350° F. Butter 4 small loaf pans or 2 large loaf pans, and dust lightly with unseasoned fine bread crumbs.

Sift together the flour, baking soda, salt, spices, and cocoa powder; set aside. In a separate bowl, beat the eggs, add the sugar and oil, and beat just to mix. Mix in the pumpkin, then the dates. Gradually add the dry ingredients, mixing only until all ingredients are incorporated. Stir in the walnuts.

Pour the batter into the prepared pans and smooth the tops. Bake for 50 minutes to 1 hour for smaller loaves, 1½ hours for larger loaves, or until a cake tester inserted into the middle comes out clean.

Cool loaves in the pans for 10 minutes. Remove loaves from the pans and cool completely on a rack before wrapping in aluminum foil. If you can wait, these cakes are best eaten the next day. They keep well refrigerated for about 1 week and freeze successfully.

TO PACKAGE

Make the wrapper a *furoshiki* tied from an orange plaid lap napkin (see page 216 for instructions).

½ cup pure vegetable oil, corn or safflower

1 pound canned solid-pack pumpkin (not pie filling) or cooked fresh pumpkin

1 cup coarsely chopped, pitted dates, about 8 ounces

1 cup coarsely chopped shelled walnuts

TOOLS

4 loaf pans, 5¾ x 3¼ x 2¼ inches, or 2 loaf pans, 9 x 5 x 2½ inches

BISCOTTI CON NOCCIOLE

YIELD: about 40 cookies

There are times when you want to give something sweet but not sugary—something that can be eaten as a mid-morning snack or with an afternoon tea. Or perhaps you are asked to bring a light dessert to accompany a friend's elaborate dinner. Each of the following recipes admirably suits these different occasions.

Nuts, never more plentiful and fresh than in the fall, provide the basic ingredient. Serve the cookies with espresso coffee or a sweet dessert wine for dunking.

Roasting the nuts for all the cookies concentrates their flavor.

In Italy, there are semisweet, crisp *biscotti* traditionally made with almonds or walnuts called *Tuscan Biscotti di Prato*. Good as these are, my favorite *biscotti* are made with *nocciole*, or hazelnuts.

METHOD

Preheat oven to 300° F. Spread the hazelnuts on a baking sheet and toast in the oven for 15 minutes. Remove the nuts from the oven and

INGREDIENTS

8 ounces shelled hazelnuts
4 ounces butter
½ cup sugar
2 eggs
½ teaspoon vanilla extract
2 cups flour
2 teaspoons baking powder
Pinch of salt

TOOLS

Baking sheet, 11 x 17 inches
Airtight containers

while they are still warm, wrap them in a clean dish towel. Let them steam for 1 to 2 minutes. Rub the nuts together vigorously in the towel to remove as much of the skins as possible. Coarsely chop nuts, leaving some whole.

Reduce oven temperature to 350° F. Cream the butter and sugar together until light and fluffy. Lightly beat the eggs with the vanilla, add to the butter and sugar, and mix well. Sift the flour, baking powder, and salt, add the nuts, and coat well with the flour mixture. Gradually, add the flour mixture to the butter mixture until well blended.

With lightly floured hands, form the dough into 2 strips, each about 12 by 3 inches. Place the dough strips on a buttered baking sheet and bake in the preheated oven for 30 minutes, or until the dough is set and lightly colored.

Remove the baking sheet from the oven and reduce the oven temperature to 275° F. With a sharp knife, slice the strips of dough on the diagonal into ½-inch-thick pieces. Cut each strip on the diagonal into about 20 cookies.

With a sharp knife, slice the strips of dough on the diagonal into ½-inch-thick pieces.

Place the cookies cut side down on the baking sheet. Toast in the oven for 15 minutes on each side or until light golden in color and slightly dry.

Stored in airtight containers, they will keep for 1 to 2 weeks.

TO PACKAGE

For a rare treat, accompany the cookies with the Italian dessert wine Vin Canto, Italy's answer to Château d'Yquem. So authentic you almost need a passport.

SWEDISH TOAST

YIELD: about 50 pieces

A real treat, similar in texture to *Biscotti con Nocciole* but characterized by the pervasive flavor of cardamom seed.

METHOD

Preheat oven to 300° F. Spread the almonds on a baking sheet and toast in the oven for 8 to 10 minutes.

Raise heat to 350° F.

Cream the butter and sugar together until light. Add the eggs and sour cream and mix well. Sift together the baking powder, salt, and flour. Fold into the batter along with the ground almonds, ground cardamom, and lemon rind. Blend well. Spoon the thick batter into a well-greased baking pan, 9 x 13 inches. Bake at 350° F. for 40 to 45 minutes.

Remove the pan from the oven and reduce the temperature to 250° F. Cool the cake for 10 minutes; slice it into 3 long strips and cut each strip on the diagonal into ½-inch pieces.

Transfer the cookies to a baking sheet, placing them on their sides. Toast the pieces at 250° F. for 30 minutes on each side, or until light golden in color and slightly dry.

INGREDIENTS

8 ounces unsalted butter, softened
    to room temperature
2 cups sugar
2 eggs, lightly beaten
1 cup dairy sour cream
2 teaspoons baking powder
½ teaspoon salt
3½ cups flour
1 cup ground blanched almonds
1 tablespoon ground cardamom
    seeds
Grated rind of 1 lemon

TOOLS

1 baking pan, 9 x 13 inches
Baking sheet

Slice the cake into 3 long strips and cut each strip on the diagonal into ½-inch pieces.

TO PACKAGE

Line a willow paper-plate holder with a 12-inch white doily. Add a layer of pastel-colored tissue paper. Arrange the cookies in the lined basket. Overwrap with clear cellophane, tying with a large bow.

HONEY CAKE

YIELD: 1 cake, 16 x 11 x 4 inches

Richly spiced and not too sweet, honey cake or *Lekakh* is the traditional cake served on the first night of the Jewish celebration of Rosh Hashanah as well as on many other sacred occasions of the Jewish faith—the birth of a child, a wedding, the Sabbath. Throughout the Bible, Israel is referred to as the "land of milk and honey," and at Jewish feasts for centuries honey has symbolically represented Israel. This cake was probably one of the very first sweet pastries since honey was the major sweetener and preservative of antiquity. (Our own familiar cane sugar was a rarity well into the Middle Ages.) Long associated with Jewish tradition, honey cake is a cake everyone will enjoy. Prepare it a day ahead so the honey and spice flavors have a chance to develop fully.

METHOD

Preheat oven to 325° F. Generously grease and flour a baking pan 16 x 11 x 4 inches. Line the bottom of the pan with wax paper. Set aside.

Sift the flour, baking soda, baking powder, and spices together. Dissolve the honey in the hot coffee. In a separate bowl beat the eggs until light. Gradually add the brown sugar to the eggs, beating all the time, then the oil. Add the dry ingredients alternately with the honey-coffee mixture to the eggs and sugar, beating well after each addition.

Mix the chopped almonds with 1 tablespoon of flour to coat the nuts. Fold the nuts into the batter with the grated lemon and orange rinds.

Pour the batter into the prepared pan and bake for 60 to 70 minutes, until a cake tester comes out clean. Cool the cake in the pan for 10 minutes. Invert the cake onto a clean surface. Remove the wax paper and place the cake right side up on a cake rack to cool completely.

Heat the corn syrup and honey together. Brush the cake with the glaze. While the cake is still warm, mark the cake with a knife in a diamond pattern and brush all over again with the heated glaze. Place 1 whole blanched almond in the center of each diamond.

To store, place a piece of wax paper over the top of the cake and then wrap cake tightly in aluminum foil. Do not eat the cake for 24 hours so the flavor has time to develop.

Wrapped tightly and refrigerated, the honey cake will keep for 2 weeks.

TO PACKAGE

This cake fits nicely into a shirt box. Paper the lid of the box with scraps of unusual wallpaper, contact paper, leftover fabric, personally stamped paper (page 221), or cover with woven ribbon (page 228). Line the inside of the box with tissue paper. Wrap the Honey Cake first in plastic wrap, then in aluminum foil, and place inside. Tie the box with colored ribbon and add a label.

While the cake is still warm, mark with a knife in a diamond pattern. Place 1 whole blanched almond in the center of each diamond.

INGREDIENTS

5 cups sifted all-purpose flour
1½ teaspoons baking soda
2½ teaspoons baking powder
1 teaspoon ground cinnamon
1 teaspoon ground allspice
½ teaspoon ground ginger
¼ teaspoon ground cloves
¼ teaspoon grated nutmeg
2 cups dark honey
1 cup prepared hot strong coffee
5 large eggs
1¼ cups firmly packed dark
    brown sugar
⅓ cup vegetable oil
2 cups coarsely chopped shelled
    almonds
Grated rind of 1 lemon
Grated rind of 1 orange
18 whole blanched almonds,
    approximately

Glaze

¼ cup corn syrup
½ cup honey

TOOLS

1 baking pan, 16 x 11 x 4 inches

MERINGUE MUSHROOMS

INGREDIENTS

Meringues

2 egg whites from large eggs
½ cup sugar
¼ cup unsweetened cocoa
    powder, preferably Dutch
    process, for dusting

Filling

1 ounce bittersweet chocolate
1 tablespoon unsalted butter,
    softened

TOOLS

Oven thermometer
Baking sheet
Pastry bag with ¾-inch plain tip
Electric mixer or whisk
Double boiler
Fine-mesh tea strainer
Airtight container

Holding the bag at a 45-degree angle, squeeze out the mushroom caps. Hold the bag straight up and squeeze out the stems by pulling straight up to form pointed ends.

YIELD: 18 mushrooms

Pop-in-the-mouth confections for picnics, or decorations for cakes or desserts. These look surprisingly like real mushrooms.

METHOD

Preheat oven to 200° F. Check the temperature with the oven thermometer; too hot an oven will color the meringues and make them tough.

Beat the egg whites until stiff but not dry. Add the sugar, all at once, beating quickly to incorporate; 5 or 6 beats should be enough. Do not overbeat or the meringues will be heavy and chewy rather than light and brittle.

Fill the pastry bag with the mixture. Hold the bag at a 45-degree angle to the pan and squeeze out 18 caps, approximately 1 to 1½ inches wide. With a wet finger, smooth away any peaks on the caps. Hold the bag straight up and squeeze out 18 stems, pulling the bag up to make the stems 1½ inches high with a pointed end.

Bake the meringues for 1½ to 2 hours, until dry but not browned. Let them cool completely.

While the meringues are baking, make the chocolate butter filling. Place the chocolate in the top pan of a double boiler, partially covered, and set over hot water on medium heat until chocolate is melted. Whisk in the butter, a little at a time, until well blended. Refrigerate the mixture for approximately 15 minutes, until the mixture begins to set. Remove from the refrigerator and beat until smooth. Set aside.

Using a sharp paring knife, gently scrape a small hole in the center of the underside of a mushroom cap. Place a small amount, about ⅛ teaspoon, of the chocolate butter filling in the hole. Carefully press the pointed end of the stem into the filling. Repeat with all caps and stems.

Dust the caps of the mushrooms very lightly with the cocoa powder by pressing it through a fine-mesh tea strainer with the back of a spoon.

Store the finished Meringue Mushrooms between pieces of wax paper in an airtight container; also they freeze well.

TO PACKAGE

For a true *trompe l'oeil* present, place the Meringue Mushrooms in a mushroom basket lined with a simple napkin.

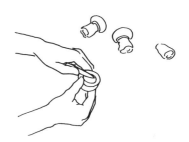

Use a sharp paring knife to carve out a small hole in the center of the underside of each cap. Fill with chocolate butter filling and insert stem.

CHOCOLATE LEAVES

A delightful fall gift to eat plain or to use as a decorative addition to cakes. You may also coat the leaves with white chocolate.

METHOD

Melt the chocolate, uncovered, in the top pan of a double boiler set over warm water over low heat. When the chocolate is melted, stir in up to ½ tablespoon of lecithin, until the chocolate is smooth and glistening.

Holding a leaf by the stem, coat one side evenly with melted chocolate. Place the leaf to dry on a baking sheet lined with wax paper. When the chocolate is thoroughly dry, peel the leaf gently from the hardened chocolate.

Store the leaves in the refrigerator. Wrap them loosely and take care not to crush them. They will keep for several weeks refrigerated and may be frozen.

TO PACKAGE

A combination of homemade Chocolate Leaves and the Crystallized Violets on page 3 makes a beautiful present for the ardent cake baker.

INGREDIENTS

6 ounces grated "real" semisweet chocolate (see Notes about Chocolate on page 142)

Up to ½ tablespoon liquid lecithin (available at health-food stores)

Camellia leaves or lemon leaves (available at florist)

TOOLS

Double boiler
Small paintbrush
Baking sheet

Choose a shiny white box with lid. Cut strips of heavy white paper and use them to divide the box into sections (see illustration). Place chocolate leaves in the center with strips of wax paper between the leaves and the violets in the corners. Tuck in a few lemon leaves for color. Decorate the lid of the box with rubber stamps (see page 221), fabric, or woven ribbon (page 228).

Remember, the chocolate leaves are fragile and should be kept refrigerated.

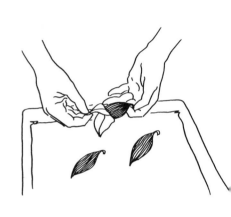

Holding a leaf by the stem, coat one side evenly with melted chocolate.

When the chocolate is thoroughly dry, peel the leaf gently from the hardened chocolate.

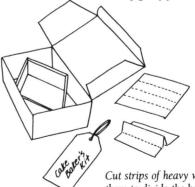

Cut strips of heavy white paper and use them to divide the box into sections.

CHOCOLATE-COVERED POTATO CHIPS

YIELD: about 1 pound

You must be kidding! But I'm not. I first saw Chocolate-Covered Potato Chips at the Penny Candy Store in Water Mill, New York. One of the oldest candy stores on eastern Long Island, it is situated midway between the famous resort towns of Southampton and East Hampton, and has an enthusiastic following of both young and old candy lovers. The chocolate-covered "chips" sit in a gallon jar right next to the cash register. They seemed to me a strange combination so I asked the owner, June Morris, if they sold well. She told me many "fancy ladies" from Southampton bought them regularly to serve at their dinner parties. I didn't think to ask if they were served with drinks, like potato chips, or for dessert, but I bought a pound and later, after having eaten them all day long—merely as a test, mind you—to see when they seemed best, I decided: definitely for dessert. But they also make a perfect snack and are utterly addictive. For the true junk food addict, there is little as heavenly as this combination of salt and chocolate.

The Chocolate-Covered Potato Chips at the Water Mill store are made by J. S. Krum, Inc. Ron Krum from that company helped me adapt this recipe for the home kitchen.

METHOD

Work in a cool room, 65° to 68° F. if possible.

Break up the chocolate into small pieces and place pieces in the top pan of a double boiler; the bottom and sides of the upper pot should be submerged in the water. Melt the chocolate over simmering water on low heat. When the chocolate is soft to the touch, stir it gently with a dry spoon and add the liquid lecithin, stirring until smooth. (The lecithin will thin the chocolate without affecting the taste.) Keep the chocolate liquid over very low heat as you proceed to dip the potato chips.

INGREDIENTS

4 ounces salted potato chips with ridges

1 pound "real" semisweet or bitter chocolate (see Note)

1½ tablespoons liquid lecithin (available in health-food stores)

TOOLS

Double boiler

2 baking sheets

2-pronged meat fork

Dip each potato chip in the chocolate deep enough to cover. Using wooden tongs or a 2-pronged meat fork, lift the chocolate-coated chip out of the chocolate and tap the tongs gently against the side of the pot to remove surplus chocolate.

Line 2 baking sheets with wax paper and place one next to the stove. Have the potato chips within easy reach.

Place 1 potato chip in the chocolate deep enough to cover. Use a 2-pronged meat fork to lift the chocolate-coated chip out of the dipping chocolate and tap the fork gently against the side of the pot several times to remove surplus chocolate. This helps to regulate the thickness of the coating.

Place the dipped potato chip on the wax paper to dry. Repeat this process until all the chips are coated.

NOTE ABOUT CHOCOLATE

"Real" or "pure" chocolate is chocolate made from chocolate liquor, not cocoa with cocoa butter or lecithin added. I use Callebaut, a Belgian chocolate available at gourmet shops. If you can't find it, choose from the following brands:

Baker's Semisweet
Lindt Extra-Bittersweet
Nestle's Semi-Sweet Morsels
Tobler Extra-Bittersweet
Tobler Tradition
Toblerone
Wilbur Dark Sweet

You might try using bittersweet chocolate on half of the potato chips and milk chocolate on the rest. Combine the two types in one package for varied munching.

TO PACKAGE

Carry this one to football games in sporty cans. Buy potato chips packaged in reusable cans with plastic lids. Decorate the outside of the cans with the sports section from a current newspaper. Cut the paper to fit the outside of the can and spray with Krylon Workable Fixatif to prevent smudging. Let the fixative dry and glue the paper onto the can with rubber cement.

When the chocolate has dried completely, replace the chips gently, one at a time, in the original can.

SPICE BAGS FOR MULLED WINE OR APPLE CIDER

YIELD: 6 bags

Nothing says welcome to friends like a warm crock of mulled cider or wine. The aroma greets guests at the door. Having these spice bags on hand makes it easy. Make lots, for everyone appreciates them. Use spice bags with apple cider or red wine, Burgundy or Bordeaux.

INGREDIENTS

6 cinnamon sticks
6 teaspoons whole cloves
6 teaspoons juniper berries
6 tablespoons grated orange peel
18 cardamom pods
¾ cup raisins
¾ cup blanched almonds

TOOLS

**Six 6-inch double layers of
    cheesecloth**
Kitchen twine
Ribbon

METHOD

In the center of each cheesecloth square, place 1 cinnamon stick, 1 teaspoon cloves, 1 teaspoon juniper berries, 3 cardamom pods, 1 tablespoon grated orange peel, 2 tablespoons raisins, and 2 tablespoons almonds.

Gather up the edges and tie each square into a neat bag with kitchen twine.

TO PACKAGE

Tie each bag with a simple bow. Tuck a sprig of holly or evergreen into the bows.

Attach the bags to jugs of apple cider or wine for gift giving. Include a recipe for mulled wine or cider. (Make sure to remove the ribbon and greens from each sack before using.) Use 1 bag per gallon of liquid.

HERB WREATH

TOOLS

**10-inch straw
    wreath**
Fern pins   available from
Florist tape   florist or garden
Florist wire   shops
Paper clips
Masking tape

The fresh scent and sentimental meaning of the aromatic dried herbs make this wreath a welcome housewarming gift. Include sage for health, thyme for bravery, rosemary for friendship and remembrance, bay leaf for success, cinnamon sticks and whole nutmeg for spice, and lavender for domestic virtues and a quiet life.

The finished wreath will be 14 to 18 inches in diameter. Create your own assortment from the following list or choose whatever dried plants and herbs are readily available.

METHOD

Use the florist tape to make small bunches of the herbs and flowers. Wrap the florist wire around the top of the wreath to form a loop for hanging.

Starting at the top of the wreath and working in one direction, alternate the bunches of herbs on the inside and outside edges of the wreath, slightly overlapping. Vary colors and textures. Work in a top layer for accent or to fill in any holes, if necessary.

Use the masking tape to hold 3 cinnamon sticks together at one end. Tape them to a flattened-out paper clip. Repeat with remaining 3 cinnamon sticks. Attach a satin bow to the base of the wreath and tuck cinnamon sticks on both sides.

INGREDIENTS

Yarrow
Globe Amaranth
Baby's Breath
Bay leaf
Chamomile
Cinnamon sticks
Dusty Miller
Pearly Everlasting
Germander
Lady's-Mantle
Lamb's Ears
Lavender
Marjoram
Whole Nutmeg
Orégano
Rosemary
Queen Anne's Lace
"Silver King" Artemisia
Southernwood
Tansy
Thyme
Lemon Thyme
Sweet Wormwood
Sweet Woodruff
Lemon Verbena
Yellow Bedstraw
Garden Sage

Use the florist tape to make small bunches of the herbs and flowers.

Starting at the top of the wreath and working in one direction, alternate the bunches of herbs on the inside and outside edges of the wreath, slightly overlapping.

Use the masking tape to hold 3 cinnamon sticks together at one end.

Attach a satin bow to the base of the wreath and tuck cinnamon sticks on both sides.

This will keep indefinitely, but it is fragile, so store it in a safe place. To keep the herbs at their best, place the wreath in a large, clear plastic bag.

To make this a housewarming gift, label the wreath with a house-shaped card. Write a message in the windows explaining the meaning of the herbs.

GIFTS
of
WINTER

Gifts of Winter

GREEN PEPPER JELLY

YIELD: five ½-pint jars

Simple to make and especially welcome during the holidays, this unique jelly is a pleasing blend of hot, sweet, and tart. Have it with crackers and cream cheese or on unsweetened *coeur à la crème,* or serve it right along with roast meats during the hectic holiday season.

I don't like to use food coloring so this jelly is more gray than bright green. If you mind a little drabness, by all means add a few drops of green food coloring to the jelly before packing it into jars.

METHOD

Place the green peppers, jalapeños, and half of the vinegar in a food processor fitted with the steel blade, or in the container of a blender, and blend until smooth. Pour the mixture into a heavy nonaluminum saucepan. Pour remaining vinegar into the processor or blender and swirl it around to pick up all the pieces of pepper. Add this vinegar to the saucepan along with the sugar.

Bring the mixture to a rolling boil that cannot be stirred down and boil hard for 1 minute. Pour the mixture into a jelly bag or a sieve lined with a double layer of cheesecloth set over a large bowl to drain. Do not squeeze or the jelly will be cloudy. Discard the pulp in the bag.

Return the liquid to the saucepan and bring it to a boil again, remove from the heat, and stir in the pectin. Stir thoroughly.

Pour the jelly immediately into hot, sterilized jelly glasses, leaving ¼-inch headspace. Seal at once with lids or paraffin (see page 235 for instruction). Cool and store in the refrigerator.

TO PACKAGE

Perfect for informal holiday entertaining—make a simple presentation of Green Pepper Jelly and Sweet Red Pepper Jam by decorating the jars with gum-backed stickers and a green-and-red-plaid ribbon. Check party or stationery store for labels with interesting Christmas designs.

INGREDIENTS

3 green bell peppers, seeded and finely chopped, about 1½ cups
4 jalapeño peppers, rinsed, seeded, and chopped, about ⅓ cup
1½ cups apple cider vinegar
4 cups sugar
3 ounces liquid fruit pectin (Certo)

TOOLS

Nonaluminum saucepan
Food processor or blender
Jelly bag or sieve lined with cheesecloth
Five ½-pint jelly jars with 2-piece lids

The classic companions are plain crackers and cream cheese. For a more elaborate gift, line a hand-painted berry basket with a lace handkerchief or napkin. Trim the basket with a plaid ribbon and fill it with a jar of each, add an individual ramekin of cream cheese, covered with clear plastic, and tie in place with more plaid ribbon. Scatter crackers around the basket. (I like Carr's Table Water Crackers or plain Bremner Wafers with this.)

SWEET RED PEPPER JAM

INGREDIENTS

**15 sweet red peppers, finely
    chopped, about 7 cups**
2 tablespoons salt
5 cups sugar
1 quart cider vinegar

TOOLS

**Nonaluminum saucepan (enamel
    or stainless steel)**
**Canning jars (see list of canning
    equipment on page 232)**

YIELD: 3 pints

This bright red jam looks spectacular, and the pleasant combination of sweet and tart is marvelous with all meats. Red pepper jam is perhaps best of all spread on cream cheese with brown bread or wheat crackers.

METHOD

Combine peppers and salt in a large bowl and let stand for 2 hours. Transfer to an enamel or nonaluminum pot, add the sugar and vinegar, and cook over medium heat, stirring frequently, until thick, about 1 hour. Pour into sterilized canning jars, leaving ¼-inch headspace. Wipe rims with clean damp cloth and seal with lids. Process in a boiling-water bath for 10 minutes (see instructions on page 231). Cool and store in the refrigerator indefinitely.

TO PACKAGE

Combine a jar of Sweet Red Pepper Jam with Green Pepper Jelly; refer to page 149 for packaging instructions.

SEVILLE ORANGE MARMALADE

YIELD: 4 cups

The Arabs introduced the bitter Seville orange, *bigarade,* to the Spanish, who in turn traded it with Britain. It was the Scots, with their great knack for preserving, who took this very expensive, ugly, and almost juiceless orange and put it to use in the best of all marmalades.

Seville oranges are available for only a brief period during January and February, but they are well worth seeking out for the marmalade lovers on your gift list. Once you have sampled this version of orange marmalade nothing else will do.

METHOD

Pierce the oranges in several places with a needle and blanch in boiling apple juice for 25 to 30 minutes. Let oranges cool in the juice until they are easily handled. Reserve the apple juice.

Quarter the oranges; remove the seeds, peel, pith, and fibrous membrane (there won't be much). Set aside the peels and discard the seeds. Put the orange pith and membrane into a food mill fitted with the medium disc and extract as much liquid as possible. Slice the peels into very thin strips.

Combine the sliced orange peels, extracted liquid, and pulp left in the top of the food mill with the reserved apple juice. Add the lemon juice and sugar. Bring to a boil, stirring, and boil rapidly until a candy thermometer reaches 220° F. To determine if the marmalade has cooked long enough, drop a tablespoon onto a cool plate. If it doesn't spread, the marmalade is set.

Transfer the marmalade to sterilized jars, leaving ¼-inch headspace. Wipe the rims clean and seal with the lids, following the directions on preserving on page 235.

TO PACKAGE

A demanding recipe to produce, so package it accordingly. A fabric "hat" cut from a Scottish plaid fabric is apropos as well as a gold-seal hand-lettered label.

INGREDIENTS

3 large Seville oranges
3 quarts apple juice
Juice of 1 lemon, strained
5 cups sugar

TOOLS

Needle
Food mill
Candy thermometer
Four 1-cup Mason jars with lids

CLOVED LEMONS IN OIL

INGREDIENTS

Lemons (quantities depend on how many jars you want to make)
Sea or kosher salt
Whole cloves
Coriander seeds
Mild olive oil

TOOLS

Stainless-steel colander
Skewer
Widemouthed jar with cork or tight-fitting lid

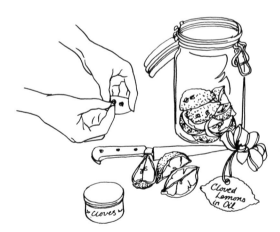

Pierce each wedge with a skewer and stud with 2 cloves. Pack loosely into French canning jars.

Serve these lemon slices with cold roasted meats, or add them to stews or soups for an unusual tart and salty taste. Elizabeth David suggests adding the preserved lemons, thinly sliced, to shredded lettuce, red onion, and mint salad. They are also delicious served after the salad course with Italian mascarpone cheese. Use the scented oil in vinaigrettes or for basting grilled fish or poultry.

METHOD

Wash and dry the lemons. Cut each lemon into 8 wedges. Place 1 layer in a plastic or stainless-steel colander and sprinkle generously with salt. Repeat until all wedges are used. Cover with a thin layer of salt. Place the colander over a bowl to catch liquid and refrigerate for 3 to 4 days, turning lemon wedges from time to time.

Remove lemon wedges from the refrigerator and rinse under cold water to remove all the salt. Wipe dry. Pierce each wedge with a skewer and stud with 2 cloves. Pack loosely in clear jars, sprinkling each layer lightly with more salt and some of the coriander seeds. Cover with olive oil. Seal jars with a cork or lid. Let stand in a cool, dark place for 3 to 4 weeks before using. Do not refrigerate.

TO PACKAGE

To call attention to the cloved lemons, present them in a clear glass jar with a tight-fitting cork or lid, tied with a few bright yellow ribbon streamers. Attach a lemon-shaped label with serving suggestions, or a favorite recipe; these lemons are used mostly in Middle Eastern or North African cuisines.

Liqueurs and Cordials

Making your own liqueurs is a lot easier than you might think and your homemade products are very inexpensive compared to the familiar commercial brands. The hard part is waiting for the home-brewed liqueurs to age. The basic process, repeated often in these recipes, involves nothing more than steeping flavorings in the alcohol base and adding sweeteners. You can easily adjust the seasonings to arrive at unique flavors that will delight the demanding connoisseurs on your gift list.

If you enjoy these recipes, refer to "Summer Fruits in Liqueurs," page 54, in the "Gifts of Summer" section. They take advantage of the plentiful fresh fruits and herbs of that season.

GINGER-HONEY CORDIAL

YIELD: 6 cups

Liqueur flavored with ginger and honey was used in colonial America as a remedy for colds, sore throats, and stomachaches. Innocent at the first sip, it leaves a powerful but pleasant aftertaste. Although I have found no scientific evidence to support its curative powers, this cordial is a warm and stimulating companion for wintry hours spent in a cozy armchair by the fire. I can guarantee that it will make any noxious cold seem almost worth the trouble. Takes about 1 month to mature in flavor.

INGREDIENTS

½-ounce fresh gingerroot, peeled and sliced into rounds, about 1 tablespoon
2 cardamom pods (discard the papery membrane)
2 whole cloves
¼ teaspoon coarsely ground pepper
1 tablespoon raisins
1 quart brandy
1½ cups honey

TOOLS

6-cup bottle with lid or cork
Kitchen funnel
Coffee filter paper

Wrap holiday spirits top to bottom in Christmas greens or tie a pretty wreath of mistletoe around the neck of the bottle. Include a gift tag with "Don't open 'til ———," if the maturing time is not up.

METHOD

Put the ginger, cardamom seeds, cloves, pepper, and raisins into a clean dry bottle that has a tight-fitting cap. Add the brandy, cap the bottle, and shake well. Store the bottle in a place where you will remember to shake it every few days. Steep for 1 week, then filter the cordial into a clean bottle, using a kitchen funnel lined with a coffee filter. Add the honey and shake well. For best results the cordial should be allowed to mature for another 2 to 3 weeks. At the end of this time, filter it again into a decorative bottle.

This cordial is very good served with the Ginger Rum Balls on page 164).

TO PACKAGE

Wrap your holiday spirits in one of the following ways:

Tie a pretty little wreath of mistletoe around the neck of the bottle and attach a label, or wrap the bottle top to bottom in Christmas greens and tie them in place with ribbon or cord. Attach a few tiny brightly colored ornaments to the ribbon.

Or, following the folding directions on page 218, create your own bottle coaster out of a large linen table napkin. Include a gift tag with "Don't Open until ———," if the maturing time is not up.

VANILLA CORDIAL

YIELD: 6 cups

The thin, dark, cigarlike vanilla bean is the unripe fruit of an orchid-bearing Mexican plant. Extract of the bean is one of our most popular flavorings; usually associated with ice cream, it enhances many recipes and has a special affinity for chocolate.

Vanilla Cordial is interchangeable with vanilla extract and is a welcome present for any baker. To make your own extract, buy fresh beans from health-food or gourmet shops where they are sold in long glass tubes or folded in jars. The beans should be soft and very fragrant. Return any beans that are dried out and stale. You may be surprised to know that although vanilla cordial has never caught on in this country, in France it is commercially made as a liqueur. Takes 1 to 2 months to ferment.

METHOD

Cut each vanilla bean into 4 pieces. Split each section lengthwise with a sharp knife. Put the pieces into a clean dry bottle that has a tight cap. Add the vodka, cap the bottle, and shake well.

Store the bottle in a place where you will remember to shake it every few days. Let it steep for 2 to 3 weeks and shake it several times a week. A sniff and a taste will help you judge when it is ready. (Don't get caught nipping on the "extract" too often or you won't have any left for a gift!) Filter the extract into a clean, decorative bottle, using a kitchen funnel lined with a coffee filter.

Make a sugar syrup by boiling the sugar and water together until the sugar is completely dissolved, 2 to 3 minutes. Cool completely.

Add the sugar syrup to the bottled extract and shake well. Add the reserved bean and cap tightly. For best results the extract should be allowed to mature for 1 month before using.

TO PACKAGE

Highlight a bottle of homemade Vanilla Extract in a Napkin Bottle Coaster (page 218), or refer to the previous cordial recipe.

INGREDIENTS

4 or 5 vanilla beans, at least 5 to 6 inches long
1 quart vodka
1 cup sugar
½ cup water
1 vanilla bean for packaging

TOOLS

6-cup bottle with tight-fitting lid or cork
Kitchen funnel
Coffee filter paper

ORANGE RATAFIA

INGREDIENTS

1 quart Armagnac
Juice of 6 oranges, about 1½ cups
Rind of 4 oranges (no white pulp, please)
1 cup sugar
1 cinnamon stick

TOOLS

2-quart jar with tight-fitting lid
Kitchen funnel
Coffee filter paper

Wrap the Orange Ratafia in corrugated paper or cardboard. Gather the paper around the neck and base of the bottle with satin cording.

YIELD: 6 cups

The term *ratafia,* often used loosely for any fruit-flavored liqueur, is thought to have derived from the Renaissance custom of drinking a toast on the ratification of an agreement or treaty. Most recipes for ratafia call for steeping the pulp, juice, and peel of fresh fruit, along with spices and a sweetening agent, in brandy—either Cognac or the earthy, less familiar Armagnac. I prefer Armagnac in this recipe for its woody assertive taste. It takes about a month for the flavor of the ratafia to develop fully.

METHOD

Place all the ingredients in a clean dry jar with a tight-fitting lid. Store the jar in a place where you will remember to shake it every few days. Steep for 3 to 4 weeks, stirring several times a week.

After steeping, discard the cinnamon stick and orange rind and filter the ratafia into a clean bottle, using a kitchen funnel lined with a coffee filter. Cap tightly before storing.

TO PACKAGE

Create a highly individual covering for any bottle by wrapping it in corrugated paper or cardboard. This underrated, humble material when used as a decorative wrapping creates a surface richness and elegance all out of proportion to its intended use. Join the seam with double-faced tape and gather the paper around the neck and base of the bottle with satin cording. Include a tag with "Don't Open until ———," if the maturing time is not up.

LEMON VODKA

YIELD: 1 quart

This is the easiest gift to make in this book. The lemon peel gives the vodka a pale yellow color and a slight but pleasant flavor of citrus.

METHOD

With a very sharp paring knife, remove the peel from the lemon in 1 long spiral, ¼ inch wide. Be sure to avoid the white pith under the skin because it will make the vodka bitter. Decant the vodka into a decorative bottle with a tight-fitting cap. Carefully place the lemon spiral in the bottle and cap tightly. Steep the peel in the vodka for at least 1 week to let the flavor develop.

TO PACKAGE

Rest the bottle in a rattan wine carrier tied with a bow—a gift in itself—to turn this into a double present.

INGREDIENTS
1 lemon
1 quart vodka

TOOLS
1-quart bottle with clamp-type lid or cork

With a very sharp paring knife, remove the peel from the lemon in 1 long spiral, ¼ inch wide.

HOT CHOCOLATE MIX

YIELD: 2 cups

A warming drink during the cold winter months

METHOD

Combine the sugar and almonds in a blender or food processor and process for several minutes into a smooth paste. Add the cocoa, cinnamon, instant espresso, and nonfat dry milk. Process for 1 minute more.

Store in an airtight container. Will keep for several months.

INGREDIENTS
¾ cup granulated sugar
¼ cup blanched almonds
½ cup unsweetened cocoa powder
1 teaspoon freshly grated cinnamon
½ teaspoon instant espresso coffee powder (optional)
3.2 ounces nonfat dry milk, enough to make 1 quart

TO PACKAGE

Present the Hot Chocolate Mix in a decorative airtight tin with a tag giving directions for making into Hot Chocolate.

For each cup of hot chocolate, bring ¾ cup water or milk to a simmer, add ¼ cup Hot Chocolate Mix, and simmer, whisking constantly, for about 30 seconds. Top with homemade whipped cream or marshmallows.

HOT FUDGE SAUCE

INGREDIENTS

3 ounces unsalted butter
6 ounces (6 squares) unsweetened baking chocolate
1 cup boiling water
1 cup sugar
⅓ cup light corn syrup
2 teaspoons vanilla extract

TOOLS

Two 1½-cup or ¾-liter sterilized French canning jars with clamp-type lids

YIELD: about 3 cups

Dark, fudgy, distinctly bittersweet, this sauce hardens slightly when spooned over vanilla ice cream. But don't limit yourself to the obvious: Use the hot fudge to enliven a wide range of desserts. Place a dollop on pound cake, meringues, or puddings. You can vary the flavoring by substituting a few drops of pure mint extract for the vanilla, or use a hint of any of these—Grand Marnier, Kirsch, rum, Cointreau, crème de menthe, or crème de cacao.

METHOD

In a heavy saucepan, melt the butter and chocolate over very low heat. Add the water, sugar, and corn syrup. Stir to blend. Gently boil the mixture, without stirring, for 8 to 10 minutes, until it is very thick and smooth. Remove the sauce from the heat and stir in the vanilla extract, or substitute any of the suggested flavorings.

Pour the hot fudge into sterilized jars. It will keep, covered and refrigerated, for several months.

To serve, heat the sauce in the top pan of a double boiler set over barely simmering water.

TO PACKAGE

Treat a hot-fudge-sundae fan to a jar of homemade sauce. To complete the gift add a white doily hat and tie an ice-cream scoop to the lid.

MAPLE WALNUT SAUCE

YIELD: about 1½ cups

A very nutty sauce for lovers of real maple flavor. Try this one on poached apples or pears as well as the usual ice cream.

METHOD

Gently heat the maple syrup in a heavy saucepan. Add the dissolved cornstarch and bring to a boil, stirring constantly. Reduce the heat, stir down the boiling liquid, and simmer, stirring constantly, until a candy thermometer reads 235° F., about 5 minutes. Remove from the heat and stir in the rum and chopped nuts. Cool.

Pour the sauce into a sterilized jar. It will keep, covered and refrigerated, for several months.

Note: If the sauce is too thick to pour when taken directly from the refrigerator, let it reach room temperature before serving, or gently heat it in the top pan of a double boiler set over barely simmering water.

TO PACKAGE

Make this part of the luscious group of sauces on pages 158–162, or place it in a ribbon-tied basket with a jar of homemade poached apples or pears.

INGREDIENTS

1 cup maple syrup
2 teaspoons cornstarch, dissolved in 2 tablespoons water
1½ to 2 tablespoons dark rum
1 cup coarsely chopped walnuts

TOOLS

Candy thermometer
1½-cup or ¾-liter sterilized French canning jar with clamp-type lid

RUM RAISIN SAUCE

INGREDIENTS

1 cup raisins
½ cup dark rum
2 cups sugar
½ cup water
½ cup heavy cream

TOOLS

Nonaluminum bowl
Metal spoon
**1-pint or ½-liter sterilized French
 canning jar with clamp-type
 lid**

YIELD: 2 cups

Full-bodied with a beautiful amber color, this sauce is my personal favorite. I would even go as far as to choose it over the luxuriant Hot Fudge Sauce on page 158.

METHOD

In a small nonaluminum bowl, macerate the raisins in the rum for 1 hour, until they are plump and most of the rum is absorbed.

Dissolve the sugar in the water in a heavy saucepan. Bring the mixture to a boil over medium heat, stirring constantly. Wash down any sugar crystals that form on the sides of the pan with a pastry brush dipped into ice cold water. Cook the syrup over medium heat, *do not stir*, until it becomes an amber-colored caramel. Remove from the heat and swirl the liquid around several times with a metal spoon.

Drain the rum from the raisins and add it with the heavy cream to the syrup, stirring to combine. Add the raisins and stir again.

Pour the sauce into a sterilized jar. It will keep, covered and refrigerated, for several months.

To serve, heat the sauce in the top pan of a double boiler set over barely simmering water.

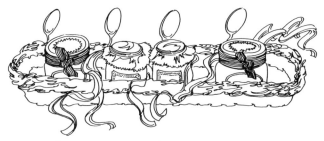

Place an assortment of ice-cream sauces in a long French bread basket and fill it with paper serpentines. Give each jar a fabric "hat," label, and serving spoon.

TO PACKAGE

This gift could be all the stimulus that's needed for an ice-cream-sundae celebration. Keep in mind that during the Middle Ages feasting during holidays was justified by the idea that occasional excess helped people achieve self-control at other times. So don't limit your friends to just one sauce; they are so easy to make, why not give several?

Place several jars in a long French bread basket and fill it with paper serpentines. (These are the curly colored papers you throw at New Year's Eve, and they are available at party supply stores.) Give each jar a fabric "hat" (page 219) cut from squares of fabric matching the shades of the serpentines. Tie a small gift tag to the metal clamp of each jar identifying the flavor.

If your budget allows, by all means add an antique silver or unusual serving spoon. The ultimate gift for an ice-cream connoisseur.

APRICOT-HONEY SAUCE

INGREDIENTS

8 ounces dried apricots, coarsely chopped, 1½ cups
1½ cups strong tea
½ cup honey
⅓ cup Grand Marnier liqueur
3 tablespoons lemon juice
Grated rind of 1 orange
2 tablespoons butter

TOOLS

Nonaluminum bowl
Food processor or blender
1-pint or ½-liter sterilized French canning jar with clamp-type lid

YIELD: about 2 cups

Not too sweet, this sauce is good hot or cold. Use it as a filling for cakes and cookies, or make a memorable apricot sundae by layering it between scoops of vanilla ice cream sprinkled with toasted slivered almonds and fresh coconut.

METHOD

In a medium-size nonaluminum bowl, macerate the apricots in the tea for 1 hour, until they are plump and most of the liquid is absorbed. In a food processor fitted with the steel blade, or in several batches in a blender, purée the apricots with any liquid not absorbed.

Combine the purée, honey, liqueur, lemon juice, and orange rind in a heavy saucepan. Bring the mixture to a simmer over low heat and cook for 3 to 5 minutes. Remove from the heat and swirl in the butter.

Pour the sauce into a sterilized jar. It will keep, covered and refrigerated, for several months.

To serve hot, heat the sauce in the top pan of a double boiler set over barely simmering water.

TO PACKAGE

Make this one part of a trio of sauces (see pages 158–162). For an individual jar, give it a fabric "hat" (page 219) and tie on cheesecloth sacks of freshly grated, toasted coconut and toasted almonds.

BUTTERSCOTCH SAUCE

INGREDIENTS
½ cup light corn syrup
1 cup light brown sugar
2 ounces unsalted butter
1½ teaspoons vanilla extract
¾ cup heavy cream

TOOLS
Candy thermometer
1½-pint or ¾-liter sterilized
    French canning jar with
    clamp-type lid

YIELD: about 3 cups

Thick, smooth but not too sweet, this sauce is heavenly spooned over vanilla ice cream.

METHOD

In a heavy saucepan, bring the corn syrup, brown sugar, and butter to a boil. Boil the mixture gently for about 5 minutes, stirring occasionally, until a candy thermometer reads 235° F. Remove from the heat, add the vanilla, and stir vigorously for 1 minute.

Let the mixture cool to warm. Add the heavy cream, a little at a time, stirring vigorously after each addition, to create a smooth, shiny sauce.

Pour the sauce into a sterilized jar. It will keep, covered and refrigerated, for several months.

To serve, heat the sauce in the top pan of a double boiler set over barely simmering water.

TO PACKAGE

A must in the trio of sauces on pages 158–162. For an individual jar, place it in the bowl of an oversized antique sundae dish lined with a white doily, overwrap with clear cellophane, and tie on a new ice-cream scoop.

SUGAR PLUMS

YIELD: about 3 dozen 1-inch balls

If you have ever wondered what the children "nestled all snug in their beds" were dreaming of, here is one version.

METHOD

Finely chop the apricots, figs, raisins, pecans, and coconut by hand, or in a food processor fitted with the steel blade. Blend the chopped ingredients together and moisten with the orange liqueur.

INGREDIENTS

½ cup dried apricots
¼ cup dried figs
¼ cup golden raisins
½ cup chopped pecans
¼ cup sweetened grated coconut
2 tablespoons orange liqueur
  (Grand Marnier or Cointreau)
¼ cup granulated sugar

TOOLS

Food processor
Airtight container

Using a 6-inch white or silver paper doily, form a cone for each Sugar Plum.

Put several confections in each doily and place in a shallow basket.

Shape the mixture into 1-inch balls, pressing gently to make sure the ingredients stay packed together. Roll each ball in granulated sugar.

Stored in airtight containers in the refrigerator, with a piece of wax paper between the layers, the sugar plums will keep for up to 1 month.

TO PACKAGE

Using 6-inch white or silver paper doilies, form a cone for each confection: Fold the doily in half, then fold in half again, twist the pointed end, and open up the cone. Put several confections in each doily and place in a shallow basket. Repeat until basket is filled. Tuck in a sprig of holly and attach a gift label.

GINGER RUM BALLS

INGREDIENTS

2½ cups gingersnap crumbs, about 3 dozen cookies
½ cup sweetened condensed milk
½ cup mincemeat
½ cup chopped nuts
⅓ cup coarsely chopped candied gingerroot
1 tablespoon Dutch-process cocoa
2 tablespoons dark rum
Confectioners' sugar, for dusting

TOOLS

Baking sheet lined with wax paper
Chinese strainer

YIELD: about 2½ dozen 1-inch balls

Ease of preparation makes these an ideal last-minute gift for the most discriminating taste.

METHOD

In a large bowl, stir together all the ingredients except the confectioners' sugar until well blended. Using about 1 rounded teaspoon of the mixture at a time, shape small balls with your hands and roll each ball in confectioners' sugar. Place the balls on a baking sheet lined with wax paper and refrigerate until firm, several hours or overnight. Store in the refrigerator until ready to use.

TO PACKAGE

What could be a better container for a gift from the kitchen than an unusual kitchen utensil?

Place 6 Ginger Rum Balls in the wire basket of a bamboo-handled strainer, to be used later in Chinese cooking. Overwrap with clear cellophane and tie with ribbon.

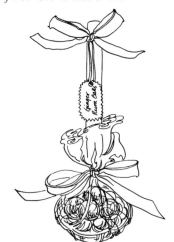

Place 6 Ginger Rum Balls in the wire basket of a bamboo-handled strainer.

CHOCOLATE AMARETTO KISSES

YIELD: about 2 dozen 1-inch balls

Another quick no-bake confection, this time redolent with almond flavor, essence of coffee, and the pure deliciousness of chocolate. While a kiss is just a kiss, these are truly a mouthful.

METHOD

Combine the chocolate bits, butter, sugar, instant coffee, and water in the top pan of a double boiler set over barely simmering water, covered, until the chocolate and butter are melted.

Stir the almond extract, cookie crumbs, and almonds into the chocolate mixture. Allow to cool. Chill.

Shape the chocolate mixture into 1-inch balls and roll in the cocoa powder.

Stored in airtight containers in the refrigerator, the confections will keep for up to 1 month.

TO PACKAGE

Since the heart is the traditional symbol of love, pack the Chocolate Amaretto Kisses into a woven heart envelope for your favorite valentine.

Using shiny red-and-white heavy paper or poster board, cut a 4- x 12-inch strip from each color of paper. Fold in half and trim the open ends in a curve (see illustration).

INGREDIENTS

6 ounces semisweet chocolate bits
3 tablespoons unsalted butter
3 tablespoons sugar
2 teaspoons instant coffee powder
1 teaspoon boiling water
2 tablespoons pure almond extract
1 cup crushed amaretto cookies
½ cup chopped blanched almonds
¼ cup unsweetened cocoa powder

TOOLS

Double boiler
Airtight container for storage

Cut an even number of slits into the folded edges of each piece, approximately 4 inches long (see illustration).

To Weave

First row: Slip row 1 into row A, slip row A into row 2, slip row 3 into row A, and slip row A into row 4.

Second row: Slip row B into row 1, slip row 2 into row B, slip row B into row 3, and slip row 4 into row B.

Third row: Row C follows the same weaving as row A.

Fourth row: Row D follows the same weaving as row B.

Adjust the rows to fit neatly. Open the heart, line with a paper doily, and place the Chocolate Amaretto Kisses, individually wrapped in tissue paper and twisted at both ends, inside.

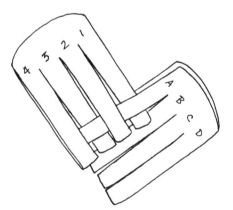

Cut a 4- × 12-inch strip from each color of paper, fold in half, and trim the open ends in a curve. Cut an even number of slits into the folded edges of each piece, approximately 4 inches long. Weave the first row.

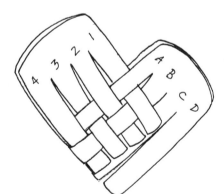

Weave the second row.

A finished heart, lined with a paper doily.

CANDIED FRUIT PEELS

YIELD: about ½ pound

Simple and inexpensive to make, this old-fashioned confection is an economical way to use up often discarded citrus fruit peels. Get rid of those tired after-dinner mints and present your host with this tart-sweet candy.

You can successfully candy grapefruit, oranges, lemons, limes, or even fresh gingerroot in this manner. The candies will keep in an airtight container in the refrigerator for several months, or may be stored in the freezer indefinitely.

METHOD

With a sharp knife remove the peel from the fruit in 4 equal pieces; if you are candying gingerroot, first peel it, then cut into ¼-inch rounds. Cut each piece on the bias into ¼-inch-wide pieces.

Place the peels or sliced gingerroot in a large saucepan and cover with water. Bring to a boil and cook for 1 minute. Drain in a colander, rinse under cold water, and repeat the boiling and rinsing twice more (3 boilings and 3 rinsings in all). After the final rinse, return the peels or gingerroot to the saucepan, cover with fresh water, and cook for 15 minutes. Drain, pat dry, and set aside.

In a saucepan, combine the sugar, ¾ cup water, and the corn syrup. Bring to a boil and boil for 2 to 3 minutes. Add the peel or gingerroot and reduce the heat to maintain a simmer. Simmer the fruit peels and syrup, stirring occasionally, until all but a spoonful of the syrup has been absorbed by the peel, about 10 minutes. Watch the peels very carefully for the last few minutes of cooking time to make sure the syrup does not burn or begin to caramelize; this would give the candy an unpleasant bitter taste.

Line a baking sheet with wax paper and cover it with 1 cup of the sugar. Arrange the peels in one layer on the bed of sugar, sprinkle on the remaining cup of sugar, and toss the peels occasionally in the sugar to coat the pieces thoroughly as they cool.

INGREDIENTS

1 large grapefruit, or 2 large oranges, or 3 lemons, or 4 limes, or about 1 pound fresh gingerroot (Use only one kind of fruit to a batch. Try making a variety and include some of each type in your gift.)
¾ cup sugar
¾ cup water
3 tablespoons light corn syrup
2 cups granulated sugar, approximately, to coat peels

TOOLS

Baking sheet lined with wax paper
Wire cake rack

Place the cooled fruit strips on a wire cake rack to dry for 24 hours.
Variation: When the fruit peels have dried out for 24 hours, you can coat one end of each peel in a chocolate coating.

4 ounces bittersweet chocolate
1 tablespoon unsalted butter

First melt the chocolate and butter in the top pan of a double boiler set over barely simmering water. Remove from the heat and stir for 1 to 2 minutes to cool slightly. Dip one end of each sugared peel into the chocolate and dry on wire rack.

TO PACKAGE

For a terrific combination present, combine the Candied Fruit Peels with Crystallized Violets (page 3) and candied gingerroot cut into shapes with aspic cutters. Show off the goodies in a shiny black-lacquer box (see page 226 for instructions). Line the box with red tissue paper and tie with red satin ribbon or cord.

With a sharp knife remove the peel from the fruit in 4 equal pieces. Cut each section into ¼-inch-wide strips.

FRENCH CHOCOLATE TRUFFLES

YIELD: 48 quarter-sized candies

This is one of the easiest candies to make and adapts readily to many variations of the basic recipe. Vary the truffles by adding coarsely chopped nuts, coconut, or rum-soaked fruit (raisins, apricots, or dates) to the centers. Instead of the Grand Marnier, add 2 teaspoons of Amaretto, Champagne, Cognac, rum, or mint or coffee extract. Use either the best semisweet or white chocolate for the coating. Start this at least 1 day before serving.

METHOD

Break the bittersweet chocolate into medium-size pieces and place in the top pan of a double boiler, covered. Melt the chocolate over hot but not simmering water. Uncover and stir. Add the butter in small pieces, stirring with a whisk after each addition until completely smooth.

Add a little of the chocolate mixture to the egg yolks and stir. Pour the yolks into the chocolate mixture in the double boiler and cook over simmering water, stirring all the time, for 2 to 3 minutes. Remove from the heat and stir in the Grand Marnier. Chill in the refrigerator for 30 minutes.

Remove the chocolate from the refrigerator and beat with a whisk or electric mixer until soft peaks form. Quickly fill a pastry bag fitted with a ¾-inch plain tip and pipe tablespoon-size mounds onto a baking sheet lined with wax paper. The truffles should be uneven, so don't try to make them perfectly round. Place the baking sheet in the freezer for 15 to 20 minutes.

While the candy centers are setting, melt the semisweet chocolate or white chocolate in the top pan of a double boiler, covered, over hot but not simmering water. If necessary thin the chocolate with the lecithin, stirring until smooth.

INGREDIENTS

Centers

12 ounces bittersweet chocolate
4 ounces unsalted butter, cut into small pieces
3 large egg yolks, well beaten, in a small bowl
2 tablespoons Grand Marnier liqueur

Coating

6 ounces semisweet chocolate or white chocolate
1 to 2 teaspoons lecithin (optional)
½ cup Dutch-process unsweetened cocoa powder

TOOLS

Double boiler
Pastry bag with plain tip
Baking sheet lined with wax paper

Fill a pastry bag fitted with a ¾-inch plain tip and pipe tablespoon-size mounds onto a baking sheet lined with wax paper.

Remove the truffle centers from the chocolate coating with a 2-prong dipping fork.

While the truffles are slightly damp, roll them in the cocoa powder.

Remove the truffle centers from the freezer and drop them one at a time into the chocolate coating. Remove them from the coating with an open mesh strainer or a 2-prong dipping fork. Return the coated truffles to the baking sheet lined with wax paper. Let the candies cool for 20 minutes. While they are still slightly damp, roll them in the cocoa powder.

If the truffles are not eaten in 2 days, store them in the refrigerator or freezer. Bring to room temperature before serving.

TO PACKAGE

In Japan there is a candy called *Futari Shizuka*. Traditionally wrapped in colored tissue paper—half the confections are wrapped in pink and half in white—the paired candies embody their name: "two persons quietly together." What could be a more charming way to wrap a Valentine gift for that special loved one?

Place 1 truffle in the center of a 4-inch square of pink tissue paper and twist upward to resemble a flower. Repeat half in pink, half in white. Weave pink and white satin ribbon through an open weave heart-shaped basket. Place the individually wrapped truffles inside. Add a valentine of your choice.

INGREDIENTS

2 cups sugar
¼ cup corn syrup
¾ cup heavy cream
**3 ounces unsweetened baking
    chocolate**
2 tablespoons butter
1 teaspoon vanilla extract
1 cup chopped pecans (optional)

MOST-LIKELY-TO-SUCCEED FUDGE

YIELD: twenty-five 1½-inch squares

For most children, the making of fudge is a rite of passage. It affords a first glimpse of the pleasures of cooking and gift giving. But, like most rites, it does not at first come easily, for making fudge is a tricky business. You will recall that fudge can harden too quickly, or it refuses to harden at all. But as unpredictable as fudge making is, Warren, a true fudge connoisseur, insisted my book would not be complete without a recipe for fudge.

There are two types of fudge lovers: those who like it smooth and creamy and those who like the sugar slightly crystallized, giving the candy a firm grainy texture. Warren falls into the latter group, for as a child he was *made* to eat poorly mixed fudge. (Someone was probably too impatient and never allowed the fudge to cook long enough before beating.)

To this day, Warren continues to crave badly made fudge, but says he has a hard time finding the type he grew up on. This recipe is for him.

METHOD

Butter the pan. Mix the sugar, corn syrup, and heavy cream together. Break the chocolate into small pieces and add to the mixture. Over low heat, stir together until the chocolate melts and the mixture begins to boil. Insert a candy thermometer and cook without stirring until the temperature reaches 238° F.

Remove the mixture from the heat, add the butter and vanilla, and stir until the butter is melted.

Cool to lukewarm, 110° F. Check with a candy thermometer. When the mixture is cooled, add the nuts and beat with a wooden spoon until the mixture begins to thicken and loses its gloss, 3 to 5 minutes. Pour immediately into prepared pans and cool.

Cut the fudge into 1½-inch squares and wrap each piece individually in plastic. Store in a tightly sealed container in a cool place. It keeps for several weeks if not eaten first.

TO PACKAGE

To start this tradition, fudge should arrive individually wrapped in a beautiful decorative tin.

TOOLS

8-inch-square pan, 2 inches deep
Candy thermometer

CHOCOLATE WREATHS

INGREDIENTS

8 ounces semisweet chocolate
    morsels
3 to 4 tablespoons unsalted butter
2 tablespoons Grand Marnier,
    rum, or any liqueur or
    flavoring (I like mint extract)

Decoration

Golden raisins
Candied cherries
Blanched slivered almonds
Whole hazelnuts
Silver nonpareils
Twelve 6-inch pieces of ⅛-inch
    double-sided satin ribbon (I
    favor red or white)

TOOLS

Baking sheet lined with wax paper
Double boiler
Pastry tube with medium star
    point

YIELD: twelve 3-inch wreaths

For the fifth day of Christmas, 12 chocolate rings

METHOD

Line a baking sheet with wax paper and set aside.

Place the chocolate pieces in the top pan of a double boiler over simmering water on very low heat. Cover and keep hot until the chocolate is melted. Uncover and stir in the butter and flavoring.

Working very quickly, spoon the mixture into a pastry tube fitted with the medium star point, and pipe thick wreath-shaped circles about 3 to 4 inches in diameter onto the lined baking sheet. Decorate with the fruits, nuts, and nonpareils. Place in the refrigerator for 1 hour, or until firm.

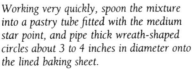

Working very quickly, spoon the mixture into a pastry tube fitted with the medium star point, and pipe thick wreath-shaped circles about 3 to 4 inches in diameter onto the lined baking sheet.

Loop a tiny satin ribbon through the center of the wreath and knot.

Carefully peel the wreaths from the wax paper. Loop a tiny satin ribbon through the center of the wreath and knot. Store wreaths between layers of wax paper in the refrigerator until ready to use.

Keeps for several weeks refrigerated.

TO PACKAGE

Use these tiny chocolate wreaths to decorate Christmas packages or take them along to a tree-trimming party. Of course, they are usually eaten before you get a chance to hang them on the tree.

Christmas Cookies

The making and giving of Christmas cookies is as much a part of the holiday season as decorating a tree and presents. This eagerly anticipated ritual is as vital today as in the past.

Most of the favored recipes for these cookies come from the countries of northern and central Europe; our word for cookie is derived from the Dutch *Koekje*. Entire books are devoted to the great variety of Christmas cookies, here are a few of my favorites. To choose from a wider selection, scan the list of cookies in the index of this book.

BUTTER COOKIES

INGREDIENTS

8 ounces unsalted butter
1 cup sugar
4 large egg yolks, beaten
1½ tablespoons vanilla extract
2¼ cups all-purpose flour
Pinch of salt

Icing

2 cups confectioners' sugar
1 egg white
3 to 4 tablespoons milk
Food coloring

TOOLS

Rolling pin
Cookie cutter or stencils
Nonstick baking sheet or baking
**   sheet lined with aluminum**
**   foil**

For decorating cookies
Toothpicks
Ribbon or wire for hanging
Pastry tube with tips
Containers to mix and hold icing
Small paintbrushes

YIELD: about 4 dozen cookies, depending on size of cutters used

I am constantly asked for a recipe for the perfect butter cookie. The dough has to be firm enough for younger cooks to handle and the cookie sufficiently buttery for adult tastes. Here is a dough that is particularly easy and delicious. You can flavor it with lemon or orange rind or a favorite liqueur if desired. Shape the cookies with fancy cutters and decorate to your heart's desire.

Keep these cookies in mind for all occasions. Make them into personalized valentines, use them to relay special messages, or use as place cards at a child's birthday party.

METHOD

In a large bowl, cream the butter with the sugar until light and fluffy. Add the beaten yolks and vanilla and beat thoroughly.

Sift the flour and salt together. Gradually add the dry ingredients to the butter mixture, blending well after each addition.

Form the dough into 2 equal balls, wrap in wax paper, and refrigerate overnight or place in the freezer for 30 minutes.

Line baking sheets with aluminum foil if not using a nonstick pan. Preheat oven to 350° F.

Working quickly with 1 package of dough at a time, place the dough between 2 pieces of wax paper and roll it to a thickness of slightly less than ¼ inch. Using cookie cutters, stencils, or an inverted water glass, cut out shapes from the dough. Arrange them on the baking sheets and refrigerate for 30 minutes. If you wish, make a hole in the top of each cookie with a drinking straw to attach string, wire, or ribbon after baking. Repeat the rolling and cutting with the second package of dough. Meanwhile, gather up any scraps of dough into a ball, wrap, and refrigerate. (Always work with chilled dough.) Roll, cut out, and arrange on baking sheet.

Bake cookies, 1 baking sheet at a time, in the preheated oven for 10 to 12 minutes, or until light brown around edges. Keep the others chilled until ready to bake. Gently remove baked cookies from baking sheet to cool.

DECORATING SUGGESTIONS

To decorate before baking, brush cookies with an egg wash of 1 egg yolk and 1 tablespoon water mixed together. Paint them with a lightly beaten egg white and top them with colored or chocolate sprinkles, chopped nuts, toasted coconut, or any favorite topping.

To decorate cookies after baking, you can paint on a Chocolate Glaze (page 178), or make the traditional confectioners' sugar icing. Beat the confectioners' sugar into the egg white; add milk 1 tablespoon at a time

Make a hole in the top of each cookie with a drinking straw to attach ribbon for hanging.

to make a thick icing. Divide the icing among several containers and, using food coloring, tint each one a different color. Ice the cookies using artists' brushes of varying widths for thick and fine lines, or pipe the icing through a pastry tube fitted with assorted tips. Baked cookies can also be rolled in cinnamon, powdered sugar, powdered cocoa, or tinted sugar. They can also be decorated with Crystallized Violets, page 3. The variations are endless.

TO PACKAGE

These cookies make unusual gift tags for all your packages or edible Christmas tree ornaments.

Use a straw to make a hole in the unbaked cutout, not too close to the edge, for attaching ribbon after the cookies are baked. Fit a pastry tube with the finest point and use the colored frosting to write names or a message on the cookies.

INGREDIENTS

2¾ cups sifted cake flour
1 tablespoon baking powder
¼ teaspoon baking soda
1 teaspoon ground cloves
1 teaspoon ground ginger
1 tablespoon ground cinnamon
½ teaspoon salt
1 egg, beaten
¼ teaspoon ground allspice
**1 cup firmly packed dark brown
    sugar**
⅔ cup dark molasses
**4 ounces butter, softened to room
    temperature**

KATHLEEN'S CHRISTMAS GINGERBREAD FAMILY

YIELD: about 5 dozen cookies of assorted sizes

This recipe was given to me by Kathleen King, owner of Kathleen's Cookie in Southampton, New York. Her cookies have made her name famous throughout Long Island and in New York City. At Christmas she makes a gingerbread man, woman, and child, each with raisin eyes and its own red satin bow tie. These figures make ideal tie-on tags for any present, appreciated by both children and adults. I have tested many recipes for gingerbread men and this one beats them all.

METHOD

In a large mixing bowl, sift together the first 7 ingredients and set aside. In a separate bowl combine the egg, allspice, brown sugar, molasses, and butter. Add the dry to the liquid ingredients, a little at a time, mixing after each addition to form a stiff dough. Gather the dough into 2 equal balls, wrap in plastic wrap, and refrigerate for 1 hour, or until firm.

Preheat oven to 375° F. Remove 1 ball of dough from the refrigerator and roll it out on a lightly floured surface to a thickness of about ⅓ inch. Cut gingerbread family members from the dough with floured cutters. Transfer cookies to a greased baking sheet. Use raisins or candied cinnamon hearts to make eyes, nose, mouth, and buttons if desired. Bake for 10 to 12 minutes, or until lightly brown. Cool on wire rack.

Note: You can frost and decorate gingerbread family members to resemble your own friends or family. Or use the dough and an assortment of cookie cutters to make cookies of unusual shapes and patterns, animals, cartoon characters, etc. Use ⅛-inch satin ribbon for bow ties.

Icing

Beat confectioners' sugar into the egg white, adding 1 tablespoon of milk at a time to make a thick frosting. Divide the icing among several containers and tint with desired food colors. Use artists' brushes of varying widths to paint the cookies, or a pastry tube fitted with a fine point tip.

TO PACKAGE

These go into cookie envelopes (page 229). Make 1 cookie for each member of the family and decorate the outside of the envelope to resemble a house.

Icing and Decoration

2 cups confectioners' sugar
1 egg white
3 to 4 tablespoons milk
Food coloring
Raisins or candied cinnamon hearts or silver nonpareils

TOOLS

Rolling pin
Cookie cutters or stencils in the shape of gingerbread men, women, children
Baking sheet
Ribbon
Several containers for icing
Artists' brushes of assorted widths

FLORENTINES

INGREDIENTS

½ cup plus 2 tablespoons sifted
all-purpose flour
1 cup mixed candied fruits (Buy
whole candied fruits and chop
them yourself.)
½ cup finely chopped walnuts
1 cup finely chopped blanched
almonds
4 ounces unsalted butter
½ cup firmly packed dark brown
sugar
2 tablespoons light corn syrup

Chocolate Glaze

6 ounces semisweet chocolate bits
2 ounces unsalted butter

TOOLS

Nonstick baking sheet, or baking
sheet lined with aluminum
foil
Cake rack
Pastry brush
Airtight container

YIELD: 2½ to 3 dozen

A true sophisticate in the world of cookies, the lacy fruit- and nut-laden florentine is rich and delicious.

METHOD

Preheat oven to 325° F. Combine the flour, candied fruits, and nuts in a small mixing bowl.

Combine the butter, brown sugar, and light corn syrup in a large saucepan. Place over low heat and stir until the butter is melted and the sugar has dissolved. Do not boil. Remove from the heat and stir in the fruit and nut mixture.

Drop the batter by scant teaspoons, 3 inches apart, onto a baking sheet lined with aluminum foil.

Bake cookies for 10 to 12 minutes, or until they are light brown around the edges. They spread very thin while cooking. Let cool on the baking sheet for 2 to 3 minutes and transfer to a cake rack covered with a layer of paper towel to cool. The paper towel will absorb any excess butter.

In a covered saucepan, heat the chocolate bits and butter over very low heat until just melted. Stir to combine. Remove from the heat. Using a pastry brush, brush the bottoms of the cookies with a thin coat of chocolate. Place them on a cake rack, chocolate side up, to dry.

Store the florentines in an airtight container so that they do not lose their crispness. They are very fragile so be sure to put a piece of wax paper between the layers of the cookies as you pack them. Stored in an airtight container, they will keep for up to 1 week.

TO PACKAGE

These should be elegantly presented in a Ribbon-Covered Box (page 228).

PEPPERNUTS

There are literally dozens of recipes for this Central European Christmas cookie. In all of them the common ingredients are pepper and spices. The cookies are called *Pfeffernüsse* in Germany, *Pepparnötter* in Sweden, and *Pebernødder* in Denmark. Wherever they are made, the evocative smell of the many spices means the Christmas season is at hand.

METHOD

Preheat oven to 350° F. Put the honey and butter in a large heavy saucepan and heat slowly until the honey is thin and the butter has melted. Do not boil. Cool to lukewarm. Add the egg and beat until well mixed.

Sift the flour with the salt, baking soda, spices, and pepper and add the mixture, a little at a time, to the honey mixture until well blended. The dough will be sticky so chill it in the refrigerator for 30 minutes, until it can be handled easily.

Gather the dough into a ball and roll it out on a lightly floured surface to a thickness of about ¾ inch. Stamp out cookies with cookie cutters. I like to cut the peppernuts into the shapes of stars, hearts, and diamonds.

Place the cookies on a lightly oiled baking sheet and bake for about 15 minutes, or until barely firm to the touch. They will be light brown around the edges. Transfer to a wire rack to cool completely before glazing.

To make the glaze, combine the egg whites, honey, and anise extract in a medium-size mixing bowl. Gradually add the sugar, beating well after each addition, until it is all used. The glaze will be fairly thin.

Using your fingers, dip each cookie into the glaze to coat all sides. Hold the dipped cookie over the bowl to let any excess glaze drip back into the bowl. Dip the top of the cookie into the candy sprinkles. Return it to the wire rack to dry completely.

Peppernuts keep for several weeks if stored in an airtight container.

INGREDIENTS

1½ cups honey
2 ounces unsalted butter
1 egg
4 cups all-purpose flour
½ teaspoon salt
1 teaspoon baking soda
½ teaspoon ground cloves
½ teaspoon ground allspice
½ teaspoon grated nutmeg
1 teaspoon ground cardamom
½ teaspoon finely crushed aniseed
1 teaspoon coarsely ground black
    pepper

Sugar Glaze

2 egg whites
2 tablespoons honey
1 teaspoon pure anise extract
2 cups sifted confectioners' sugar

Silver or colored candy sprinkles

TOOLS

Rolling pin
Cookie cutters
Baking sheet
Wire rack
Airtight container

TO PACKAGE

Place 2 cookies, flat sides together, and wrap in a square of printed or plain tissue paper, twisting both ends. Place the cookies in a Tied Paper Bag (page 220) or in decorated boxes or tins (page 226 or page 221), using stickers or cutouts to create a Christmas scene.

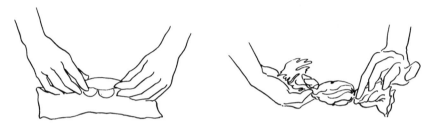

Place two cookies, flat sides together, and wrap in a square of tissue paper, twisting both ends.

SPECULAAS

YIELD: about 4 dozen 3-inch cookies

December 6 is St. Nicholas Day on the calendar, the day when the patron saint of children and sailors makes his rounds to reward "good" children with goodies from his big sack. In Holland and Belgium, where this recipe originated, the bag is sure to contain a large supply of these delicious cookies.

These Dutch cardamom-spiced cookies, knows as *Speculos* in Belgium, are traditionally rolled and pressed into wooden molds or rolling pins patterned with a variety of pictures or shapes. Their name derives from the Latin word for mirror and refers to the technique of imprinting, or mirroring, on the cookie the pattern from the molds. Make Speculaas at least a day ahead; their flavor improves as they sit.

METHOD

Sift the flour with the spices, baking powder, and salt and set aside.

In a large mixing bowl, cream the butter and brown sugar together until light and fluffy. Add the egg and beat until smooth.

Add the flour mixture, a little at a time, to the butter mixture, beating thoroughly after each addition. Add the chopped almonds with the last addition of flour. The dough will be quite stiff. Form the dough into several balls, wrap each one in wax paper, and refrigerate for several hours.

Preheat oven to 350° F. Lightly oil several baking sheets. Remove 1 ball of dough from the refrigerator and roll it between 2 pieces of wax paper to a thickness of about ¼ inch. If you have them, press floured molds or patterned rolling pin firmly into the dough. Remove mold and cut with a knife between the designs, or cut the dough into shapes with cookie cutters or a sharp knife.

Transfer cookies to a prepared baking sheet and bake for 20 to 25 minutes, until cookies are golden around the edges. Remove to a wire cake rack and cool completely. Reroll trimmings and repeat the baking until all the dough is used.

The Speculaas will keep for several weeks if stored in an airtight container. They also freeze very well.

TO PACKAGE

Give these cookies in decorated bags (page 220) or boxes (page 226). Team them with a wooden cookie mold as a special surprise.

INGREDIENTS

3 cups all-purpose flour
2 teaspoons ground cinnamon
1 teaspoon ground ginger
1 teaspoon ground cardamom
¼ teaspoon grated nutmeg
⅛ teaspoon baking powder
⅛ teaspoon salt
8 ounces unsalted butter
**1 cup firmly packed light brown
  sugar**
1 egg
**½ cup almonds, blanched and
  finely chopped**

TOOLS

Rolling pin
**Wooden cookie molds or
  patterned rolling pin
  (optional) or cookie cutters**
Baking sheets
Wire cake rack
Airtight container

Carefully remove the dough from the Speculaas molds and cut with a knife between the designs to form cookies.

INGREDIENTS

6 ounces unsalted butter

¾ cup sugar

4 hard-cooked egg yolks from large eggs

2 tablespoons raspberry-flavored liqueur or Kirsch, or 1 teaspoon vanilla

2 cups sifted all-purpose flour

⅛ teaspoon salt

Red raspberry jam (If you mind the seeds use jelly instead.)

Confectioners' sugar

TOOLS

Rolling pin

Wire strainer or egg ricer

1 large and 1 small heart-shaped cookie cutter

Baking sheet

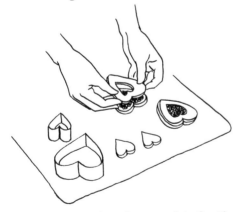

To assemble the cookies, spread the flat side of each large heart-shaped cookie with jam and top the jam with a heart ring.

EIER KRINGEL

(Raspberry-Filled Cookies)

YIELD: about 3 dozen cookies

The addition of cooked egg yolks to the dough gives this classic German cookie its rich taste. I like to make *Eier Kringel* in the shape of hearts for St. Valentine's Day. Filled with raspberry jam and dusted with powdered sugar, they will help win any reluctant suitor.

METHOD

In a large mixing bowl, cream the butter and sugar together until light and fluffy. Press the egg yolks through wire tea strainer or egg ricer into the butter-sugar mixture. Add the liqueur and mix well. Gradually add the flour and salt, mixing as you go, to form a firm dough.

Divide the dough into 3 balls, wrap in plastic wrap, and refrigerate for several hours or overnight.

Preheat oven to 350° F. Remove the chilled balls of dough, one at a time, from the refrigerator and roll between 2 sheets of wax paper to a thickness of about ¼ inch. Gently remove the top layer of wax paper. Using 1 large and 1 medium-size heart-shaped cutter, cut the cookies according to these directions: Cut pairs of large hearts from the dough; then, using the medium heart cutter, cut out a heart shape from the center of half the cookies to form heart-shaped rings; be careful to stay away from the edges so the cookies remain strong. Save the smaller hearts cut from the rings and bake with the larger hearts and heart rings. Gather up dough scraps into a ball and refrigerate. Bake the hearts and heart rings on an ungreased baking sheet for 8 to 10 minutes, until the edges are lightly browned. Cool on a rack. Repeat the entire process with each chilled ball of dough.

To assemble the cookies, spread the flat side of each large heart-shaped cookie with jam and top the jam with a heart ring, flat side down. Dust the top with sifted confectioners' sugar and fill the center with additional jam. Sandwich the smaller hearts, cut from the heart rings, together with jam and dust the tops with confectioners' sugar.

TO PACKAGE

Because these cookies are quite fragile and no one wants a broken heart, package them in metal cookie tins lined with large paper doilies. Decorate the tops of the tins with the familiar small candy hearts inscribed with romantic messages.

FORTUNE COOKIES

YIELD: about 3 dozen cookies

Crisp Chinese wafers spiked with pure almond flavor, these cookies are nothing like the tough soggy cookies found in most Chinese restaurants. These lend themselves to many occasions; simply vary the messages of "fortunes" you include to suit your friends or any special occasion. A large basket of them at a New Year's party or for an open house on New Year's Day would be fun. Make sure you have the messages prepared ahead of time for, once the cookies are baked, the fortunes must be slipped into place quickly. Type or write the messages in permanent ink.

METHOD

Preheat oven to 350° F. Cut 3 dozen strips of white paper ¼ inch wide and 1½ inches long. Write appropriate messages or fortunes on the papers and fold each in half. Set aside.

Beat the egg whites until frothy and gradually beat in the sugar and salt until dissolved. Stir in the melted butter, flour, and almond extract, and beat until well blended.

Drop the dough in rounded teaspoons about 3 inches apart onto an ungreased baking sheet.

Bake for 8 to 10 minutes, until the edges of the cookies are golden brown. Working very quickly, remove 1 cookie at a time from the baking sheet. Hold the cookie in the palm of your hand and place 1 folded

INGREDIENTS

3 egg whites
¾ cup sugar
Pinch of salt
4 ounces unsalted butter, melted
½ cup sifted flour
2 teaspoons pure almond extract

Place 1 folded fortune in the center of each cookie. Fold the cookie in half.

Drape the folded cookie over the handle of a wooden spoon.

TOOLS

White paper
Pen
Scissors
Baking sheet
Rolling pin

For packaging cookies

Chinese food container
Gold cord
Gift label

fortune in the center. Fold the cookie in half. Drape the folded cookie over the handle of a wooden spoon. Fold the corners around the spoon to meet and gently press together. Slide the cookie off the spoon. Repeat with remaining cookies.

Note: If the cookies became too brittle to fold as you work, return them to the oven for a minute to soften.

TO PACKAGE

Fortune cookies call for a suitable Oriental packaging. Most Chinese restaurants will give you a few "take-out" containers, or colorful printed cardboard containers are available at novelty party shops.

Decorate the outside of plain white containers with Chinese characters or rubber stamps. Wrap each cookie individually in a square of tissue paper and pack them into the container. One container holds approximately 8 cookies. Fold the lid together, place a gold or red seal over the opening, and tie with satin cord.

CHRISTMAS STOLLEN

YIELD: 2 large loaves

Stollen, a sweet fruit-laden and frosted bread, originated in Germany but has become a popular Christmastime specialty in America as well. The word *Stollen* means "stick" or "post" in German and this bread symbolizes the Christ Child's wooden manger. Serve it at breakfast or anytime. It is always a welcome gift, and it freezes well.

METHOD

In a large mixing bowl combine glacéed fruits, raisins, cherries, pineapple, and brandy and let stand for at least 1 hour. This can be done the night before.

Combine the yeast and 1 teaspoon sugar in a large mixing bowl. Add the warm water and stir until yeast is dissolved. Let proof for about 5 minutes. Add the milk and 2 cups flour and beat until smooth and elastic, 2 to 3 minutes. Cover and let the sponge rise in a warm place, 72° to 75° F., for 15 minutes.

Stir the sponge down and add the eggs, 6 ounces melted butter, ½ cup sugar, and the salt. Add 3 more cups of flour and beat until a soft dough is formed. Place the dough on a lightly floured surface and knead in about ½ cup more flour, a little at a time. Knead the dough until smooth, 6 to 8 minutes.

Add the almonds to the fruit mixture. Dust the nuts and fruits with ¼ cup flour and knead them into the dough. Place the dough in a buttered bowl and turn to coat all surfaces. Cover and let rise in a warm place until about doubled, 1½ to 2 hours.

Punch dough down and divide into halves. Shape each half into a circle about 12 inches in diameter and ¾ inch thick. Brush each one with some of the 2 ounces melted butter and sprinkle with granulated sugar. Fold each circle in half and press the edges together to seal. Place the loaves on lightly greased baking sheets, cover, and let rise for about 1 hour, or until not quite doubled.

Preheat oven to 425° F. Brush stollen again with melted butter and bake for 10 minutes. Reduce heat to 350° F, and continue baking for 25 to 30 minutes more. If the stollen browns too quickly, cover loosely with aluminum foil.

Take loaves from the oven and brush them again with melted butter, dust with confectioners' sugar, and drizzle on more brandy.

The stollen freezes well if it is not eaten within a day or two of baking.

TO PACKAGE

Wrap each stollen in a heavy linen dish towel and tie with a wide polka-dot ribbon. Attach a holly sprig or wrap Japanese style in a *furoshiki* (see directions on page 216).

INGREDIENTS

1 cup mixed glacéed fruits
½ cup golden raisins
½ cup seedless dark raisins
½ cup glacéed cherries, halved
¼ cup diced glacéed pineapple
½ cup brandy
2 envelopes dry yeast
1 teaspoon sugar
¼ cup warm water, 105° to 115° F.
1 cup warm milk, 105° to 115° F.
5½ to 6 cups all-purpose flour
2 eggs, beaten
6 ounces butter, melted and cooled to room temperature
½ cup sugar
1 teaspoon salt
1 cup slivered almonds, lightly toasted at 400° F. for 5 minutes
2 ounces butter, melted
Granulated sugar
Confectioners' sugar
Brandy

TOOLS

Baking sheet

PRETZEL BREAD

INGREDIENTS

1½ cups half-and-half
1 envelope dry yeast
1 tablespoon sugar
3 egg yolks, beaten
3½ to 4 cups flour
⅓ cup sugar
1 teaspoon salt
4 ounces unsalted butter, chilled

Filling

7 ounces almond paste
½ cup sugar
1 egg white
1 teaspoon ground cinnamon
1 teaspoon almond extract
¾ cup chopped almonds

Topping

Sugar
1 egg white mixed with 1
    tablespoon water
Sliced almonds

TOOLS

Rolling pin
Baking sheet

YIELD: 1 large bread

During the Middle Ages it was customary throughout Europe to prepare a special bread called a *Bretzel* to celebrate the winter solstice. The bread was circular like the sun but twisted in the center to form a cross representing the four seasons. Today the *Bretzel* shape is retained in what we know as a pretzel, but the seasonal connection has been lost. The pretzel is now for all occasions. This variation calls for a rich, briochelike dough filled with almond paste and nuts. It is 2 days in the making. Slice the bread very thin and serve it with coffee or at teatime.

METHOD

Heat the half-and-half to lukewarm, 105° F. Combine the yeast and 1 tablespoon sugar and add the lukewarm half-and-half. Stir until the yeast and sugar are dissolved. Let proof for about 5 minutes.

Add the egg yolks and 1½ cups flour, and beat 2 to 3 minutes to activate the gluten. Cover and let rest for 15 minutes.

In a separate bowl, combine remaining flour, ⅓ cup sugar, and the salt. Cut in the butter until the mixture resembles oatmeal. Fold in the yeast sponge and beat for 2 minutes. Cover with plastic wrap and refrigerate overnight.

The following day, combine the almond paste, ½ cup sugar, the egg white, cinnamon, and almond extract, and blend into a smooth paste.

Remove the dough from the refrigerator, dust it lightly with flour, and knead on a smooth surface for 2 to 3 minutes. Allow to rest for 5 minutes before rolling it into a rectangle 24 x 18 inches. Sprinkle the rectangle with sugar and flip it over.

Spread the filling evenly over the dough to within 1 inch of all the edges. Sprinkle on the chopped almonds and tightly roll up the dough into a long cylinder. Roll the cylinder between your palms until it is about 36 inches long.

Place the dough on a greased baking sheet and shape it into a large pretzel. Brush it with the egg white and water, sprinkle with sugar and sliced almonds, cover, and let rise for 1 hour.

Preheat oven to 375° F. Bake the bread for 45 minutes to 1 hour, until it is golden in color and a cake tester comes out clean. If the bread colors too quickly, cover it loosely with aluminum foil.

Remove the bread from the baking sheet and allow it to cool completely before packaging.

Wrapped tightly in aluminum foil, the pretzel bread will keep in the refrigerator for a week. It freezes very well.

TO PACKAGE

The prettiest way to wrap the pretzel bread is to place it on a round wooden bread board and overwrap with clear cellophane and a ribbon bow. Tie on a few sprigs of dried or fresh flowers.

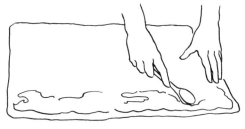

Spread the filling evenly over the rectangle of dough, 24 × 18 inches, to within 1 inch of all the edges.

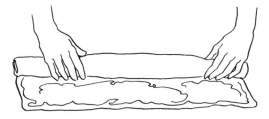

Roll the dough into a long cylinder.

Shape the dough into a large pretzel.

ENGLISH PLUM PUDDING

Christmas comes, he comes, he comes,
Ushered in with rain of plums!

INGREDIENTS

1 cup dried currants
1 cup golden raisins
¾ cup dark raisins
½ cup mixed candied peel,
    coarsely chopped
½ cup walnuts, coarsely chopped
Rind of 1 lemon, coarsely chopped
¼ teaspoon salt
1 tablespoon ground cinnamon
1½ teaspoons ground ginger
1 teaspoon grated nutmeg
1 teaspoon ground allspice
½ cup strawberry preserve
1 cup sugar
1¾ cups fresh bread crumbs
½ pound suet, chopped fine
4 eggs
½ cup brandy

TOOLS

Two 1-pound coffee cans
Aluminum foil
Kitchen twine
Steamer rack

YIELD: two 2-pound cakes, 20 to 24 portions

Despite its name, this old-fashioned bread pudding has no plums. The English use the word "plum" in reference to many dried fruits, especially raisins and currants. Like American fruitcakes, English plum puddings are known for their incredible keeping capacity: It is not unusual to make a pudding 6 months to a year in advance. Traditionally, however, they are made the Sunday before Advent, which is about 5 weeks before Christmas and is known as "stir-up" Sunday, a name which derives from the first line of the collect in earlier Books of Common Prayer for that Sunday: "Stir up, we beseech thee, O Lord, the wills of thy faithful people." For good luck have all members of the family give a stir before cooking the pudding.,

This recipe is baked in 2 clean 1-pound coffee cans. The cans make perfect containers for wrapping, storing, and reheating the cakes. Plum pudding is usually flamed with brandy and accompanied by hard sauce, for which a recipe follows.

METHOD

Combine the currants, both raisins, candied peel, walnuts, lemon rind, salt, spices, strawberry preserve, sugar, bread crumbs, and suet in a large mixing bowl. In a separate bowl, beat the eggs until very thick, stir in the brandy, and add this mixture to the fruit mixture. "Stir-up" until well mixed.

Thoroughly grease 2 clean 1-pound coffee cans and dust them with flour. Pack the pudding mixture firmly into the 2 cans. They should be about three-quarters full. Cover the cans tightly with greased and floured aluminum foil tied in place with kitchen twine.

Place the cans on a steamer rack in a very large deep kettle. Pour boiling water into the kettle to reach halfway up the sides of the cans.

Cover the kettle with a tight-fitting lid and cook at a gentle boil for 2½ hours, adding more boiling water to the kettle during cooking as needed.

To store: Refrigerate the puddings, still in the cans, wrapped in clean aluminum foil, for several weeks, a month, or as much as a year. Keep the cake moist by periodically adding more brandy.

TO PACKAGE

For a change from all the red and green at Christmas try using a combination of silver and white. Ordinary aluminum foil wrapped around the cans creates a functional and beautiful container. Overwrap with clear cellophane; attach a large white satin bow and a few tiny silver Christmas balls. Add a tag with instructions for reheating and serving as follows:

Place the foil-covered can on a steamer rack in a deep kettle. Pour boiling water to reach halfway up the sides of the can. Cover the kettle and keep the water at a gentle boil for 1 hour. Remove the can from the water and run a knife all around the inside edges of the mold to loosen the pudding; unmold onto a serving platter. Pour several tablespoons of brandy over the pudding. Heat an additional ½ cup in a saucepan until vapor starts to rise. Ignite and pour the flaming brandy over the pudding. Serve flaming with Hard Sauce.

Place the cans on a steamer rack in a very large deep kettle. Pour boiling water into the kettle to reach halfway up the sides of the cans.

HARD SAUCE

YIELD: about ¾ cup

A little Hard Sauce goes a long way. This quantity should be enough for 1 pudding. Keep the sauce refrigerated until you are ready to use it, then remove it from the refrigerator to soften slightly before serving.

INGREDIENTS

**4 ounces unsalted butter, softened
to room temperature**
½ cup confectioners' sugar
Grated rind of 1 large orange
2 tablespoons good brandy

TOOLS

Electric mixer

METHOD

In a small bowl, cream the butter until light. Gradually beat in the sugar until fluffy. Mix in the orange rind and brandy. Store covered in the refrigerator.

TO PACKAGE

Place the Hard Sauce in a small, beautiful bowl. Cover with plastic wrap and tie in place with ribbon.

MARZIPAN-WRAPPED FRUITCAKE

INGREDIENTS

Cake

1 cup dark seedless raisins
1 cup dried currants
1 cup golden raisins
2 ounces lemon peel, chopped
2 ounces orange peel, chopped
**6 ounces candied cherries or
Candied Cranberries
(page 120)**
6 ounces candied pineapple, sliced
2 ounces citron, thinly sliced
**1½ cups shelled pecans, coarsely
chopped**
**2 cups shelled hazelnuts, coarsely
chopped**
1⅔ cups flour
¼ teaspoon baking soda
1 teaspoon ground cinnamon
1 teaspoon ground allspice

YIELD: 2 loaves

This is my family's treasured fruitcake recipe. Loaded with fruits and nuts, it is very rich. I have added the marzipan icing because I love its flavor and I happen to be partial to a cake with an icing. You can make the cake as much as a month before you give it. Keep in mind the farther ahead you make it, the more often you get to drench it with Cognac. The icing should be added a day or so before presentation.

METHOD

Oil and line the 2 loaf pans with wax or parchment paper cut to fit the bottom of the pan. Set aside.

Combine the fruits and nuts with ⅓ cup of the flour. Set aside.

Sift remaining flour, measure 1⅓ cups, and add the baking soda and spices. Sift again.

Cream the butter until light, gradually add the brown sugar, and beat until light and fluffy. Beat the egg yolks and add; mix well. Add the molasses to the combined fruits and nuts.

Fold the dry ingredients into the fruit and nut mixture, adding a little at a time. Beat the egg whites until stiff but not dry. Add ½ cup of the batter to the egg whites and then fold the egg whites into the batter.

Divide the batter equally between the 2 paper-lined pans. Tap the pans several times on the counter to distribute the batter evenly. Cover the cakes with oiled parchment paper extending 1½ to 2 inches over the edges of the pans. Tie in place with kitchen twine. Place the pans several inches apart in a roasting pan. Pour boiling water into the roasting pan to a level halfway up the loaf pans.

Steam cakes in a 350° F. oven for 2½ hours, adding more water if needed. When cakes are done, a cake tester should come out clean.

While the cakes are baking, make the sugar glaze. Combine the brown sugar, corn syrup, and Cognac in a saucepan. Bring slowly to a boil over low heat. Boil for 3 minutes. Remove from the heat and add the lemon juice. Remove the cakes from the water bath. Uncover and brush with half of the sugar glaze.

Cool cakes for 20 minutes before removing from the pans. Carefully peel off the paper. While the cakes are still warm, brush tops and sides with remaining sugar glaze. Use it all.

Wrap the cakes in a double layer of cheesecloth that has been soaked in Cognac. Pour Cognac slowly over the wrapped cakes until all is absorbed. Place several apple slices on the cakes to keep them from drying out, and wrap airtight in heavy aluminum foil. Store the cakes in the refrigerator for 10 days, adding more Cognac to the cheesecloth if desired. If the cakes are not iced, they can be stored in the refrigerator indefinitely. Just unwrap the foil and soak the cheesecloth again in Cognac once a month to keep the cakes from drying out. The cakes can also be frozen.

After the cakes have marinated for at least 10 days, cover them with the marzipan icing. Combine the marzipan, confectioners' sugar, and egg whites in the bowl of an electric mixer. Blend with the mixer or beat by hand until smooth.

Unwrap the cakes and spread the icing ¼ inch thick on the tops and sides. For a professional look, dip a spreading knife in ice water and smooth it in one direction over the icing. Decorate with candied fruits, nuts, and chocolate leaves.

½ teaspoon grated mace
½ teaspoon grated nutmeg
5½ ounces butter
⅔ cup firmly packed light brown sugar
4 eggs, separated
⅓ cup molasses
¾ cup Cognac
Apple slices

Sugar Glaze

1 cup light brown sugar
⅔ cup corn syrup
⅔ cup Cognac
1½ tablespoons lemon juice
Additional Cognac

Marzipan Icing

21 ounces marzipan (three 7-ounce logs)
1 cup confectioners' sugar
3 egg whites

Decoration

Candied fruits (red and green cherries, orange peel)
Whole nuts
Chocolate Leaves (page 139)

TOOLS

2 loaf pans, 8½ x 4½ x 2½ inches
Wax paper or parchment paper
Roasting pan
Kitchen twine
Cheesecloth
Electric mixer

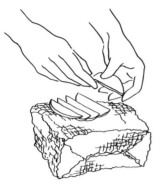

Wrap the cakes in a double layer of cheese cloth that has been soaked in Cognac. Pour Cognac slowly over the wrapped cakes until all is absorbed. Place several apple slices on the cakes to keep them from drying out.

TO PACKAGE

The iced cake looks beautiful when presented on an antique platter or long wooden bread board, but a less expensive and equally attractive presentation can be achieved if you take several layers of heavy cardboard 4 to 5 inches longer and wider than the cake and cover the cardboard with aluminum foil, shiny side up. Place the cake in the center of the foil-wrapped cardboard. Tuck lemon leaves under the cake and decorate the base with additional candied fruits and nuts.

Gently wrap the cake and board in clear cellophane. As a final touch, wrap a red satin ribbon around the entire package, making a large bow over one end of the cake.

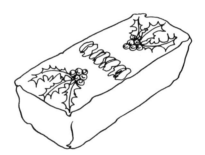

Decorate the iced cake with candied fruits, nuts, and chocolate leaves.

MIXED FRUIT AND NUT CAKE

YIELD: 2 cakes

There are many people who say they don't like fruitcake but what they actually mean is that they do not like the candied fruits and citron in the cake. This fruitcake is really a dried fruit and nut cake with almost no batter. The salted nuts, especially the peanuts, are a surprise. The best news: no candied fruits and no citron. The cake should be sliced very thin with a serrated knife.

METHOD

In a very large bowl or pasta pot, combine the fruits and Cognac. Let stand for 15 to 20 minutes, until the liquid is absorbed.

Line the 2 pans with aluminum foil, pressing out all wrinkles, allowing 1 inch of foil to overlap the edges of the pan all the way around.

Reserve 1½ cups of the mixed nuts and set aside. Add remaining nuts to the fruit mixture. Add the flour, sugar, and baking powder to the fruit and nut mixture and stir until well combined. Pour the eggs over the mixture and mix well. (I use my hands to do this; the mixture is almost too heavy for a spoon.)

Divide the batter into 2 equal parts and pack in the foil-lined pans, firmly, to eliminate air pockets. Sprinkle the reserved nuts on top, pressing them firmly into the batter.

Bake in a preheated 300° F. oven for 1½ hours for large cakes, until a knife inserted into the center of a cake comes out clean.

Cool the cakes in their pans for 30 minutes. Use the overlapping edges of foil to lift the cakes from their pans. Carefully peel off the foil. Cool the cakes completely on a cake rack before wrapping tightly in foil. Refrigerated, the cakes keep for 1 month.

TO PACKAGE

Wrap the fruitcakes Japanese-style in a *furoshiki* (see page 216 for folding instruction). In Japan this ubiquitous square of cloth is used to make almost anything portable. Tie on a sprig of holly and a few tiny Christmas balls.

INGREDIENTS

10 ounces figlets (small dried figs)
12 ounces pitted prunes
10 ounces pitted dates
10 ounces muscat raisins
½ cup Cognac
1½ pounds salted mixed nuts
6 ounces whole pecans
1½ cups flour
1 cup sugar
1 teaspoon baking powder
6 eggs, beaten

TOOLS

Large bowl
2 loaf pans, 8½ x 4½ x 2½ inches
Wire cake rack

Materials

Two 24-inch-square pieces of fabric

TWELFTH NIGHT CAKE

INGREDIENTS

8 ounces butter, softened to room
temperature
2 cups sugar
6 medium-size eggs
½ cup light honey
Rind of 2 lemons, finely chopped
1 tablespoon freshly ground black
pepper
1 tablespoon finely grated fresh
gingerroot
3¼ cups flour
1 teaspoon salt
¼ teaspoon baking soda
1 cup buttermilk or plain yogurt
(If you don't want a half-
carton of buttermilk lying
around, try using plain yogurt
instead.)
1 coin wrapped in aluminum foil

Decoration

½ cup light corn syrup
2 tablespoons rum
Whole blanched almonds
Assorted glacéed fruits

TOOLS

1 tube pan, 8- to 10-cup volume
Wire cake rack

YIELD: 1 large cake

For centuries it has been the custom for Christians to celebrate the 6th of January or Twelfth Night with a cake containing a hidden coin, or favor. The belief holds that when the cake is cut, whoever finds the buried gift will have luck in the coming year. This Twelfth Night Cake celebrates the feast of Epiphany, a festival held on the twelfth day after Christmas to honor the coming of the Magi to Bethlehem. The cake is also of ancient origin and figured in both Greek and Roman rites held at the same time of the year: The Greek bread of St. Basil contained a coin for foretelling the future while Roman rulers used the hidden coin to draw lots for kingdoms.

Many versions of the Twelfth Night Cake have come down to us. Some cakes are made of flaky puff pastry, some of yeast dough. They are either filled with raisins and citron or heavily spiced. Traditionally the cake was not iced but decorated with glacéed fruits and blanched almonds in a pattern resembling a crown. This version is a rich, buttery, and spicy pound cake.

METHOD

Preheat oven to 325° F. Grease and flour the tube pan.

Cream the butter and gradually add the sugar, beating until light. Separate the eggs. Beat the yolks with the honey until thick and add a little at a time to the butter mixture, beating all the time. Add the lemon rind, black pepper, and gingerroot.

Sift the flour, add the salt and baking soda, and sift again. Add the flour mixture in 3 parts to the butter mixture, alternating with the buttermilk and ending with a portion of the flour. Beat the egg whites until stiff but not dry. Fold the whites into the batter. Fold in the foil-wrapped coin and pour the batter into the prepared pan. Bake for 1 hour and 25 minutes, until the cake tester comes out clean.

Cool in the pan for 10 minutes. Gently run a knife around the inner and outer edges of the cake. Turn out on a rack and cool.

Heat the corn syrup with the rum until warm. Brush the top of the cake with the syrup and decorate with nuts and fruits. Pour remaining syrup over the cake.

If wrapped tightly in aluminum foil, the cake will keep for 3 to 4 days.

TO PACKAGE

Wrap the cake in red or green cellophane (the kind used to wrap Easter baskets) and tie with a red-and-green-checked ribbon. Attach a label that explains the Twelfth Night custom.

PEAR MINCEMEAT BOXING DAY TARTS

According to Lorna J. Sass's wonderful book on Christmas folklore and history, *Christmas Feasts from History,* in the seventeenth century, mincemeat pies were baked in rectangular shapes to symbolize the Christ Child's crèche and filled with spicy mincemeat, thought to represent the gifts of spices from the Magi. During the Reformation the Puritans, objecting to these religious associations, for a short time outlawed the serving of mince pies. They were renamed "Christmas pies" and have been part of Christmas ever since.

Mincemeat tarts are traditional English holiday favorites, once boxed and presented to the servants at the end of the Christmas season, a custom that gave its name to Boxing Day. Few of us have servants these days but these tarts, beautifully boxed, are always welcome. If you are exhausted from the holidays, simply make the pear mincemeat and include instructions for making up the tarts. The mincemeat is also delicious over ice cream or as an accompaniment to roast meat.

PEAR MINCEMEAT

INGREDIENTS

2 pounds firm pears (Anjou or
    Bartlett), peeled, cored, and
    coarsely chopped, about 4
    cups
1 green apple (Granny Smith),
    peeled, cored, and coarsely
    chopped, about 1 cup
Grated rind and juice of 1 lemon
Grated rind and juice of 1 orange
½ cup dried currants
1 cup golden raisins
½ cup brown sugar
1 teaspoon ground cinnamon
1 teaspoon grated nutmeg
¼ teaspoon ground ginger
Pinch of salt
¼ cup coarsely chopped shelled
    walnuts
¼ cup Cognac

TOOLS

Four 1-cup Mason jars with lids

YIELD: about 4 cups, enough for 12 tarts

More in keeping with the way we eat now, this recipe does not contain either meat or suet and is therefore simpler to prepare and not as heavy or rich as traditional mincemeat. Use the pear mincemeat as a filling for pies or tarts (see following recipe) or as a topping for ice cream, pudding, or poached fruit.

METHOD

Combine the pears, apple, lemon and orange rinds and juice, currants, raisins, brown sugar, spices, and salt in a heavy saucepan. Cover and simmer for about 45 minutes, stirring occasionally. Lower the heat, and continue cooking uncovered for 30 to 40 minutes more, stirring occasionally until very thick. Add the walnuts and Cognac and cook for 5 minutes more.

If the mincemeat is to be preserved, pack it into hot sterilized jars, leaving ½-inch headroom. Wipe the rims clean and seal with lids. Process for 10 minutes (see instructions on page 231).

BOXING DAY MINCEMEAT TARTS

YIELD: 12 tarts

METHOD

Preheat oven to 375° F. Measure the flour and salt into a bowl. With your fingers, or with a pastry cutter, work rapidly to blend the flour, salt, and chilled butter together until the mixture has the texture of oatmeal.

Add the ice water a little at a time and gather the dough into a rough ball.

Knead the dough on a lightly floured surface for 1 minute to distribute the butter evenly. Gather into a ball and wrap in plastic. Refrigerate for at least 1 hour before rolling out.

Roll the dough into a large circle about ¼ inch thick. Using a 2-inch-round cookie cutter, cut circles from the dough. Gather up the scraps and reroll the dough until all of it is used. You should get twelve 2-inch circles from each batch of dough.

Place a heaping tablespoon of cooled Pear Mincemeat in the center of 1 circle. Place another circle on top and pinch the edges together. Prick the top in 3 places with a fork and place tarts on a greased baking sheet. Brush with egg wash. Repeat until all circles are used.

Bake the tarts in the preheated oven for 35 to 40 mintues, until golden brown. Remove to a wire rack to cool completely before packaging.

Wrapped individually in wax paper, the tarts will keep in the refrigerator for 2 or 3 days. The tarts are best eaten warm, reheat them in a 325° F. oven for 15 to 20 minutes before serving.

INGREDIENTS

For best results, make pastry in small batches. It is easier to handle and produces a flakier crust. You will need 2 batches of this dough to make 12 tarts.

1½ cups flour
⅛ teaspoon salt
5 ounces unsalted butter, chilled, cut into ½-teaspoon pieces
4 tablespoons ice water
4 cups Pear Mincemeat (preceding recipe), or any homemade or canned mincemeat

Egg Wash

1 egg, lightly beaten with 1 teaspoon water

TOOLS

Pastry cutter (optional)
Rolling pin
2-inch round cookie cutter
Pastry brush
Wire cake rack

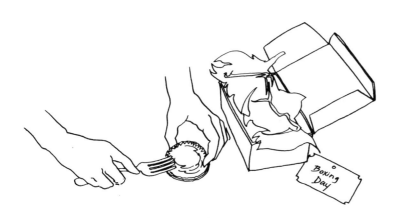

Pinch the edges together with the back of a fork.

TO PACKAGE

To carry on the custom of Boxing Day in a contemporary way, place each tart in the center of a square of tissue paper and twist upward to form a flower shape. Place the individually wrapped tarts in a personally stamped box (see instruction page 221). Include a tag with heating instructions and, before a fight breaks out, an explanation of Boxing Day.

Frozen Assets

One of the most felicitous food gifts that Devon Fredericks, my friend and partner at Loaves and Fishes, ever came up with was a freezer full of all-in-one-dish meals for her sister and husband. Both of them were working and going to school and had very little time to cook. For Christmas, she filled their freezer with entrées which they could thaw and cook in less than an hour. She included a menu so they knew what was available and happily they ate all winter long, frequenting the grocery store only for salad, bread, and wine.

These were three of their favorites.

TO PACKAGE

Pack the "frozen assets" into a Styrofoam ice chest along with a frozen cooler pack or dry ice to prevent spoiling. This will keep the food cold for several hours.

Using a red Magic Marker, hand letter the words "Frozen Assets" in a decorative pattern on several financial pages of the newspaper. Spray with Krylon Workable Fixatif to prevent smudging. Let dry. Use the paper to wrap up the ice chest. Tie with thick red yarn.

SPINACH LASAGNE

YIELD: 6 individual servings

METHOD

To prepare the tomato sauce: In a large saucepan, heat the oil, add the onion and garlic, and sauté for 2 to 3 minutes, until onion is limp and translucent but not browned. Add the mushrooms and cook for 3 to 4 minutes more, until all the liquid has evaporated from the mushrooms. Add the basil, orégano, and parsley to the saucepan and cook for 1 minute. Add the tomatoes with the purée, breaking up the whole tomatoes with the back of a wooden spoon. Toss in the bay leaves, season with salt and freshly ground pepper to taste, and stir. Pour in the beef broth, wine, and Worcestershire sauce and give another stir. Simmer uncovered over low heat for 25 to 30 minutes, until quite thick. Discard the bay leaf.

To make the filling: Cook the spinach according to directions on the package and drain in a colander, making sure to press out *all* liquid. Heat the oil in a skillet, add the onion and garlic and sauté lightly. Add the drained spinach and cook for 1 to 2 minutes more.

Set aside ¼ cup of the grated Romano cheese.

In a medium-size bowl, combine the ricotta cheese, remaining Romano cheese, the spinach mixture, and the beaten eggs. Flavor with the parsley and nutmeg and season with salt and plenty of freshly ground black pepper.

Cook the lasagne noodles according to the directions on the box and drain under cold water, separating the noodles.

To assemble the lasagne: Oil the individual baking dishes. Cut the lasagne noodles into halves. Arrange one layer of the lasagne noodles on the bottom of each pan, spread about 2 tablespoons of the ricotta cheese mixture over it, sprinkle with grated mozzarella, and cover with a thin layer of the tomato sauce. Repeat these layers twice more, finishing with a layer of sauce. Sprinkle with remaining Romano or Parmesan cheese and any mozzarella that is left over.

TOOLS

Large saucepan
6 individual baking dishes
Heavy-duty aluminum foil
Stick-on labels

INGREDIENTS

Tomato Sauce (Makes 2 quarts)

½ cup olive oil
1 onion, finely chopped
4 garlic cloves
1 pound mushrooms, finely
    chopped
¼ cup fresh basil, or 1 tablespoon
    dried
2 tablespoons dried orégano
¼ cup finely chopped fresh
    parsley
2 cans whole tomatoes, 1-pound,
    12-ounce size, with thick
    tomato purée
2 bay leaves
Salt and freshly ground pepper
2 cups beef broth
1 cup red wine
1 teaspoon Worcestershire sauce

Lasagne Filling

2 packages (10 ounces each)
    frozen chopped spinach
2 tablespoons olive oil
1 onion, finely chopped
2 garlic cloves
1 pound ricotta cheese
½ pound Romano or Parmesan
    cheese, grated
2 eggs, lightly beaten
2 to 3 tablespoons finely chopped
    fresh parsley
½ teaspoon grated nutmeg
Salt and freshly ground pepper

½ pound lasagne noodles
2 pounds mozzarella cheese,
    grated

INGREDIENTS

¾ cup flour
2 teaspoons salt
½ teaspoon freshly ground pepper
2 teaspoons thyme leaves
2 frying chickens, cut into 16
    pieces
¼ cup olive oil
4 ounces butter
½ cup dry white wine
2 garlic cloves, crushed
1 bay leaf

Cover the baking pans with heavy-duty aluminum foil, crimping the edges tightly. Use stick-on labels for freezing and baking directions.

To bake the lasagne: Preheat oven to 450° F. Bake the frozen lasagne, covered, for 30 minutes; remove the foil and bake, uncovered, for another 15 to 20 minutes.

CHICKEN MARENGO

YIELD: 8 servings

Legend has it that this distinguished dish was created for Napoleon following the Battle of Marengo. Try this invaluable "frozen asset" after your own battles of the day.

METHOD

Preheat oven to 350° F. Mix the flour, salt, pepper, and thyme, dredge the chicken pieces with the mixture. Reserve remaining flour mixture.

In a large skillet heat the olive oil and 2 ounces of the butter, add the chicken, and brown on all sides. You may need to do this in 2 batches. Place the chicken in a heavy casserole. Add reserved flour to the fat and drippings in the skillet, add the wine and cook, gathering up all chicken drippings and stirring constantly, until the sauce is smooth and thick. Pour the sauce over the chicken in the casserole and add the crushed garlic, bay leaf, and tomatoes. Cover the casserole and bake for 45 to 50 minutes, or until the chicken is tender.

While the chicken is cooking, sauté the onions and mushrooms in the remaining butter. When the chicken is done, transfer it to a platter. Add the Cognac, mushrooms, and onions to the sauce and heat thoroughly.

Place 1 breast, 1 wing, 1 leg, and 1 thigh in each aluminum container. Divide the sauce, mushrooms, and onions equally among the containers. Sprinkle each one with parsley and wrap tightly in heavy-duty aluminum foil, crimping the edges tightly.

Use stick-on labels for freezing and baking directions.

To bake the Chicken Marengo: Preheat oven to 450° F. Bake the frozen Chicken Marengo, covered, for 30 minutes; remove the foil and bake uncovered for another 30 to 40 mintues. Serve with buttered noodles or rice.

2 cups Italian-style tomatoes with
    their juice
16 to 20 small white onions
1 pound small whole mushrooms
1 ounce Cognac
Chopped parsley

TOOLS

Large casserole with lid
Four 7¾-inch-square aluminum
    baking containers, 2 inches
    deep (each contains 2
    servings)
Heavy-duty aluminum foil
Labels

CHILI

YIELD: about 4 quarts
    The third perfect freezer meal, always a winner

METHOD

Heat the olive oil in a very heavy soup kettle, preferably enameled. Add the onions and cook over low heat, covered, until tender but not brown, about 10 minutes. Break the sausage meat and ground chuck into small pieces and add to the onions. Cook over medium heat, uncovered, stirring often, until the meats are well browned. Drain off as much fat as possible.

Stir in the pepper, tomato paste, garlic, cuminseed, chili powder, hot pepper flakes, salt, orégano, tomatoes, wine, parsley, and kidney beans. Stir well and simmer, uncovered, for about 45 minutes. Taste and correct seasoning.

TOOLS

Large soup kettle
Quart-size freezer containers
Labels

INGREDIENTS

¼ cup olive oil

2 large yellow onions, coarsely
  chopped, about 4 cups

1 pound sweet Italian sausage
  meat, removed from casing

4 pounds beef chuck, ground

1 tablespoon pepper

1 12-ounce can tomato paste

2 tablespoons minced garlic

2 tablespoons ground cuminseed

2 tablespoons chili powder

½ teaspoon hot pepper flakes

2 tablespoons salt

2 tablespoons crumbled dried
  orégano

3 2-pound, 3-ounce cans Italian
  plum tomatoes, drained

½ cup red wine

¼ cup chopped fresh parsley

2 16-ounce cans dark red kidney
  beans, drained and rinsed

Cool and pack into quart-size plastic freezer containers, sealing with tight-fitting lids. Use stick-on labels for freezing and baking directions.

To serve: Thaw in the refrigerator overnight. Warm over low heat until heated through. Keeps frozen for 2 to 3 months.

Herb Blends

These custom-blended spices are so superior to the ready-mixed varieties that they will make a gourmet cook out of almost anyone. Give all six blends as the ultimate present for the accomplished cook.

TO PACKAGE

Put the spices in recycled glass spice jars or any small jars that you have on hand, such as baby food jars. The jars do not need to all be the same. Label each jar and cover the lid with a flattened, foil candy cup, glued in place with rubber cement.

Pack the spices into a wooden crate and tie with ribbon.

BOUQUETS GARNIS

YIELD: 12 small herb bouquets

One of the secrets of French cooking is the classic *bouquet garni.* It is simply sprigs of herbs, either dried or fresh, tied in a bunch or gathered in cheesecloth. Intensely aromatic when dropped into stews or sauces, the volatile oils of the herbs are released and their flavors added to the dish. Many herbal combinations are possible, but the classic combination of parsley, bay leaf, and thyme lends itself to the most uses.

METHOD

Place 2 parsley sprigs, 1 bay leaf, and ⅛ teaspoon thyme in the center of each piece of cheesecloth. Gather up the edges of the cheesecloth, wrap a length of twine around the bundle, and knot it. Repeat with the remaining herbs and cheesecloth.

TO PACKAGE

As an individual gift, place the *bouquets garnis* in a widemouthed glass jar with clamp-type lid. Decorate with a French provincial printed fabric "hat" and ribbon streamers (page 219), or see page 202.

INGREDIENTS

24 small parsley sprigs
12 bay leaves
1½ teaspoons dried thyme leaves

TOOLS

Twelve 3-inch squares of cheesecloth
Twelve 4-inch lengths of kitchen twine

For packaging

Two 1-pint glass jars with clamp-type lids

ÉPICES FINES HERBES

YIELD: about 1 cup

Nothing can touch this for flavoring pâtés or meat loaves.

METHOD

Place all of the ingredients in an electric spice or coffee grinder or a blender (I found the grinder did the best job) and pulverize to a fine powder. Store in an airtight jar or self-sealing plastic bag.

TO PACKAGE

See page 202.

INGREDIENTS

1 tablespoon each of whole cloves; freshly grated nutmeg; cinnamon stick, broken into pieces; grated mace; paprika; thyme
2 teaspoons each of dried basil, ground allspice, orégano, marjoram, sage, savory, ground ginger
3 bay leaves
1½ teaspoons whole peppercorns

CHILI POWDER

INGREDIENTS

2 large dried *pasilla* chiles, seeds
    and stems removed
2 large *ancho* chiles, seeds and
    stems removed
1 tablespoon cuminseeds
¼ teaspoon whole cloves
½ teaspoon ground coriander
¼ teaspoon ground allspice
2 tablespoons dried orégano
1 teaspoon garlic powder

YIELD: ⅓ to ½ cup
  For Mexican food enthusiasts

METHOD

Crush the chiles and combine them with the remaining ingredients. In an electric spice or coffee grinder, or in a blender, pulverize the mixture to a fine powder. Store in an airtight jar or self-sealing plastic bag.

TO PACKAGE

See page 202.

INDIAN SWEET SPICES

(Garam Masala)

INGREDIENTS

3 cinnamon sticks
2 tablespoons cardamom seeds,
    removed from their pods
2 tablespoons whole cloves
6 tablespoons coriander seeds
4 tablespoons black peppercorns

YIELD: about 1½ cups
  To flavor Indian dishes

METHOD

Crush the cinnamon sticks on a clean kitchen towel with a kitchen mallet or the end of a rolling pin. Heat the spices in a 2000° F. oven for 15 minutes. Pulverize the mixture to a fine powder in an electric spice or coffee grinder, or in a blender. Store the spices in an airtight jar or self-sealing plastic bag.

TO PACKAGE

Again, make this part of a spice group (page 202), or as a gift of just 1 spice, place 1 tablespoon of the mix in the center of a square of plastic wrap and tie at the top with kitchen twine or twist tie. Fold each individual bundle in a square of rice paper or any decorative paper and wrap a contrasting strip of hand-lettered paper around the bundle. Stack the packages together and tie with ribbon. Attach the spice package to a favorite Indian cookbook—anything by Madhur Jaffrey.

CURRY POWDER

YIELD: about 1 cup

METHOD

In a heavy skillet combine coriander seeds, cuminseeds, mustard seeds, fenugreek seeds, peppercorns, and red peppers. Roast the spices over very low heat for 15 minutes, stirring occasionally. (Your house will smell wonderful.)

Remove the skillet from the heat and add the cardamom seeds, cinnamon, cloves, and turmeric. Pulverize the mixture to a fine powder in an electric spice or coffee grinder, or in a blender.

Store in an airtight jar or self-sealing plastic bag.

TO PACKAGE

Substitute curry powder for half of the Garam Masala packages in the previous recipe, or give as part of a spice blend (see page 202).

INGREDIENTS

3 tablespoons coriander seeds
1½ tablespoons cuminseeds
1 tablespoon mustard seeds
2½ teaspoons fenugreek seeds (optional)
1 tablespoon peppercorns
3 small dried red hot peppers, crumbled
1 teaspoon cardamom seeds, removed from their pods
1 tablespoon ground cinnamon
1 tablespoon ground cloves
¼ cup ground turmeric

CHINESE FIVE-SPICE BLEND

INGREDIENTS

**1 tablespoon Szechuan
    peppercorns**
1 tablespoon black peppercorns
2 tablespoons ground cinnamon
2 tablespoons fennel seeds
6 whole star anise

YIELD: about ¾ cup
    To season Oriental dishes

METHOD

Place all of the ingredients in an electric spice or coffee grinder, or in a blender, and pulverize to a fine powder. Sieve the powder into a small bowl and store in an airtight jar or self-sealing plastic bag.

TO PACKAGE

Substitute Chinese Five-Spice Blend for Garam Masala in the packaging on page 205, or include it as part of the blend of spices on page 202.

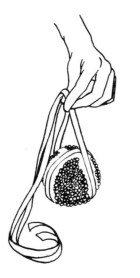

Leave open strips on the fruit to fit narrow satin ribbons between the rows of cloves.

CLOVE-STUDDED POMANDER BALLS

Attach these fragrant spice balls to any gift. Tuck them into linen closets and drawers. The sophisticated mixture of scents from the balls can be savored for several years.

METHOD

Starting at the top of the fruit, make holes with the large darning needle so that the cloves can be pushed easily into the skin. Place the cloves as close together as possible. Continue studding the fruit in a circular pattern.

Mix the ground spices in a paper bag. Add the clove-studded fruit and shake several times to cover with the spices. Place the spiced pomanders in a cool, dry place to dry out for 3 weeks.

For a more decorative effect, leave open strips on the fruit to fit narrow satin ribbons between the row of cloves. Add the ribbon when the fruit is dry. Use florist pins to attach juniper branches and berries, tiny dried flowers, or pine cones to the top of the pomander along with an additional ribbon for hanging.

TO PACKAGE

Tie these onto packages, or wrap individually in clear cellophane.

A finished Pomander Ball.

INGREDIENTS

Use an assortment of thin-skinned lemons, limes, oranges, tangerines, grapefruit, apples, and pears.

Whole cloves

Spices to scent and dry 6 small fruits:

2 ounces ground cloves
2 ounces ground cinnamon
2 ounces grated nutmeg
2 ounces ground allspice
2 ounces grated mace
2 ounces ground ginger
2 ounces orris root (available at health-food stores or from your pharmacy. Orris root is a powder used as a fixative for the other spices.)

TOOLS

Large darning needle, 50 gauge
Paper bag
Narrow satin ribbon
Florist pins

HAUTE CANINE DOGGIE BISCUITS

YIELD: 10 biscuits

I tasted every recipe in this book at least once, except for this one. However, any gourmet dog will like these biscuits as well as if not better than any you can buy. A man's best friend will appreciate your effort and

INGREDIENTS

1¾ cups whole-wheat flour
½ cup cornmeal
½ cup uncooked oatmeal
¼ cup rye kernels (available at
    health-food stores)
½ teaspoon garlic powder
½ teaspoon salt
3 tablespoons liver powder
    (available at health-food
    stores)
½ cup meat drippings (bacon,
    hamburger, etc.) or butter,
    margarine, or shortening
1 egg
½ cup beef or chicken stock

TOOLS

Bone-shaped cookie cutter or
    stencil
Baking sheet
Wire cake rack

be healthier without the additives, chemicals, artificial coloring, and preservatives found in commercial dog biscuits. Present the biscuits in a decorative "wreath for Rover."

METHOD

Preheat oven to 350° F. Combine flour, cornmeal, oatmeal, rye kernels, garlic powder, salt, and liver powder. Add meat drippings or fat. Blend until mixture resembles oatmeal. Mix in the egg and enough of the stock to form a ball.

Knead the "dough" for 1 to 2 minutes, and roll out on a floured board to ½-inch thickness. Cut into bone-shaped cookies freehand, or with a bone-shaped cookie cutter (available at good kitchen or gourmet shops). Place the biscuits on an oiled baking sheet. Prick the biscuits with a fork 2 times to make a line down the middle. Reroll scraps and make more cutouts until all the dough is used.

Bake biscuits for 25 to 30 minutes. Remove from oven and cool on wire cake rack.

Overwrap with the green grosgrain ribbon, tucking the dog biscuits between the ribbon and wreath.

TO PACKAGE

Present the biscuits in a decorative wreath.

Wind the wide red satin ribbon around the wreath, overlapping so that no straw shows through. Secure the ribbon to back of the wreath with a row of straight pins and cut off any excess.

Overwrap with the green grosgrain ribbon, tucking the dog biscuits between the ribbon and wreath. Keep the ribbon pulled tight at all times. Secure in place with straight pins. Use remaining red ribbon to form a large bow and attach it to the top of the wreath with a straight pin. Attach the gift tag with the greeting "Bone Appétit."

Materials

A 10-inch straw wreath (available from a florist or crafts supply shop)

Approximately 6 yards of 1½-inch-wide red satin ribbon

4 yards of 1-inch-wide green grosgrain ribbon

3 yards of 2-inch-wide red ribbon for a large bow

Straight pins

SHORTBREAD

YIELD: 24 wedges

While most countries celebrate Christmas with special cookies, shortbread plays an even more prominent part in Scotland's celebration of New Year's Eve, or Hogmanay. According to tradition the first dark-haired man to enter the door on New Year's Day, or "first-footer," bears a gift of shortbread. Like the Hoppin' John recipe that follows, it also symbolizes good luck and prosperity for the household.

There are endless variations on this simple short pastry, but for the purist, only butter, sugar, and flour are indispensable.

With a little careful handling shortbread is easy to make. Clean hands—never a mixer—and fresh cold butter are the secrets.

INGREDIENTS

8 ounces lightly salted butter
½ cup superfine granulated sugar
2 cups all-purpose flour

TOOLS

6-inch-round cake pan
Wire cake rack

METHOD

Preheat oven to 325° F. Using your hands and working quickly, in a medium-size bowl cream the cold butter until it is soft but not melting. Add the sugar and blend together with the tips of your fingers until all the sugar is dissolved. Add the flour, and still using your fingers, mix together until smooth. Gather the dough into a ball and knead on a lightly floured surface for 1 to 2 minutes to blend the butter further. Do not let the dough become oily. Return dough to the refrigerator to chill before this happens or the shortbread will have an unpleasant oily surface when baked.

Divide the dough into 3 equal balls. Wrap 2 in plastic wrap and refrigerate. Pat the third into the 6-inch-round cake pan. It will be about ⅜ inch thick. Crimp the edges with a fork and mark the circle with a knife into 8 triangular wedges without cutting through to the bottom. These are known as "petticoat tails." Prick each triangle in 3 places with a fork. Chill in the refrigerator for 30 minutes before baking.

Bake for 30 minutes. Do not open the door of the oven during this time. When the 30 minutes are up, check the shortbread. Turn the pan in the oven to ensure even baking and bake for 5 to 10 minutes more. Shortbread should be pale! Perfectly baked shortbread is light, with only a golden tint to the edges. Do not overbake. Remove the large round cookie from the pan and cool on a wire rack. Repeat with remaining dough.

The dough will keep in the refrigerator for several days and may be frozen.

To store the shortbread, wrap it tightly in aluminum foil, or store it in airtight containers. It also freezes well.

TO PACKAGE

Carry the shortbread on New Year's Day in a gaily decorated cookie tin lined with yellow cellophane. Tie with ribbon.

HOPPIN' JOHN

(Black-Eyed Peas Vinaigrette)

YIELD: 12 or more portions

In the past no Southerner would let New Year's Day pass without eating Hoppin' John, for this Low-Country delicacy, brought to America by African slaves, assures good luck throughout the year to all who savor it on New Year's Day. Traditionally, a silver dime is dropped into the finished dish and the guest who discovers it in his portion can claim the "fortune," great good luck and health in the upcoming year.

METHOD

Rinse and pick over the peas. Place them in a large kettle with 8 cups water, the onion stuck with cloves, whole garlic clove, bay leaf, parsley sprigs, and celery tops. Bring to a boil, reduce heat, and simmer uncovered for 45 minutes to 1 hour. Do not overcook. Let the peas rest in their water for 10 minutes. Remove the onion, garlic, parsley, and celery, and discard. Drain the peas in a colander.

Put the peas in a large mixing bowl. Add the chopped red onion, minced garlic, and chopped parsley. Toss to distribute ingredients evenly.

Combine the vinegar, mustard, and olive oil and mix until well blended. Pour the dressing over the peas and gently toss the mixture with your hands to coat the peas evenly with dressing. Season to taste with coarse salt and lots of freshly ground pepper. Wrap a coin in aluminum foil and bury it in the finished dish.

Serve lukewarm or at room temperature.

TO PACKAGE

Carry the Hoppin' John to a New Year's buffet in a covered casserole dish. Make sure to tape the lid on tightly. Overtie the casserole with wide ribbon to hide the tape, making a large bow on top. Place the casserole in a pie box for easy transport.

INGREDIENTS

1 pound dried black-eyed peas
8 cups water
1 onion, stuck with 2 cloves
1 garlic clove, peeled
1 bay leaf
A few parsley sprigs
A few celery tops
½ cup finely chopped red onion
1 teaspoon minced garlic
½ cup finely chopped parsley
6 tablespoons red-wine vinegar
1 tablespoon prepared Dijon
   mustard
½ to ⅔ cup olive oil
Coarse salt
Freshly ground pepper

TOOLS

Large kettle
Colander
Coin wrapped in foil

The trumpet of a prophecy! O Wind,
If Winter comes, can Spring be far behind?

Percy Bysshe Shelley,
Ode to the West Wind

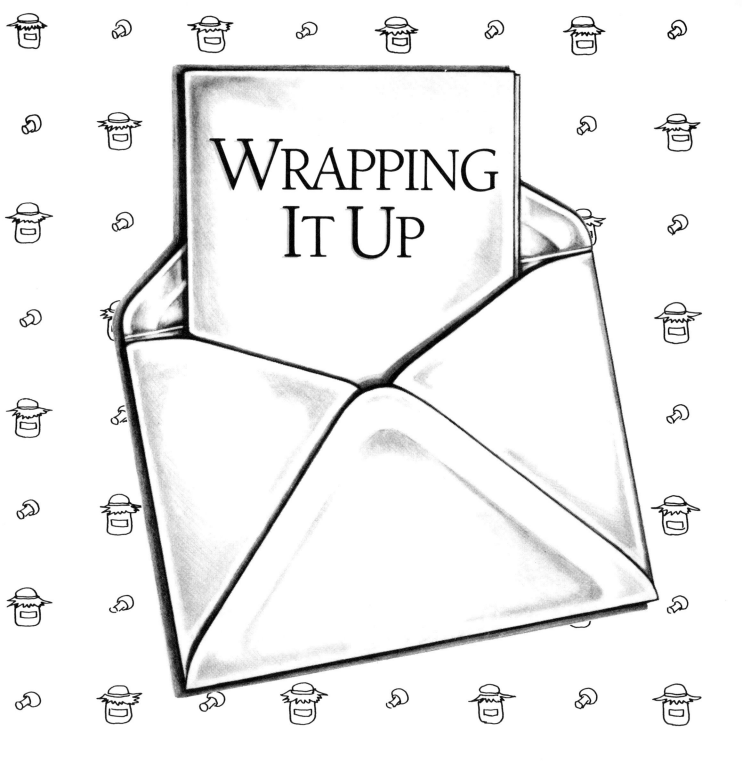

Wrapping It Up

Wrapping It Up

❀

TIPS FOR EASY WRAPPING

1. Make sure all containers are clean or sterilized.
2. Wrap cookies, cakes, breads, and candies individually in plastic wrap and store in airtight containers for maximum freshness.
3. Wrap fragile candies and cookies individually in tissue paper to prevent breakage.
4. Fill containers with shredded tissue paper or packing straw to keep fragile gifts from breaking.
5. Use freezer tape or fabric tape to seal the lids of containers that might open or spill.
6. Keep perishable foods refrigerated or frozen until the last minute.
7. Label everything.

CONTAINERS

Chosen with care and imagination, containers along with the wrapping and a label become an integral part of your food gift. They give pleasure even before they are opened, and in many cases may be reused and enjoyed long after the gift of food is gone.

Opportunities for finding unusual containers are many. Some are easily available, while others take time and a collecting mentality.

I have found a well-stocked hardware store to be the most versatile supplier. They carry everything you need from assorted jars and bottles to corks and flowerpots. Along with a special kitchenware store or catalog, you should be able to come up with all the basics.

For more esoteric containers, look in florist shops for odd-shaped vases and terra-cotta pots. Frequent antiques and thrift shops for unusual china, bottles, and boxes. Try stationery and card shops for desk accessories or toy stores for pails, hats, or open-back trucks.

If you have a Chinatown near you, make a special trip to scavenge for crates, boxes, and newsprint.

But most important, keep an imaginative, open mind for objects that can easily and cleverly be converted into containers for your food gifts.

LABELS

It is very important to label every food gift, saying what it is and the date when made.

Whenever necessary, give information on storing, shelf life, freezing, reheating, or any appropriate accompaniment or serving suggestion. You might include your own special recipe for Chicken Curry with home-made Curry Powder or the history of Mothering Sunday with a Simnel Cake. For an extra bonus include a copy of the recipe.

Don't limit yourself to the plain white, stick-on labels found in boxes of canning jars. Cut and decorate your own, taking your cue from the contents of the jar—a lemon for Cloved Lemons in Oil, a carrot for Fourteen-Carat Marmalade, fruits or berries for jams and preserves. If you can't draw, cut pictures from magazines, old greeting cards, post-cards, or collect old-fashioned gift tags from antiques shops. Explore office-supply and stationery stores for gold or red seals, luggage tags, or metal-rimmed tags.

Vary your lettering by using gold or silver metallic pens, calligraphy pens, chisel-tip Magic Markers, or Outliner pens. If your handwriting is illegible, use rubber stamps or Prestype (available at art supply stores in the graphic art section).

FUROSHIKI

The *furoshiki* is a square of cloth that is used throughout Japan to wrap practically everything to make it portable. The simple folding technique produces a beautiful design and also a handle for carrying.

DIRECTIONS

Fold the cloth diagonally in half, forming a triangle. Place the cloth so the fold is along the bottom edge. Place the food or container in the center of the triangle.

Fold the top pointed edge over the top of the food or container and tuck it firmly under the food gift.

Lift up the 2 long edges of the triangle, and tie in a knot at the center of the food gift. You now have a handle for carrying. Attach an appropriate label.

MATERIALS

1 piece of cloth, 30 x 30 inches, or a large lap napkin, or a scarf (Softer fabrics are easier to work with.)

Fold the cloth diagonally in half, forming a triangle. Place the cloth so the fold is along the bottom edge.

Fold the top pointed edge over the top of the food or container and tuck it firmly under the food gift.

Lift up the 2 long edges of the triangle.

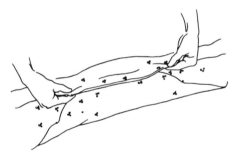

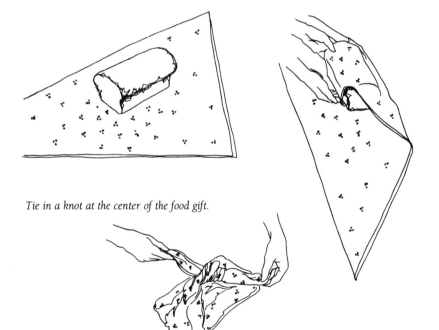

Tie in a knot at the center of the food gift.

You now have a handle for carrying.

NAPKIN BOTTLE COASTERS

MATERIALS

**1 napkin, 20 x 22 inches, or a
square piece of cloth, woven,
not printed, per bottle (for
cans and jars use a slightly
smaller rectangle)**

A simple way to show off the beautiful contents of a bottle or jar is to wrap it in a big cheerful lap napkin. The effect is stunningly simple and speaks of sophistication. Great for picnics, where you can always use an extra napkin.

DIRECTIONS

Fold the napkin diagonally in half, forming a triangle. Fold up the bottom edge approximately 1½ inches. Repeat, folding up the bottom edge another 1½ inches.

Fold down the top layer of the triangle over the folded band at the bottom. Place the bottle in the center of the top triangle.

Place both triangular pieces against the bottle. Lift the band and tie the ends together into a knot against the bottle, making sure to catch the triangle at the back, between the knot and the bottle.

Fold the napkin diagonally in half, forming a triangle.

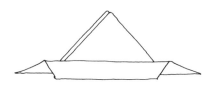

Fold up the bottom edge approximately 1½ inches.

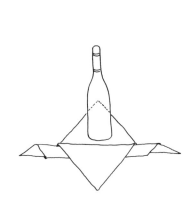

Fold down the top layer of the triangle over the folded band at the bottom. Place the bottle in the center of the top triangle.

Lift the band and tie the ends together into a knot against the bottle, making sure to catch the triangle at the back of the bottle.

TOP IT OFF HATS

One of the simplest and most festive ways to decorate bottles, cans, and jars is to give them paper or fabric "hats." These can be made from plain or colored paper, tissue paper, doilies, or fabric remnants. Use pinking shears to finish the edges with a decorative zigzag pattern which will prevent raveling.

Your choice of material should be guided by the contents of the jar or used to signify the nature of the occasion. You might use a small berry-print fabric on a jar of Sunshine Strawberry Preserves, page 60, or emphasize the earthiness of Windfall Apple Butter, page 97, by topping it off with a rough square of burlap tied in place with sisal cord. Assorted red and green fabrics and ribbons are a natural for Christmas.

The hats may be held in place with ribbon, lace, rickrack, silk cord, twine, string, or, if you wish, may be placed under the rim of Mason jars.

DIRECTIONS

For each jar, use pinking shears or scissors to cut a 6-inch square or circle 6 inches in diameter from the fabric or paper of your choice. Center the material over the lid of the container and secure in place with a rubber band. If you wish, carefully remove the rim of a canning jar, but be sure not to break the seal. Center the material over the seal and gently screw the rim into place. Tie on a ribbon and add a label and any additional decoration you desire.

Top It Off Hats.

MATERIALS

A 6-inch square or a circle 6 inches in diameter will fit the lid of most canning jars. You will need one for each jar. For larger containers, measure the top and cut the fabric 2 inches larger; for example, if the lid of a coffee can measures 4 inches in diameter, cut a circle 6-inches in diameter for the "hat."

Choose from white or silver doilies; flattened, fluted silver cupcake papers; any decorative paper, such as Chinese rice paper, gold or silver foil, enamel origami paper, Chinese prayer paper; or decorate your own with rubber stamps (see Personally Stamped Containers on page 221); antique linen or lace handkerchiefs or tea napkins.

Use tissue paper, plain or stamped, or fabrics like calico, checks, plaids, prints, taffeta moiré, burlap.

You also need pinking shears or scissors to cut the fabric, ribbon, twine, cord, rickrack, old lace, shoelaces, rubber bands to hold the "hats" in place, and a label (see page 216 for suggestions).

TIED PAPER BAGS

MATERIALS

Assorted plain bags, any size, white or brown, with or without handles, clear or opaque plastic

Hole puncher

Assorted ribbon, such as satin, grosgrain, lace, eyelet, shoe strings, rickrack, gold or silver cord, rope

No need for wrapping paper when you can make these super sacks. Just collect plain paper bags, either white or brown, in an assortment of sizes and shapes.

Decorate bags in various ways before filling.

Use Magic Markers; experiment with all types—gold and silver metallic markers, chisel-tip markers, Outliner pens as well as standard markers. Try Paint Pens and rubber stamps or make a see-through panel by cutting through the top layer and lining it with colored cellophane.

DIRECTIONS

Fill bag with your food gift, leaving several inches at the top of the bag for folding. For fragile gifts, first stuff the bag with shredded tissue paper or packing straw.

Fold down the top of the bags in various ways (see illustration).

Make holes with puncher through folded layers.

Weave ribbon through holes (see illustrations).

Attach appropriate label (see label section on page 216).

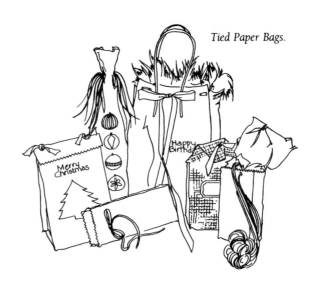

Tied Paper Bags.

PERSONALLY STAMPED CONTAINERS

Rubber stamps come in a variety of motifs and letters and the ink pads in an amazing spectrum of colors. (See Sources, page 238, for mail ordering stamps, or purchase them from stationery shops or gift shops.) Use the stamps to customize your package for a special occasion or to create a personal message.

DIRECTIONS

Place the paper on a smooth, flat surface. Using desired rubber stamps and colored ink, stamp designs as you choose over paper. Let dry.

Cut paper to fit outside surface of container or box, adding approximately ¼ inch to all edges to fold under for a neat edge.

Place paper over container, fold under edges, and secure in place with double-faced tape.

For mushroom or strawberry boxes, stamp directly onto the containers.

MATERIALS

Rubber stamps
Ink pads
White shelf-lining paper, plain butcher or brown paper
Double-faced tape
Sturdy boxes, any size; use shoe boxes, cigar boxes, shirt boxes, candy boxes, etc., or
Sturdy containers; use clean empty cardboard or metal containers that nuts or pet food was packaged in, coffee cans, cracker cans, or mushroom or strawberry boxes.

Personally Stamped Containers.

Line container or box with doilies, tissue paper, or napkins. You may also decorate the doilies or tissue paper with stamps; just make sure the ink is dry before using.

Arrange the food inside the container or box. Attach an appropriate label. (See label section on page 216.)

WAX-SEALED BOTTLES

The model for this packaging comes from the expensive vinegars and oils found in gourmet shops. The effect is stunningly simple and at the same time speaks of sophistication. To break the seal, pull the cord upward.

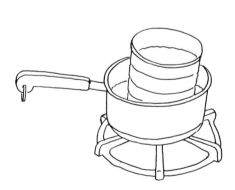

Melt the sealing wax, crayons, or colored paraffin in the metal can, set in the saucepan, half filled with water, over low heat.

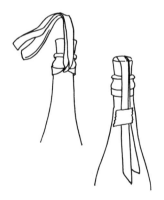

Tie a knot around the neck of the bottle, making sure the 2 ends hang down the front of the bottle in approximately equal lengths Overlap the 2 ends and lift them over the cork.
Hold them in place with the masking tape.

DIRECTIONS

Melt the sealing wax, crayons, or colored paraffin in the metal can set in the saucepan, half filled with water, over low heat. Do not let the paraffin smoke.

Take the ribbon and tie a knot around the neck of the bottle, making sure the 2 ends hang down the front of the bottle in approximately equal lengths.

Place 1 end of ribbon over the other and lift over the cork. Hold them in place with the masking tape.

Dip the bottle into the softened wax so that it covers the rim and about ¼ inch of the neck of the bottle. Let the wax dry. You may need to dip the bottle again to cover any spots missed the first time. Remove the masking tape. Attach an appropriate label (see page 216) by punching a hole in one corner of a label and slipping the ribbon through the hole.

To open bottle, pull up firmly on the ribbon, breaking the wax seal.

MATERIALS

For each bottle or jar:
24-inch-long piece of ¼-inch-wide ribbon—you choose the color; or for a more rustic look, use hemp rope or cording. Test the ribbon to make sure it will take the wax without resisting.
Sealing wax, wax crayon (all paper removed), or colored paraffin
Clean metal can (soup, coffee, etc.)
Small saucepan
Masking tape

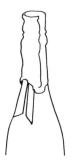

Dip the neck of the bottle into the melted wax, making sure the wax covers the rim and about ¼ inch of the neck of the bottle.

To open bottle, pull up firmly on the ribbon, breaking the wax seal.

WAX FABRIC CONTAINERS

These unique containers are easy and fun to make and can be used again and again. Choose fabric according to the season and your food gift.

MATERIALS

Scraps of cotton fabric, depending on size of container to be covered

Household paraffin wax, available in most groceries and hardware stores in 1-pound boxes. Use 2¼-pound blocks for 1 container, depending on size of container.

Tongs

Rubber gloves

Medium-size saucepan, one you don't mind discarding or are keeping just for this purpose

Flame-Tamer (see page 235 for description)

Pinking shears

Baking sheet

Wax paper

Spray vegetable oil

Containers to be wrapped—loaf pans, jars, pie plates, etc.

Newspaper

DIRECTIONS

Cover a cleared surface (table or counter) with newspaper and yourself with an apron.

Place desired container upside-down on a baking sheet lined with wax paper. Using the pinking shears (these give the edges of the cloth a finished edge and prevent raveling), cut the fabric to cover the outside surface of the container. Remove the fabric. Spray a light coat of vegetable oil over the surface of the container.

Place the saucepan on the Flame-Tamer and melt the paraffin over low heat. Do not let it smoke. Use the tongs to dip the cut fabric into the melted paraffin, gently moving it around to make sure all surfaces are covered with paraffin. Carefully remove the fabric from the paraffin and drape it over the desired container. Working quickly (the coated fabric will cool and harden quickly), mold the fabric to the container, folding or gathering sides as desired.

Allow fabric to dry completely before removing from the container. Use a kitchen knife to loosen any sides that stick.

Line the container with a napkin, doily, or tissue paper. Place desired food gift inside. Do not place warm or hot food gifts in these containers, for the paraffin would melt. Attach an appropriate label (see label section on page 216).

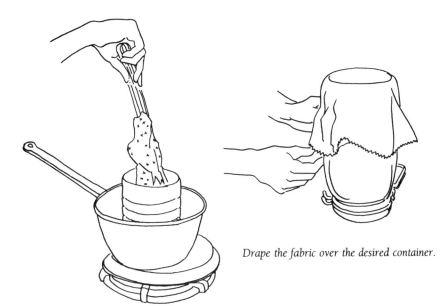

Use the tongs to dip the cut fabric into the melted paraffin.

Drape the fabric over the desired container.

Working quickly, mold the fabric to the container, folding or gathering sides as desired.

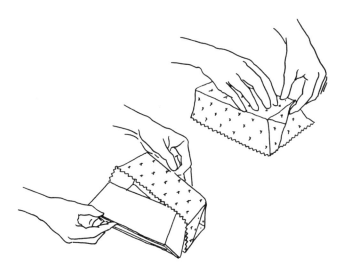

Allow fabric to dry completely before removing from the container.

Line the container with a napkin, doily, or tissue paper. Place desired food gift inside.

PAINTED WOODEN BOXES

Hand-painted boxes are a forgotten craft. These strikingly attractive containers are just the thing for packaging all types of food gifts. When lined with a padded fabric, these boxes cushion fragile cookies and candies. The boxes, of course, are meant for use after the goodies are gone. Choose one of the following materials to decorate adaptations of Shaker boxes, pint- or quart-size wooden berry baskets, or mushroom baskets.

A FEW HINTS

For a sophisticated look limit yourself to 2 or 3 colors.

Keep patterns and designs very simple; use dots, stripes, broken lines, or simple geometric shapes.

For best results, work with the grain. Remember the paint or ink will bleed vertically. Experiment before attempting a finished product. Try all the techniques to see which you do best.

Painted Wooden Boxes.

Cover your work surface with newspaper and yourself with an apron. Use one of the following:

CHISEL-TIP WATER-SOLUBLE MAGIC MARKERS

These give you both a thick and fine water-color line. The Magic Marker bleeds vertically into the wood, forming an ikat look. Seal with butcher wax, Krylon Workable Fixatif, or spray polyurethane.

TESTORS ENAMELS

Kids use these to paint models. Purchase them by the individual color, or buy several and mix your own. They will give the box a lacquered look.

Use pieces of sponge or a comb, dipped into a contrasting color, to create a textured look.

Keep the paint thin around the edges of the box, so the lid will fit when replaced.

Make sure the paint is completely dry before lining or filling the box.

PAINT PENS

One of the newest ideas for craft projects, these pens paint on any surface and dry to a permanent, high-gloss finish that will not fade. Use them like a paintbrush to create simple designs, write names or messages. Available in a variety of colors.

TO LINE THE BOX

These boxes are easily lined with fabric or paper. For more fragile food gifts use quilted fabric or cotton batting.

Cut a strip of fabric or paper to fit around the inside edge of the box or container. Allow an additional ¼ inch to all edges for turning under. Glue in place with white craft glue, folding under all seams. Adjust fabric if necessary. Let dry for 20 minutes.

Cut a piece of fabric to fit over the bottom of the container, allowing an additional ¼ inch to all edges for turning under. Glue in place, smoothing fabric and folding under all edges. Let dry.

RIBBON-COVERED BOXES

Plain boxes, resplendently decorated, are appealing and useful as gifts in themselves, long after the goodies have been eaten.

MATERIALS

Assorted ribbon, any width: Use contrasting colors, textures, and widths. Choose from polka dots, checks, plaids, satin grosgrain, eyelet, old or new lace, rickrack, and so on.
Sturdy boxes, any size: Use shoe boxes, cigar boxes, shirt boxes, candy boxes, and so on.
Masking tape
Rubber cement

DIRECTIONS

Cut desired ribbon into strips long enough to cover the top of the box vertically, including sides, adding ½ inch to each strip for securing to inside of box. Repeat with contrasting ribbon, cutting enough to cover the top of the box horizontally including sides, adding ½ inch for securing to inside of box.

Place cut vertical strips on the top of the box, side by side, as close together as possible and secure end to the box with masking tape on the inside edge of the box, leaving the opposite edges of the ribbons free.

Place cut horizontal strips on the top of the box, side by side, as close together as possible and secure ends to the box with masking tape on the inside edge of the box, leaving the opposite edges of the ribbons free.

Working with one horizontal strip at a time, weave the ribbon over and under vertical ribbons, leaving ends free.

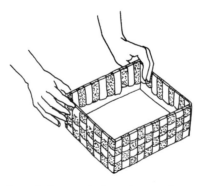

Turn the box upside down. Remove the masking tape. Adjust the ends until tight and even. Hold in place with rubber cement or masking tape.

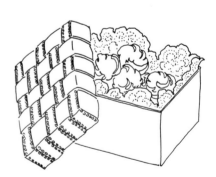

Finished Ribbon-Covered Box.

Working with one horizontal strip at a time, weave the ribbon over and under vertical ribbons, leaving ends free. They will be secured later. Repeat with all horizontal pieces.

Turn the box upside down. Remove the masking tape. Pull the ends of the ribbon tightly over the box, adjusting until even and tight. Fold the ends under and hold in place with rubber cement or masking tape. If using glue, allow it to dry before filling boxes.

Line boxes with tissue paper, doilies, or napkins. Place food inside, replace lid, and attach appropriate label. (See label section for suggestions.)

COOKIE ENVELOPES

Ordinary poster board is used imaginatively to create these functional, forthright containers. Use them to present one special cookie or to hold several candies. They make ideal party favors.

DIRECTIONS

For each envelope cut 1 rectangle, 13 x 8½ inches, from a sheet of poster board. Draw a rectangle, 6 x 4½ inches, in the center of the larger rectangle. Draw round-cornered flaps to connect the smaller rectangle to the outside edges of the larger rectangle (see diagram).

Cut out the envelope and fold along dotted lines forming the inside rectangle (see diagram).

Place a doily on the inside of the envelope, add the cookies or candies, and fold in the side flaps to meet. Fold in the top and bottom flaps.

Seal with an appropriate sticker, tucking one 2-inch piece of ribbon, folded in half, under the bottom edge of the sticker, as you press it down (see diagram).

Use a gold or silver metallic pen to label with name or message.

Note: If you wish, the dimensions of the envelope may be doubled or tripled to hold larger cookies.

MATERIALS

Poster board, available in shiny white or colors. Each 22-inch x 28-inch board will make 5 envelopes.
Ruler
Scissors
6-inch doilies
Gum-backed labels, available at party supply or stationery stores. Choose from circles, stars, or any decorative shape or design to suit your occasion.
Ribbon cut into 2-inch lengths

Cookie Envelope Pattern

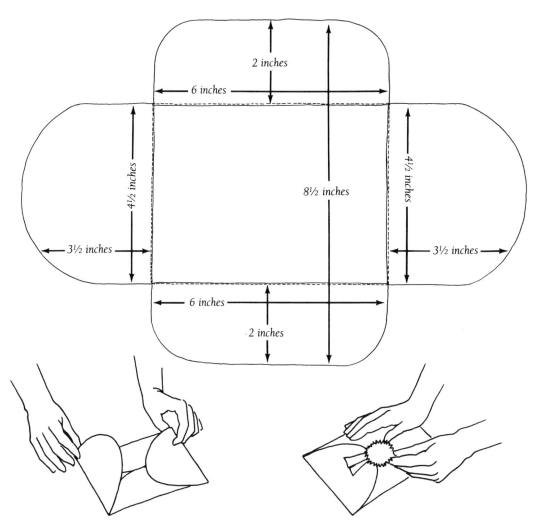

2 inches

6 inches

4½ inches

4½ inches

8½ inches

3½ inches

3½ inches

6 inches

2 inches

Fold in the side flaps until they meet.

Fold in the top and bottom flaps, seal with a decorative sticker, tucking in a 2-inch piece of ribbon.

Some Cooking Hints

⊙ ✷ ⊙

HOT-WATER BATH CANNING

Many recipes in this book call for the preparation of high-acid foods such as most fruits and many vegetables into jellies, jams, conserves, relishes, pickles, and chutneys. These foods must be properly processed and sealed to prevent spoilage if they are not refrigerated and eaten within a few days. This is not a complicated undertaking, but a few words of explanation and some tips on how to succeed with home preserving of foods will help you with the recipes.

With the exception of the jellies, recipes requiring canning in this book call for a boiling-water bath, a method recommended by the U.S. Department of Agriculture for the preserving of all high-acid foods. (Jellies may be either processed or sealed with paraffin wax, then covered tightly with a lid, plastic wrap, or cloth. See instructions for sealing with paraffin on page 235.) I am not going to discuss canning in tin cans since the many recipes for jams, jellies, pickles, and relishes in this book should only be home-canned in glass.

When I "can" at home, I proceed in this order:

STEPS FOR HOT-WATER BATH CANNING

1. Assemble ingredients for recipe.
2. Assemble equipment, checking jars for cracks or nicks and lids for dents or rust.
3. Prepare recipe.
4. While recipe is cooking, sterilize jars and lids and place in oven to keep warm.
5. Fill water-bath canner and begin heating. Start another pot of water to boil (to be added to water bath later), or begin melting paraffin.
6. Fill jars.
7. Process in canner for specified time or seal with paraffin.
8. Cool and check for seal.
9. Label and package.

These steps are explained in some detail in this section. Please read it in full before proceeding. If you have a problem or further questions on the whys and wherefores of the canning and pickling processes, there are many books on the subject. I consider the following three to be the best and at least one of them should be part of every culinary library.

Ball Blue Book. Muncie, Indiana: Ball Corporation, 1905.

Ruth Hertzberg, Beatrice Vaughn, and Janet Greene, *Putting Food By*. Brattleboro, Vermont: The Stephen Greene Press, 1977.

The Complete Book of Canning. San Francisco: Ortho Books, 1982.

Equipment

As in most projects, good planning is a key factor in successful canning. A checklist of needed equipment follows. Much of what you need is standard in today's kitchens. What you don't have may be bought at good hardware and kitchen stores. Their stock is often thin at the height of the canning season, so try buying what you need in advance. It is maddening to have quarts of molding berries on your hands just because the stores have run out of canning lids. (I know. I've done it.)

- Assortment of spoons, including measuring, wooden, slotted spoons, and large ladle, at least 8-ounce size
- Measuring cups, both dry (metal stacking) and wet (glass), ranging from ¼ cup to 4 cups
- Food brushes; stiff bristles are the best for washing fruits and vegetables. "Cleanliness is next to Godliness."
- Colander and strainer, enamel, stainless steel, or plastic; no galvanized aluminum, please
- Jar-lifter or tongs with rubber ends
- Jelly bag and stand
- Cheesecloth
- Scales

- Candy thermometer
- Timer
- Food mill
- Rubber gloves
- Pot holders
- Dish towels
- Saucepans for heating lids
- 6- to 8-quart kettle for preparing foods. Nonreactive pots of heavy enameled metal or stainless steel are best. Do not use galvanized aluminum or cast iron; these kettles react with the acid and salt, causing unpleasant colors and taste.
- Widemouthed funnel
- Water-bath canner rack. The height of the canner is important. Jars placed in the rack must be covered by 2 inches of water, with an additional 2 inches of free air space above the jars to permit boiling.
- Assorted jars and lids

A Note About Canning Jars

The four most popular types of canning jars come in a variety of sizes and are made so the closures seal tightly. The glass is specially tempered to withstand the heat of sterilizing and processing. Don't reuse commercial containers like mayonnaise, peanut butter, or pickle jars; they are for single use only and generally will not withstand the heating process nor will their lids form a proper seal.

Jars are available in half-pint, pint, and quart sizes, with either narrow or wide mouths. I find the smaller jars best for jellies, jams, and preserves and the larger widemouthed size better suited for whole fruits and vegetables. But use what you like best.

There are several types of glass jars in use today. Mason or Ball jars, with self-sealing lids held in place by screw-on metal ring bands, are the most common type of jar used for home canning. You can reuse the jars and the ring bands but not the self-sealing lids.

Clamp-type jars have hinged glass lids held tightly in place over a rubber ring by metal clamps. I like this style for canning whole fruits, pickles, and mustards. There are some beautiful ones on the market with enamel tops in a variety of colors. Check the lids for chips before each use.

"Lightening" jars are the most old-fashioned of the canning jars and have domed glass lids that clamp down over rubber rings. I generally don't use them because replacement rubber rings are hard to find. If you decide on these jars, read the manufacturers' instructions since I do not cover them in this section.

The fourth type of jar is a zinc-cap jar with a porcelain-lined zinc cap fitted over a rubber ring. These are not widely available and, like the lightening jars, have a rubber ring that is not reusable. Again, make sure to follow manufacturers' directions for sealing them before using. I don't cover this style of jar in my instructions.

Sterilizing the Jars

Jars must be clean and hot when ready to be filled. Wash them in hot soapy water and rinse well in hot water. Place them in a large kettle and cover with hot water. Bring to a boil and boil for 15 minutes. Many canning books recommend leaving the jars in the hot water until you are ready to use them and then inverting them onto a clean dish towel to dry just before filling. This is too confusing and fussy for me. I find it more convenient to place the sterilized jars upright on a rack in a preheated 180° to 200° F. oven. This keeps the jars hot as well as dry and elimi-

nates waiting for them to dry or worrying if they have cooled down too much while drying. If you are using clamp-type jars, fit the rubber rings onto the rims of each lid before placing the jars in a warm oven.

Sterilize the jar lids according to the manufacturers' instructions. Do not boil them. Generally, 5 minutes in slow simmering water is enough to scald them and soften their sealing compound.

While the jars and lids are sterilizing, place the canning rack in the canner half filled with water and begin to heat the water. Do not let it boil.

Filling the Jars

Jars should be filled while they are hot. It is a good idea to handle hot jars with heavy, well-fitting rubber gloves. They will protect your hands from the heat of the jars and from any spills and they will enable you to keep a firm grip on the jars while filling them.

Pack the food into the jars, bearing in mind that you must always leave *headspace* when filling jars; headspace is space between the contents and the lid of the jar. Headspace allows the contents to expand during processing. Each recipe tells you the correct amount. Wipe the rim of each jar with a clean, damp cloth to ensure a tight seal.

Place the lids on the mouth of the jar so that the rubber sealing compound rests on the top edge of the jar. Screw the band down firmly but not too tightly, just as much as you can tighten comfortably with your hands.

Processing the Jars

Using your jar-lifter, lower the sealed jars into the hot water onto the canning rack. This rack is divided so that the jars will not bump into one another or fall over in the boiling water. Add more boiling water, enough to cover the jars by 2 inches, and place the lid on the canner.

Bring the water to a brisk boil and begin counting processing time from the point when the water begins to boil. Each recipe specifies correct processing time.

Cooling and Checking the Seal

After the suggested processing time, remove the canner from the heat and cool the jars to room temperature in the water. With the jar-lifter remove the jars from the canner by lifting them straight up, making sure not to tip the contents. Place the jars on a clean towel to cool for 8 to 12 hours. As the jars cool, you may hear a loud popping or pinging noise. This sound indicates that a jar has sealed. To test for a proper seal, wait 12 hours and then gently press the center of the lid with your finger. If the lid stays down, the jar is sealed.

Once the jars have sealed, the flat lids will adhere tightly to the jar rims. If a jar fails to seal, refrigerate it and eat the contents within a week.

Labeling and Storing

It is amazing how soon I forget what each jar contains and the time when I canned it. Get into the habit of labeling each product with the date and the name of the recipe as you go along. There are many labeling suggestions throughout this book from which to choose.

Properly sealed jars should be stored in a cool, dark, dry place. Stored this way, they will keep for about a year. Once opened, canned foods should always be refrigerated.

SOME NOTES ON MAKING JELLY AND OTHER SEMISOFT SPREADS

Jellies, jams, preserves, marmalades, conserves, and chutneys are all sweet and sticky semisoft spreads made in about the same manner. They all contain fruit, sugar, and fruit juice and are jellied to various degrees, but there are differences between them and I have defined them below so you will know the distinctions. Processing of the soft spreads is by the boiling-water-bath method for full safety, but the jellies can be put up successfully without this step.

The fruit for the spreads is crushed, chopped, or left whole, then boiled with sugar and its own juice to the *jell point,* the point at which the fruit thickens. The crucial factor is getting the right proportion of fruit, sugar, liquid, and natural or commercial pectin and cooking the mixture to just the right stage. If our grandmothers could do this without much worry, so can we. First, you must determine the jell stage. This is reached when the temperature of the mixture is 9° F. higher than the boiling point of water (for soft spreads) and 8° F. higher (for jellies). The boiling point of water varies slightly, depending on atmospheric conditions and altitude; it is somewhere around 212° F. To ensure success it is important to check it in your own kitchen before making any of these recipes. To find the boiling point of water, use a candy thermometer to determine the actual temperature at which water breaks into a boil. Add 8 or 9 degrees to this and you will have the temperature at which the spread will set up. It will be around 220° F. for jelly and 221° to 225° F., for jams, in recipes without commercial pectin added.

Hints for Jelly Making

Make sure you have the right equipment. A large 8- to 10-quart kettle is essential. This size permits the jelly to come to a full rolling boil without spilling over. Boiled over jelly is a real mess to clean up!

If you plan to make a lot of jelly, you might invest in a jelly bag and stand, though an adequate substitute can be made by lining a colander with several layers of closely woven cheesecloth and suspending this over a large bowl. Never squeeze the bag or put pressure on the fruit; a cloudy jelly will result.

A watch or clock with a second hand is a must for timing jelly made with pectin. If you are not using pectin, the most dependable way to tell when jelly has reached the right temperature is with a candy thermometer: about 220° F. for jelly and 221° to 225° F. for jams.

The jelly point can also be tested using the sheet method. Dip a cool metal spoon into the boiling jelly. Lift the spoon out and tip it so the jelly falls off the spoon back into the pot. At first the mixture will be light and syrupy and run off the spoon. Later the mixture thickens and falls from the spoon in separate drops. The jelly is done when it forms 2 drops, then falls from the spoon in a steady sheet.

Only prepare one batch at a time. A small batch is easier to handle and preserves the flavor of the fresh fruit; doubling the recipe may prevent it from setting properly.

Select fruit that is fresh and unblemished. Damaged fruit should be discarded. Include some underripe but not green fruit for its higher pectin content. Avoid overripe fruit; it has lost some of its natural pectin and will not jell properly.

Never use puréed fruit. It adds too much juice for a good jell.

It is important to use the full amount of sugar called for in the recipe. If you don't like sugar, don't eat the jellies. Reducing the amount may prevent the recipe from setting up. The same rule applies for commercial pectin.

Sealing Jelly with Paraffin Wax

When sealing jelly with paraffin wax, almost any size or shape of jar or glass may be used as long as it can be sterilized in boiling water and is not scratched or chipped.

Melt the paraffin wax in a disposable container (I like to use a clean metal soup can) set in a pan of hot water over very low heat. Do not let the paraffin smoke and *never* melt it in a saucepan over direct heat; it is highly flammable and spatters easily. This is a good time to use a Flame-Tamer, an asbestos plate used directly over the stove flame, which allows you to control heat with greater ease.

Ladle the jelly into sterilized jars (see page 233 for instructions on washing and sterilizing jars), making sure to leave ½ inch headspace. Wipe the rims clean. Immediately pour over the hot jelly a thin layer of melted paraffin about ⅛ inch deep. A thin layer of paraffin makes a better seal than a thick one. To ensure a good seal, the paraffin must touch all sides of the jars. Wear rubber gloves or use a pot holder to hold the jar firmly and rotate it slowly, forcing the paraffin to adhere to the jar at all points. Prick any air bubbles that appear in the paraffin as they rise to the top. Air bubbles will cause the seal to break, so pop them all.

Cool the jars at room temperature until the contents are completely cool and the paraffin sets. As the paraffin cools and hardens, it will become opaque in color and sink slightly in the middle.

When the jelly has cooled and the paraffin has set, cover the jars with plastic wrap or a clean cloth held in place with a cord, ribbon, or rubber band. This will prevent dust from settling in the paraffin and causing it to mold. If you are using commercial jelly glasses, use the snap-on plastic lids that come with the glasses for this purpose.

Label each jar with the date and name of the recipe. Store jellies in a cool, dark, dry place. They should be eaten within 6 months. Once opened, jars must be refrigerated.

Hints for Jams and Other Soft Spreads

Most of the hints for jelly making apply as readily to the making of soft spreads. But with the soft spreads you have a choice to make about the consistency of the finished product. I prefer recipes made without commercial fruit pectin; they retain a truer fruit flavor and color and are slightly soft and sticky. I like jams, preserves, and the like just to fall off the spoon onto muffins and toast. I don't want to struggle to spread "tough" jam in the morning. (If a recipe does call for pectin, use it. The fruit used in the recipe has a low pectin content and the commercial pectin is needed to ensure the proper jelling and consistency.)

Remember that powdered and liquid pectin are not interchangeable. Use the one called for in the recipe and read the label for directions on use.

Measure the fruit, sugar, and any spices into a large kettle and bring to a boil. Cook the mixture until a thermometer reads 9° F. higher than the boiling point of water (see directions on page 235). This will take between 15 and 45 minutes, depending on the amount of natural pectin in the fruit you are using. If the preserve still looks soft when the temperature is reached, remember it will thicken more as it cools. Rather than overcooking low-pectin fruit, which only makes a tough spread, be satisfied with the softer one or use a recipe calling for commercial pectin.

Some Definitions

Jelly is the juice of fruit cooked with sugar (more pectin or acid such as lemon juice is added if necessary) until the mixture will hold its shape.

Jams are made from mashed fruit and sugar cooked to the jell point. Depending on the pectin content, their consistency varies from thick to runny.

Preserves are made from whole or coarsely chopped fruit and sugar cooked together to the jell point. Depending on the pectin content, the consistency varies from thick to runny.

Conserves are mixtures combining two or more fruits with nuts or raisins. They are made similarly to preserves or jams.

Marmalades are softly jellied jams containing the flesh and the peel of citrus fruit. They are generally more cloudy than jellies although they are prepared by a similar method.

Fruit butters and *honeys* are made from cooked fruit which has been put through a food mill and then cooked again until the fruit pulp becomes a thick sauce. They are made with sugar and are often highly seasoned.

Chutneys are condiment-type preserves, a spicy combination of chopped fruits, vegetables, herbs, and spices in a thick sweet-sour syrup.

Ketchups are condiment-type jams or sauces.

Relishes are chopped vegetables, sometimes fruits, pickled with vinegar and sugar. They range in taste from hot or mild to sweet or tart.

Sources

The following sources will provide special ingredients or equipment mentioned in this book:

Williams-Sonoma
Mail-Order Department
P.O. Box 7456
San Francisco, CA 94120

Dean & Deluca, Inc.
121 Prince Street
New York, NY 10012
or
46 Newton Lane
East Hampton, NY 11937

Bridge Kitchenware Corp.
214 East 52nd Street
New York, NY 10022

Zabar's Gourmet Foods
249 West 80th Street
New York, NY 10024

For dried herbs:
Aphrodisia Products, Inc.
282 Bleecker Street
New York, NY 10014

For rubber stamps:
Rubber Stamps of America
Box 67
Saxton River, VT 05154

Bizzaro Rubber Stamps
P.O. Box 126
Annex Station
Providence, RI 02961

For unique papers and art supplies:
New York Central Art Supply
62 Third Avenue
New York, NY 10003
catalog and swatches
available

Index